"Donald Spoto offers a mature ... millennium. At times the ho... the catechist and at times the r... he is not satisfied with merely finding nuggets of truth embedded in ancient tales."
—*The Los Angeles Times*

"Spoto...cannily weaves literary criticism, historical research and theological scholarship into his story of the life and work of history's most enduring figure. Written with impressive clarity and pace."
—*Publishers Weekly*

"A probing work that examines its subject from the point of view of both a Christian apologist and a sympathetic and careful observer. This book focuses on the life and message of Jesus in an intimate and sobering way."
—*Library Journal*

"Spoto...applies his impressive research skills in this book, a Christian's personal quest into the ultimate meaning and enduring impact of Jesus of Nazareth."
—Amazon.com

"Spoto saw clouds gathering over the life of Jesus of Nazareth. He saw debunkers chipping away at the divinity of Jesus while zealots stripped him of his humanity. And finally Spoto had enough."
—Portland *Oregonian*

"This isn't the blue-eyed, sweet-talking Jesus of movies, the dreamy mystic of New Age vision or the placid babe of Christmas carols. *The Hidden Jesus* of Donald Spoto's new biography charges through his brief lifetime, challenging and rebuking the accepted order at every turn."
—Sally MacDonald, *Seattle Times*

Also by Donald Spoto

Diana: The Last Year

Notorious: The Life of Ingrid Bergman

Rebel: The Life and Legend of James Dean

The Decline and Fall of the House of Windsor

A Passion for Life: The Biography of Elizabeth Taylor

Marilyn Monroe: The Biography

Blue Angel: The Life of Marlene Dietrich

Laurence Olivier: A Biography

Madcap: The Life of Preston Sturges

Lenya: A Life

Falling in Love Again: Marlene Dietrich (photo essay)

The Dark Side of Genius: The Life of Alfred Hitchcock

Stanley Kramer: Film Maker

Camerado: Hollywood and the American Man

The Art of Alfred Hitchcock

THE
HIDDEN
JESUS

A NEW LIFE

DONALD
SPOTO

ST. MARTIN'S GRIFFIN 🐘 NEW YORK

DESIGN BY JAMES SINCLAIR

Library of Congress Cataloging-in-Publication Data

Spoto, Donald.
  The hidden Jesus: a new life / Donald Spoto.
    p. cm.
  Includes bibliographical references and index.
  ISBN 0-312-19282-7 (hc)
  ISBN 0-312-24333-2 (pbk)
    1. Jesus Christ—Biography—History and criticism.   2. Bible.
N.T. Gospels—Criticism, interpretation, etc.—History—20th
century.   I. Title.
BT301.9.S65 1998
232.9'01—dc21
[B]
                                                          98-18703
                                                          CIP

First St. Martin's Griffin Edition: September 1999

10 9 8 7 6 5 4 3 2 1

With loving gratitude to

Irene Mahoney
Elaine Markson
John Darretta

Nunc scio quid sit amor.
—Vergil

CONTENTS

Contents

"Skip the exegesis," Didymus broke in weakly. "I can do without that now. Read the verse."

—J. F. Powers, "Lions, Harts, Leaping Does"

INTRODUCTION

For almost fifty years, since I first heard them as a schoolboy, I have been haunted by phrases from the ancient Easter liturgy:

"Christ yesterday and today, the beginning and the end, Alpha and Omega. All time belongs to him, and all the ages."

For the early Christian community, those words summarized belief in the permanent presence of the Risen Jesus among them—not just a vague spirit, living on among those who believed in him and his teachings, but his being, his total self, alive and accessible to everyone. For me, the proclamation has always been the carrier of a meaning I can never fully fathom but whose power I can never shake off: *Ipsius sunt tempora*, "All time belongs to him . . ."

All time, it has become clear to me, means not only time as a universal construct, but *the* time—the particulars of every moment—of every human being, of *my time*: everything that comprises my life and relationships, my work and even my death. Everything relates to my relationship to God. My life, I have come to see, is not so much about learning *who* I am but about understanding and living in light of *Whose* I am. Everything I think of as mine belongs to and relates to God, for, as Paul wrote to the Corinthians, "you belong to Christ, and Christ belongs to God."

Over the last twenty-four years, I have been working mostly as a biographer. But for twice that length of time, the deepest concern of my life, the one thing that has sustained, prodded, enlivened, nurtured, bothered, convicted, terrified and gladdened me, has been the mysterious journey that is faith in God. It has, therefore, been a singularly wonderful experience—and a frightening and humbling one—to join my vocation as a writer to the task of articulating questions and concerns of ultimate significance.

Clinging in trust to God's self-disclosure in Jesus of Nazareth is quite literally, however frequent the darkness and profound the personal inadequacy, a matter of life and death. It must be obvious already, then, that *The Hidden Jesus: A New Life* is a work rooted in belief, which is neither an intellectual pose nor a poetic fancy, nor is it a thing one possesses, like an academic degree or a language fluency. Faith is an attitude about reality—a context in which one perceives and acts, and a process in which one grows. The attitude, the context and the process are, for me, adumbrated by the early Christian proclamation reflected in the New Testament.

But we do not place our faith in writings, nor in the necessary classic credal formulas through which orthodox Christianity struggled to articulate belief in the critical early centuries. Much less do we place our faith in the statements of theologians or the contributions of Bible scholars, however fascinating and useful they can be. No, the only real object of Christian faith is the living, present Jesus, who stands above, behind and infinitely beyond any human expression about him and the God he reveals.

––––––––

Authors, I am told, should never begin their books with negative statements. That is the first tradition I am breaking. *The Hidden Jesus: A New Life* is not for the theological expert or the professional biblical exegete, though I owe a great debt to the best among them. Although each chapter takes into account many of the fine points of this century's biblical scholarship, the book is intended as a series of meditations on the significance of Jesus of Nazareth. It is for the general reader who is intrigued by him, and while it may have special interest for Roman Catholics, I have written with all people of good will in mind.

There are many fine works of literary and historical criticism that will take you deeper into relevant matters of history, ancient culture, linguistic analysis and archaeology, to name but a few of the fields that impact on contemporary biblical studies. Many of the works I consulted are cited in the Bibliography, and many essays and articles are listed in the Notes, which also contain reflections of more scholarly interest.

Although this is not a textbook, then, I hope to have brought to these reflections my years of training as a New Testament theologian and as a teacher of New Testament Studies. In that context, I have enormous admiration for the great scholars and exegetes of this century whose labors have tilled the ground in which the modest seeds of this book took root.

I must, therefore, explicitly acknowledge two professors under whom I studied when I took my doctorate in New Testament theology at Fordham University, for they and their writings have contributed greatly to the formation of my thinking. Myles M. Bourke and Raymond E. Brown are internationally respected scholars whose achievements are well known to people familiar with contemporary biblical studies. Anything worthwhile in this book owes much to their tutelage.

And while I am expressing gratitude and admiration:

Robert Weil, senior editor at St. Martin's Press, has believed in and encouraged this project and its author from day one. A man of extraordinary insight and understanding, he is every writer's dream of an ideal publisher, and I am emboldened by his kindness to anticipate our continuing collaboration. This partnership, the inspiration of my dear friend and unfailingly perceptive agent, Elaine Markson, is but another example of her superb guidance of my career.

How pleased I am, too, that a long-term mutual hope to work together has at last been realized: Sally Richardson, the wise and energetic president of St. Martin's Press, has been my constant and supportive ally at every stage of this project.

In Bob Weil's office, I must thank Andrew Miller, who patiently and with unfailing good grace dispatches a daily tangle of responsibilities. Steve Snider designed the impressive cover.

Gregory Dietrich, who worked with me so efficiently and effectively for four years as research assistant, has now begun a promising career as a writer. I acknowledge with gratitude his devoted and valuable collaboration.

———

The Bible was, of course, written by human beings—it is the word of God in the words of men. Although those writers (and this author) affirm that they had been touched by transcendent realities, they were nevertheless bound by the constraints of their own languages. All human discourse is metaphor—that is one of my major themes—and so any utterance about God must necessarily be provisional and incomplete, limited by the structures of language and the ideologies that constitute culture. For all that, I think that trying to speak of God is neither misguided effort nor lunacy.

Jesus was as hidden to his contemporaries as he seems to us today. Many Christians and others of good will, regardless of their faith or lack of it, feel that if they had been able to walk the hills of Galilee with Jesus, to see and hear him, they would be able to decide for themselves. I doubt it. Being there might not have made a difference at all.

Look at that motley crew of disciples, a not very impressive lot who walked, talked, ate and lived with Jesus of Nazareth. They trudged around those rough hills and scorching deserts with him for the best part of two years and yet, as late as the time of his death, they failed to grasp the greatness. One of the most poignant aspects of Jesus' final hours is the complete abandonment he suffered: he was truly alone at the end.

The realization of Jesus' significance began to dawn on his friends only gradually, after the first Easter. By virtue of a series of remarkable experiences, they came to see that the fullest truth about the man had been hidden during his life. And they were convinced that he was not bound by death—instead, they proclaimed that he had entered into a completely different mode of existence, a totally new life despite the fact that he was now invisible. Jesus, for the first Christians, was still hidden, but paradoxically he had become more present and more accessible than ever. Hence my title.

———

The original witnesses to Jesus and the writers about him did not set out to provide a historical biography. For them, he was not a figure of history but a living one, very much present and real. However invisibly and mysteriously, he was approaching them and they were meeting him in the specificity of their lives and situations.

The Gospels, therefore, although completed a half-century after the original events, were not documents of the past, for the past. They were written for people in critical new situations, people trying to find the meaning of faith, coping with pain and with political and social ostracism, striving despite their own foolishness and lack of clarity, grappling with their divisions and self-interests. The Gospels responded to community needs and corresponded to their experiences of the Risen Jesus—the one believed and preached, the same person who had once lived and died in the flesh and was now alive forever.

God still remains, it so often seems, the hidden one; and Jesus, whatever one thinks of him, also was and remains the hidden one. But it is in his new life—and in the new life he imparts—that he is alive and present, and that he offers meaning where there is only muddle.

The inquiry, the problems, the questioning and the astonishment that these issues evoke are at the core of *The Hidden Jesus: A New Life*. I offer nothing like definitive answers. I would simply like to propose that the humility and hiddenness of Jesus, then as now, may be the key to understanding the deepest meaning of his new life. And mine, and yours.

D.S.
Los Angeles: 27 January 1998
The Feast of Saint Angela Merici,
Founder of the Ursulines

THE
HIDDEN
JESUS

A NEW LIFE

CHAPTER ONE

THE MUSIC OF SILENCE:
THE BIRTH OF JESUS

Anewborn baby lies in a manger lined with straw. His parents kneel beside him. Nearby are an ox and a donkey, perhaps some lambs and a few shepherds, and three strangely attired, exotic men offering treasures to the infant.

The cast and setting are familiar. The birth of Jesus, whether described in hymns and oratorios or depicted on canvas, in plaster or in wood, grandly or simply, remains perhaps the most widely known religious icon in the world.

So presented, the artistic rendering of the birth of Jesus originated not in the New Testament but with Saint Francis of Assisi and a few companions, and it has survived for more than seven hundred years. In 1223, Francis presented a kind of panorama for Christmastide near the village of Greccio in Italy. Because the Gospel according to Luke mentions that the child was placed in a manger (an animal feed-box), one of Francis's company said there must have been oxen, horses and mules in a stable. To Francis, the man's remark about animals recalled a verse from the prophet Isaiah—"The ox knows its owner, and the donkey knows the manger of its master"—and so some livestock were hauled in for the *tableau vivant* and carefully tethered next to a local family, who stood in for the original trio. And because the Gospel according to Matthew specifies a visit of an undetermined number of soothsayers or astrologers (the meaning of *magi*) and Luke mentions the presence of shepherds, Francis asked friends to represent them, too. From his devout spirit came the picturesque iconography of Christmas night.

Taking Francis's lead, artists representing the nativity since his time have often combined all the Gospel elements into a single lively scene.

1

In the texts, each detail and each event is offered by either Matthew *or* Luke: except for the Bethlehem setting, the accounts vary in virtually every detail and are impossible to harmonize. But this poses no problem once we recall that each writer had a specifically religious purpose in constructing the event—a goal that reflected perfectly the faith of the community for and from which he wrote.

Only Ebenezer Scrooge, before his change of heart, would dare to tamper with the simple, moving beauty of the artists' scene of the nativity as rendered down through the ages. But like all art, it points to truths both within and beyond its components. Few people, after all, are unmoved by the situation of a poor, rural family and a helpless baby in distressed circumstances. Still, it is astonishingly rewarding to consider the various events and episodes constructed by the two Gospel writers who aimed to present the significance of Jesus at his coming.

A decree went out from Emperor Augustus that all the world should be registered. Joseph went from the town of Nazareth in Galilee to Judea, to the city of David called Bethlehem, because he was descended from the house and family of David. He went to be registered with Mary, to whom he was engaged and who was expecting a child.

Set in the hills and equidistant between the Lake of Galilee and the Mediterranean, Nazareth was an obscure, sixty-acre village whose residents depended on agriculture for their livelihood. Tenant farmers, slaves and some transient day laborers worked the soil of a few wealthy landowners, whose domains (thanks to a temperate climate and adequate rainfall) produced healthy crops of fruits, grains and vegetables.

The most respected members of the community were not farmers, however, but merchants and manufacturers: goldsmiths, masons, tentmakers, potters, stonecutters, sandalmakers and—at the pinnacle of the trades—carpenters, who not only carved doors and furniture but also constructed and installed beams, roofs and staircases for homes and for the local synagogue (the religious meetinghouse), where the faithful met to read, pray and discuss Scripture and its written and oral interpretations.

Most private homes of the poor and middle class consisted of a room or two, each measuring twenty or thirty square feet, and the floor was the earth. With walls of straw and bricks, this small, dark, usually windowless cottage was usually connected to neighbors' dwellings. In a central courtyard were communal ovens, cisterns and millstones, a livestock barn and a storehouse for oil, wine and provisions.

Dietary staples included bread; roasted wheat, cooked into a kind of porridge; corn; lentils and barley; and grapes, peppers, dates, berries and olives. Fish from the Mediterranean and the Lake of Galilee were plentiful and salted to preserve against spoilage, but poultry or meat was a luxury. People drank water, goat's milk, diluted vinegar, date juice, a kind of beer fermented from barley, and a potent, filtered wine that had to be diluted with water. Still, few escaped repeated, debilitating bouts of dysentery, and very often people died from contaminated food. Few families had access to effective herbal remedies.

Among their few household possessions, most people had a lamp, made of clay and fueled by olive oil, and a storage chest, which served for clothes and setting up meals. Two or three plain floor mats were the typical bed; stones or wood fragments were used for pillows, and cloaks doubled as blankets.

On the other hand, Bethlehem, five miles south of Jerusalem, was profoundly sacred to the Jewish people as the family home of King David and the place where he was anointed. But after the Matthean and Lukan infancy narratives, Bethlehem is never mentioned again anywhere in the New Testament, and Jesus is called "of Nazareth."

A primary proclamation about him in light of his Resurrection and new life was his reigning Messiahship or Lordship of the universe—an assertion beyond anything ever hoped for from the royal line of David. It is entirely possible, then, that the first Jewish Christians placed Jesus' birth in Bethlehem to affirm his status as the true Davidic King, especially since it is well attested that Jesus was descended from the line of David. Thus Jesus is proclaimed by faith as the representative personality of the new Israel.

As for the census decreed by the Emperor Augustus for "all the world"—a mandate that supposedly brought Mary and Joseph to Bethlehem in the first place—this was, according to Luke, "the first registration taken while Quirinius was governor of Syria." But in fact Augustus never registered the entire Empire (much less the whole world), and the Judean census, which would not have included natives of Nazareth in any case, was actually called by Quirinius when Jesus was about eight years old. In a small matter of fact, while attempting to establish a specific date in history, Luke has erred.

> Wise men from the East came to Jerusalem, asking, "Where is the child who has been born king of the Jews? For we observed his star at its rising and have come to pay him homage." When King Herod heard this, he was frightened . . . [The wise men] set out, and there, ahead of them, went the star . . . until it stopped over the place where the child was . . . On entering the house, they saw the child . . . and they knelt down and paid him homage . . . offering him gifts of gold, frankincense and myrrh . . . Now after they had left, an angel of the Lord appeared to Joseph in a dream and said, "Get up, take the child and his mother and flee into Egypt . . . for Herod is about to search for the child, to destroy him" . . . Herod sent and killed all the children in and around Bethlehem who were two years old or under.

These dramatic episodes are found only in Matthew: according to Luke, the circumstances of the birth are all peaceful and auspicious—shepherds come to worship the babe, angels sing, the child is named, and the parents travel peacefully to Jerusalem before returning to their own town, Nazareth. In Luke's account, there is no visit of wise men, no wondrous star, no flight to Egypt, and no slaughter of children by Herod, terrified of losing his primacy.

Every year at Christmastide, newspapers and magazines present imaginative articles by astronomers or Bible readers, attempting to find once and for all which star (or comet, or conjunction of planets) was followed by the wise men, came to rest over the birthplace of Jesus and was later recorded by Matthew. But to look for an astral phenomenon is to miss the point of the sublime literary and religious character of the text and of the deep truth it conveys.

First of all, there is no notice of such a dramatic astronomical spectacle in the records of the times. If indeed a star had attracted exotic characters from a distant land and miraculously marked the spot of Jesus' birth, why did this event have no impact on contemporary history, much less on anyone's later knowledge or impression about extraordinary circumstances at the time of Jesus' birth? Why had it no effect on his life or that of his family and friends? And if Herod the Great—the nominally Jewish King of Judea who was fiercely loyal to Rome—took such steps against Jesus, why did his son Antipas later have no knowledge of Jesus until late in Jesus' ministry? The answer lies in an appreciation that the star and the wise men are elements of religious truth, and their significance for faith is not found by arguing for their literal historicity.

At the time of Jesus, the motif of a symbolic star was linked by Jewish stories to the birth of Abraham. On the day of that patriarch's birth, according to a contemporary midrash (a meditation in light of rabbinic teaching), astrologers announced they had seen a star rise; just so, writes Matthew, the magi follow a star to Jesus—whom Matthew had announced in the first verse of his Gospel as "son of Abraham."

Furthermore, in the Hebrew Bible's Book of Numbers, the strange magician and astrologer Balaam spoke of the birth of King David and his victory over the enemies of Israel: "A star shall come out of Jacob, and a scepter shall rise out of Israel." And the tradition of Isaiah hoped for the restoration of Jerusalem's fortunes after the Babylonian Exile: "Arise, shine, for your light has come . . . Nations shall come to your light, and kings to the brightness of your dawn." The star, in other words, represents not only a kingly individual but also the nation whose hopes he will fulfill: "The wealth of nations [i.e., of the Gentiles] shall come to you . . . They shall bring gold and frankincense and shall proclaim the praise of the Lord."

Jesus fulfills all those hopes, Christians believed, and so his presence is signified by a rising star. With wondrously skillful use of traditional motifs in common Jewish currency, Matthew presents the faith of a community who believed Jesus to be the one whom all had awaited for centuries. In his new life after death, Jesus had fulfilled (indeed, surpassed) every expectation of ancient Israel. More to the point, after Easter, even the Gentiles—represented by the wise men—had come to adore. Jesus came for the Jews, proclaims Matthew in his first chapter, announcing the conception to Joseph after listing the Abrahamic genealogy; but, Matthew continues in his second chapter, Jesus is also for non-Jews—thus the point of "wise men from the East."

Matthew, writing from and for a Jewish Christian community, naturally turned to the rich traditions of Judaism. These were summarized by Flavius Josephus in his first-century history of the Jewish people, but they had long circulated and were already well known when Matthew's Gospel was composed (probably in the ninth decade of the first century A.D.). The stories concerned Moses' father, Amram, a sojourn in Egypt, the Pharoah's consultation with sages, a massacre of Hebrew boys and the escape of the infant Moses in the Egyptian wilderness. Taking as a starting point the Book of Exodus, in which the Egyptian Pharaoh threatens to kill Moses, Josephus's account documents a popular meditation on the holy destiny of Moses even from his conception, and on the apprehension he causes among the enemies of God:

> Amram's wife was with child, and he was in grievous perplexity . . . God appeared to him in his sleep, exhorting him not to despair of the future . . . "This child [God said] will escape those who are watching to destroy him . . . and he shall deliver the Hebrew race from their bondage in Egypt . . ." One of the sacred scribes—persons with considerable skill in accurately predicting the future—announced to the king that there would be born to the Israelites at that time one who would abase the sovereignty of the Egyptians and exalt the Israelites . . . Alarmed thereat, the king ordered that every male child born to the Israelites should be destroyed.

But Moses and his people were spared—thus the original Passover—and the fulfillment of God's promise was seen by the first Jewish Christians as the ultimate accomplishment of what was begun in the sojourn of their ancestors in Egypt, and their deliverance in the Exodus, many centuries earlier. Hence Jesus recapitulates the history of God's people in his entire life, death and destiny. Matthew has introduced the meditations on the significance of Jesus' life—culminating in the actual historical events of his ministry, death and Resurrection—with typically Jewish reflections of deep insight, in which Jesus is presented as the true Israel and the new Moses.

As for the family's precipitate journey to Egypt and their residing there for, it seems, two years—a period to which no reference is made anywhere else in the New Testament—this, too, is very likely Matthew's religious reflection, for it is incompatible with Luke's account of the peaceful, uneventful return from Bethlehem to Nazareth. More to the point, the slaughter of Jewish babies (a horrific act supposedly decreed at the time of Jesus' birth and impossible for Herod to hide, says Matthew) is not even alluded to in the writings of Josephus, who documents, usually with gleeful relish, the king's every reprehensible deed. Especially during the last years of his reign, Herod treated many people appallingly—it is all the more odd, therefore, that Josephus would have made not even the vaguest reference to Herod's atrocity against the children of Judea.

Instead, the religious background for Matthew's meditation is the Old Testament account of Pharoah's slaughter of children, Moses' in-the-nick-of-time escape and the Lord's subsequent oracle to Moses: "Go back to Egypt, for all those who were seeking your life are dead"—clearly fulfilled in Matthew's report of the order to Joseph, "Go back to the land of Israel, for those who were seeking the child's life are dead." Thus, as the family resettles in Nazareth of Galilee (not in Judea, for now Herod's son is ruling there), Matthew quietly ends his dramatic two-chapter prelude and begins the Gospel proper with the person and proclamation of John the Baptist.

While they were there, the time came for her to deliver her child. And she gave birth to her firstborn son and wrapped him in swaddling clothes and laid him in a manger, because there was no place for them in the inn. In that region, there were shepherds living in the fields, keeping watch over their flock by night. Then an angel of the Lord stood before them, and the glory of the Lord shone around them, and they were terrified. But the angel said to them, "Do not be afraid; for see—I am bringing you good news of great joy for all the people: to you is born this day in the city of David a Savior, who is the Messiah, the Lord. This will be a sign for you: you will find a child wrapped in swaddling clothes and lying in a manger." And suddenly there was with the angel a multitude of the heavenly host, praising God and saying, "Glory to God in the highest heaven, and on earth peace among those whom he favors!" . . . So the shepherds went and found Mary and Joseph and the child lying in the manger . . . And when [Mary and Joseph] had finished everything required by the law of the Lord [the circumcision and naming of Jesus and the purification ritual of Mary], they returned to Galilee to their own town of Nazareth. The child grew and became strong.

The Lukan account, of course, is the story read on Christmas night in churches around the world—a text of dazzling beauty yet touching simplicity. Yet how divergent it is from Matthew's colorful mini-drama of wealthy astrologers, royal mayhem and a dangerous excursion to Egypt. But Luke is no less rich in his complementary proclamation about the significance of Jesus, expressed with different emphases for another Christian community.

The firstborn son, we are told, is wrapped in swaddling clothes and placed in a manger. How many people have wondered about the exact meaning of those clothes—and does it not seem strange that a mother would blithely place her newborn in an animal's feed-box? What is going on here?

As a matter of fact, Saint Francis's meditation on a verse from Isaiah was on target: "the donkey knows the manger of its master." For Luke, shepherds (not wise or rich men) are sent to find the Lord, who is the source of joy for "all the people." Contrary to the complaint of the prophet Jeremiah, who asked God why He seemed to have abandoned His people "like an alien, like a traveler who lodges in an inn," now the Lord and Savior of Israel does *not* stay in lodgings, does *not* stay in an inn, but comes as the nourisher and food of His people (in a manger) and dwells at last fully among them. The swaddling bands do not indicate abject poverty, but are (as Luke says) a "sign"—and they refer directly to Solomon, the wealthiest of Judah's kings: "I was nursed with care in swaddling bands, for no king has any other way to begin at birth."

———

And so Jesus, born in the royal city of David, is not found in an inn, like a transient alien, but in a manger—as the very sustenance of his people; and here Jesus is wrapped in the raiment of the true king.

The entire magnificent passage tells us, therefore, much more than *what happened:* Luke is not at all interested in the ordinary circumstances of labor and of birth. Rather, he tells us the *meaning* of this birth—God has a new relationship with His people. Finding the child in these circumstances leads the shepherds not to mourn for a poor traveling family forced into a stable; rather, they proclaim the glory of God, for He reveals Himself as a sustaining king in the life, death and Resurrection of the Jesus introduced by this overture to the Gospel.

———

And who are these people to whom the first announcement of the birth is made? Shepherds were not thought of in Judaism as sweet, sentimental pastoral figures, gently leading their flocks. Quite the contrary: they were the most common example of unscrupulous embezzlers, for they routinely led their sheep to others' lands, stole from neighbors and returned at night with more animals than they had in the morning. Like tax collectors of that time, they got rich by dishonesty. "For herdsmen and tax collectors, repentance is hard" ran a common Jewish saying of the time. More important still, the word "shepherd" became virtually a synonym for "sinner," and anyone engaged in herding flocks was denied civil rights and could be ostracized and even dragged into court. Yet it is these men who are the first to learn about the birth of a Savior: outcasts and sinners are welcomed, even the first to be invited into the presence of the Lord. And—shockingly, it must have seemed to the first hearers—they respond with simple piety and adoration.

Finally, the Lukan birth account has given us one of the most famous lines of Scripture, the angelic hymn—which has unfortunately been so long subjected to mistranslating, either as "Peace on earth, good will to men" or "Peace on earth to men of good will." But Luke's verse, based on a preexisting Hebrew and Coptic literary source, is properly rendered as "Peace on earth be to men who follow God's good will." Centuries later, precisely the same sentiment was expressed by Dante: *E'n la sua volontade è nostra pace*—"In His will is our peace." The divine will is not a restriction imposed on us, a destiny from which we cannot escape: it is a loving reality far more benevolent, and far more effective on our behalf, than our own will could ever effect.

The sense of the joy surrounding the entrance of God's son into the world is, then, related to the notion that peace comes to those who seek the compassionate presence of God, Who approaches us only to embrace and to forgive, to bestow meaning and to save. That is what, of all people, the sinner-shepherds hear and understand, for at once they rush to worship, as so many Gentiles and sinners came to know Jesus in his risen life. The herdsmen are Luke's equivalent of the Matthean astrologers—those outside Judaism by virtue of nationhood or sin. For them as for the devout Jews represented by Mary and Joseph, there is indeed "good news of great joy for *all* the people."

That exultation is directly connected to the name given by Joseph and Mary to their infant eight days later at the traditional Jewish rite of circumcision. By way of the Greek *Iēsous*, "Jesus" derives from a shortened form of the Hebrew name Joshua (Yehosua), who was the successor of Moses; the name means "Yahweh is salvation," or "God saves."

After the return of the Jewish people from exile in Babylon in the sixth century B.C., Jesus became a common name—for Yahweh had indeed, they believed, again saved His people from extinction. It remained popular until the second century A.D., when the quickly growing Christian faith led the Jews to abandon it and revert to the original longer form, Joshua.

But in the first century A.D., the name was so common that a description of origin was normally added in order to distinguish, for example, "Jesus of Nazareth" from the many who had the same given name. As early as the 50s A.D. (within twenty years of Jesus' death), Paul included in his letters many references to the widely known title "Christ" to designate Jesus. This word is a description: the Greek *Christos* translates the Hebrew word for Messiah, God's "anointed one" for whom all Israel awaited.

By the end of the first century, "Christ" had become so widespread that it was virtually a second name. Jesus, the one who saves, is proclaimed the Christ, God's anointed: such was the settled faith of those who had come to know him in his risen life. To this day, "Jesus Christ" is the form by which he is known—the label for this man whom the process of history may reject but whom it cannot ignore. "Jesus Christ," if nothing else, has entered all Western languages as, at least, a common exclamation of shock or anger, a universally recognized pair of cuss words. But to those who consider him not a dusty figure of the past but the one who is truly alive, the name is, as Bernard of Clairvaux said in the twelfth century, "a shout of joy and music to the ear."

————

The accounts of the birth of Jesus that we read in Matthew and Luke were created by them as transitions as well as curtain-raisers—or, to continue the literary-theatrical metaphor, they are like intermezzi linking the hopes of the Old Testament to the ministry of Jesus in the New. Hence they used Old Testament narratives and allusions to clarify the meaning of the Jesus event. Matthew presents Joseph (about whom virtually nothing is known from the Bible) as the father of Jesus—the spiritual heir of his namesake Joseph, the great patriarch of the Old

Testament. In dreams, God speaks to Joseph about the birth and destiny of Jesus and leads him to Egypt in order to save the child and his mother; just so, the patriarch Joseph had been (thus the book of Genesis) "the dreamer" who went down to Egypt, where he saved his people from famine. Can it be accidental that Jesus' father Joseph is portrayed as the major New Testament figure to hear revelations in dreams—and is the only person to go to Egypt?

Later, to exterminate the children of Israel, the wicked pharaoh slaughtered male infants; Moses, however, escaped and led his people from bondage in Egypt. Just so in Matthew: the wicked Herod kills Hebrew babies, but the infant Jesus, the new Moses at the head of a new Israel, escapes and returns from Egypt to save his people. During Moses' journey to the promised land, Balaam, the magus from the East, proclaimed that the star of a Davidic king would rise in Israel. Jesus is indeed that saving king, announces the faith of the community addressed by Matthew: hence the conversion of foreigners, represented by Matthew's magi from the East who see the rising star of the true king. Revealed in secret to Joseph, Jesus is made known through the magi; Christ's identity, hidden and invisible, is to be proclaimed far and wide through the life of faith.

With Luke it is much the same. The Old Testament parents, Abraham and Sarah, are portrayed indirectly, in the figures of Zechariah and Elizabeth, parents of John the Baptist: the angelic announcement that infertility will be reversed; the querulous doubt; the ultimate rejoicing of the mother—Luke brilliantly re-creates the old in a revised version. As he was writing, it was clear that only through faith in what Jesus *has already become* by virtue of his ministry, death and Resurrection can the former dispensation of the Hebrew covenant be shown as preparation for the new.

And the ancient Christian hymns of praise put on the lips of Mary, of Zechariah and of Simeon (the temple prophet), are taken almost line for line from Old Testament verses in the psalms or the prophets. As Hannah brought her son Samuel to present him to the Lord and he was received by the aged Eli, for example, so Mary brings the infant Jesus to the temple, where he is received by the aged Simeon. Revealed in secret to Mary, Jesus is made known through the proclamation of the shepherds; once again, Christ's identity, hidden and invisible, is to be proclaimed far and wide through the life of faith.

How different all this is from the typical greeting-card idea of Christmas, with a perpetually smiling infant so tender and mild, sleeping in heavenly peace. I do not mean to be churlish or snide about our loveliest traditions in the West—it would be a shame even to try to do away with the humble Franciscan crib—but the exaggerated, bucolic sweetness of the seasonal images unfortunately masks the strong message of the Gospels. A romantic emphasis on treasures offered to the babe in the manger has so long drenched a rank commercialism that the deeper, richer significance of Matthew and Luke has been all but drowned.

These Gospels state that God has embraced humanity and entered into its suffering with unimaginable love. His Christ is the one who arrives not in royal purple but in silence and simplicity, far from the cheers that attend Augustus and Herod. A king he surely is—hence the swaddling bands and the treasures that are his due—but a new sort of king who makes no claim to worldly authority. In infancy as during his life on earth (and since), he arouses antipathy and even, by his person and message, provokes outright hostility from those who covet earthly supremacy. He comes to the shepherds, to the dissolute, to impolite society—thus, from the start, identifying himself with outcasts, the poor and the humble.

This is the Jesus whom Luke proclaims throughout his Gospel and announces in the first chapters. Instead of bestowing the great titles (King, Lord, Son of God) invented for earthly potentates, they are ascribed by Matthew and Luke to this humble child who, the authors knew, was later known to be God's ultimate spokesman, the healer, the one who utterly transforms human expectations and human destiny. To reduce the Christmas message to a comforting story of a baby, therefore, is to rob the Bible narratives of their strength and of their revolutionary character. The paradox of it all is precisely the message: real power lies not where the world either values or sees it.

In the event we celebrate each Christmas, it is indeed a historical moment that is honored—but no historical account, even if we had the eyewitness details, could do justice to an event that can only be perceived through faith. In Jesus' entrance into history, God has once and for all broken the clouds of obscurity and entered concretely into history. The self-disclosure of God, which began in creation, continued through the call of the patriarchs, accompanied the wandering of the people and was heard in the cries of the prophets and the longing of the psalmists—that revelation reached its zenith in the enfleshment of God in human nature.

And herein lies the crucial distinction between the Judaeo-Christian tradition and the other great religions of the world. Only in the continuum that reaches its fulfillment in Jesus is the relationship between God and man a *downward* motion. This is of course patently metaphoric language, but by it is indicated something quite real, quite concrete: that God enters definitively into the sphere of the human—that He takes seriously the reality of what He has made. God acts within history, not apart from it in splendid, transcendent isolation. He takes human suffering seriously, too.

And in Jesus of Nazareth God shows a human face. With tenderness that is literally unimaginable, He shines on the world an infinite compassion. Despite all the greed, political chaos, social dissension, great deceptions and local hostilities that characterized life then and continue to infect it now, mercy arrives like the stillness of night.

Nor is our suffering, our selfishness, our perversity—all of it emblematic of our need of God—trivialized by Him. God comes in silence, shrouded in darkness, to a world sunk in enmities whose sources it scarcely remembers. He claims us for His own and promises a final triumph—which, the Gospels announce and faith proclaims, has already been achieved and awaits only our acceptance.

The created order, according to Christianity, is not an illusion, not a vague representation of another perfect world, nor a dream that will one day vanish into oblivion when a sleeping deity awakens. No, it is a matter of something far more specific. God is the ground and basis of all reality—one might say that He is the ultimately *real* reality, alive and dynamic in everything that is. God provides the world and everything and everyone in it with a reference point, a goal and a meaning. He does not accompany the world alongside it, much less "above" it: from creation to the present, God acts *within* history, and within the most intimate points of our lives and activities.

That is the meaning of the incarnation, the enfleshment of God in the human dimension. "From Him we come," wrote the medieval English mystic Julian of Norwich, "in Him we are enfolded, to Him we return." That is the complete cycle: creation, incarnation, salvation. God makes, He takes what He has made for His own, He loves what He has made and saves it forever. That is gospel: good news.

Christmas is not, then, a time when we merely offer and receive material gifts: it is a season to acknowledge that God makes *Himself* His gift to us—and not just once but each day, each moment of always, and especially when our inner life grows old and jaded and seems to die. Whenever we turn to this reality, we know the good news to be true: we are forever befriended.

———

Two words of Luke's nativity account (with no parallel in Matthew's) are often ignored, but they are full of meaning. When the shepherds learn of the birth of Jesus, they are keeping watch over their flocks "by night."

The background for this small detail is the ancient Hebrew experience of God's saving act in their history. On the first Passover night, when God acted to save His people from destruction by liberating them from Egyptian slavery, He sent His omnipotent, salvific word—the "agent" of the divine judgment: "While gentle silence enveloped all things," we read in the Wisdom of Solomon, "and night in its swift course was now half gone, your all-powerful word leaped down from heaven, from the royal throne."

Jesus' birth at night thus marks the moment of God's ultimate "leap" from obscurity to full disclosure. And his birth, life and death are (in the words of Ignatius of Antioch, writing at the end of the first century) "resounding mysteries, wrought in the silence of God." A "mystery," it is worth pointing out, is not something infinitely unknowable or forever incomprehensible—it is, quite the contrary, something always to be further grasped, more deeply known. To put it another way, a "mystery of God" is something of the divine that knows and grasps you and me, that invites us into the life of God.

Good old Ignatius of Antioch: he knew something of the "silence of God," which speaks more loudly that any human speech or music or noise. Perhaps he had in mind the words of the New Testament's Letter to the Colossians, which referred to "the mystery that has been hidden throughout the ages and generations but has now been revealed" to those who make themselves accessible to God's whisper—those who heed God in silence. This deserves some reflection, for the moments when God acts in history on our behalf, and the moments in which we reach out to Him, seem to occur mostly in silence.

Human discourse and writing about God and the things of God— yes, even the best of it, the Scriptures held sacred by Jews and Christians—are always inexact analogues, precisely because they are expressions limited by the specifics of culture. However necessary as a guide for faith, the Bible itself represents the attempts of human beings to express what is finally inexpressible: the identity, the nature, the *meaning* of God for the world. Behind the words are experiences that (faith insists) were manifestations of God within history. But the experiences occurred, were understood and were perceived as meaningful in silence—just as their meaning is plumbed by us in silence today.

In every case, human discourse is less clear and less creative than the silence of God. "While gentle silence enveloped all things," God made Himself known. And so He continues to do. "The Lord is in His holy temple," announced the prophet Habakkuk. "Let all the earth keep silence before Him."

This silence is not nothingness, it is not denial. God alone, who is our absolute future, remains (in the words of Karl Rahner) "the incomprehensible mystery to be worshipped in silence." Our fulfillment in His eternity remains, too, "a mystery which we have to worship in silence by moving beyond all images into the ineffable"—into that of which we cannot speak. Many earnest people throughout history have found a deep security and comfort in this, for we can say only what God is *not*, since He is beyond all human conceptions of Him. Hence, by rejecting false images, we can say that God is not a stern accuser, not a rich uncle, not a demanding accountant, not a passive spectator.

But it is possible to say something rather than only to deny the negatives—as long as we understand that our language is always metaphoric. It is at least possible to say that God approaches us not when we are babbling away about Him, but when we force ourselves to remain still: when we not only refrain from speech, glances, gestures and any form of communication, but when we try to let thoughts become quiet and emotions calm.

Deep interior silence is listening, heedful attentiveness, and it is the condition of prayer; it does not mean attending nothing, but becoming aware of the enveloping Presence that makes breath and life possible. This kind of quiet attention is not only essential for a discovery of who we are, what we are thinking, where we are going with our lives. It is also an absolute requirement if we are to allow God to be God for us, for in His presence we are all of us passive, all of us receivers. In His presence, we experience our contingency, our total dependence; that, too, is part of the good news, for we know that we simply cannot heal all our wounds, that for all our ideals and all our goals, we cannot provide ultimate meaning for our life, we can only recognize it. The source of it is elsewhere. "Be still, and know that I am God," the psalmist hears.

Silence makes thought and feeling possible, and thought and feeling give birth to articulation. Relationships—both revelations of relationships and insights into them—occur in silence; speech is the response to them. Hence we do not *create* with language: we belong to it and are limited by it, even in a way subordinated to it. It is in silence that we know we are beheld, in silence that we know how to respond. Writing or speech is our response to the prior reality established and discovered only in silence.

At the end of the twentieth century, it seems that we have made the noisiest, loudest society in the history of the world—and the most confused. An orgy of noises robs us of portions of our very being: announcers shout; music, movies and plays are overamplified; traffic becomes noisier each year; advertisements become more intrusive in the media. The effect of exaggerated sound and constant noise on the central nervous system of humans and animals is only just beginning to be felt: it seems to be a kind of madness, a dislocation of ourselves from ourselves.

Related to this is the speed and volume of communication and of travel, all of which is thought necessary simply because it is possible. Today we have the information superhighway, the communications explosion, the Internet, the ubiquitous probing of the media—asking questions, telling us things to frighten us or things to shock us or things to make us envious. We have constant commentary on just about everything, endless chatter and that modern artifact, the "talk show"—a curiosity in itself, for now "talk" has become a matter for "show." Yet despite the incessant noise, as numbing as background music in stores and elevators, there is very little depth and less reality in relations: for all the talk, there is precious little communication.

The creative life of the artist, like the inner life of everyone, depends on silent intuition and reflection before anything can be put into words or images, sounds or lines. In this regard, we can see that silence is not the *absence* of something, it is the most powerful *event,* the precondition for reality. "While gentle silence enveloped all things, your all-powerful word leaped from heaven." By putting distance between us and the time and space that usually control us, we enter into a creative moment of silence that makes effective our relationship with God. Saint Augustine was quite right: *Verbo crescente, verba deficiunt*—When the Word appears, words fail.

This is, of course, no new knowledge. In the Old Testament, the prophet Elijah is told to go onto the mountain. "Now there was a great wind . . . but the Lord was not in the wind; and after the wind an earthquake, but the Lord was not in the earthquake; and after the earthquake a fire, but the Lord was not in the fire; and after the fire, a sound of sheer silence."

And with that, Elijah—literally stricken with awe—wraps his mantle about his face, aware that he is, in the sound of sheer silence, in the presence of God.

CHAPTER TWO

UNEXPECTED CHILDREN:
THE MARVELOUS CONCEPTION
OF JESUS

For all its differences, the world into which Jesus was born was in
some ways remarkably like our own: fragmented, angry and full
of international and domestic suspicions. It was also, like ours,
subject to political and religious institutions that many regarded as jaded,
incompetent, irrelevant or downright hypocritical when it came to the
human needs they were meant to serve.

From 37 B.C., and with Rome's vigilant tolerance, the Jewish state of
Judea was ruled by Herod the Great, the grandfather of Antipas. Imposing
and athletic, loyal to Rome and an advocate of Gentile culture, Herod
was brutally intolerant of any opposition and eliminated anyone who
questioned his authority. Cunning, cruel, insatiably ambitious and at
the end mentally unstable, he eventually counted ten wives and fourteen
children; some of these he executed out of mere caprice or petulance.

Herod also courted Rome's approval—and that of the Jewish
priests—by a massive program of public works, including a complete
rebuilding of the Jerusalem temple, a magnificent thirty-five-acre project
begun in 19 B.C. and not completed until more than thirty years after
the death of Jesus. Seven years later, in A.D. 70, Roman forces leveled
it during the futile Jewish revolt.

Though he was their king, Herod really despised the Jews: he had no
interest in the Hebrew portion of his ancestry (which was only partially
Jewish in any case), and nothing in his conduct qualified him as one
who identified with the situation of Judaism. In addition to paying for
the temple, heavy taxes financed splendid new cities and massive for-

tresses throughout Palestine, and theaters, hippodromes and spas pro-liferated under Herod's regime. Meanwhile, the poor languished, ignored and powerless.

After ordering the deaths of several relatives, friends, enemies and a number of leading citizens during his final illness—so that his funeral would be accompanied by widespread public grief—Herod died, prob-ably in early spring of the year 4 B.C., when Jesus was, contrary to popular notions, about two years old. The words "probably" and "about" occur often when we discuss ancient history, but this is not surprising. Almost nothing can be known about the birth and early years of almost every historical figure in the ancient world, and the birth dates of the last Roman emperors cannot be indisputably fixed by historians. We can even study the sixteenth century and have a lack of certitude: of Sir Walter Ralegh's youth, virtually nothing is known—the records of his life began when he was about thirty (about the year 1583).

Regarding Jesus, the most likely date of his birth was sometime in 7 or 6 B.C., a fact that often causes the wrinkling of brows: how could Jesus be born several years before he was born?

Roman historiographers traditionally dated events from the founding of the capital city, and this calendar system was in general use until A.D. 533, when the scholar Dionysius Exiguus reckoned that the 754th year after Rome's establishment corresponded to the year of Jesus' birth. But it later became clear that Dionysius miscalculated: Herod actually died 750 years after the founding of Rome, or in the year we now call 4 B.C. The New Testament is quite clear that Jesus was born toward the end of Herod's reign, which was a time of civil and religious unrest in Pal-estine. In about the year 7 or 6 B.C., then, a young woman of twelve or thirteen conceived a son. Her Hebrew name was Miryam or Marah—Maria in Greek and Latin, Mary in English.

She lived in Nazareth, where she was engaged to a man whose name was Yosep, or Joseph. "Engaged" can be a misleading word in this case, for in Judaism at that time it meant "married." The Jewish engagement or betrothal ceremony, arranged by the couple's parents, usually took place when a girl was twelve, but it often occurred earlier; most husbands were a year or two older than the bride. At that time, a contract was signed before witnesses, signifying that a true marriage had taken place and that a man had legally acquired a woman as his property. Thus began the process of the legal conveyance of a girl from her father's jurisdiction to her husband's—a formality that lasted a year. Although the couple continued, during that year, to live apart with their own parents, the new husband had virtually complete rights over his wife. Should the man die, she would be considered his widow; she could be rejected by him through a writ of divorce; and if unfaithful, she could be executed for adultery.

One of the many elements in Jewish life that varied according to geography was the issue of sexual relations after the betrothal. In certain parts of Judea, a betrothed couple could consummate the relationship during this year. But in Galilee, the virginity of the bride was customarily preserved until her formal entry into her husband's home. A year after the betrothal, another ceremony was held for the typical Jewish couple, after which the girl was fully transferred from her father's power to her husband's. The groom then took the bride home, and he assumed full financial and legal support for her.

In return for support, a Jewish wife became completely servile: she was expected to obey without question and to address her husband as *rab*, or "master." She was also required to fulfill all household duties, to submit to her husband's every whim and demand, to bear and nurse his children, to turn over to him anything she found, to bathe him and to tolerate whatever concubines he might like to have cohabiting with them. She had no right to her own possessions, and she could not initiate a divorce unless her husband demanded something that caused public humiliation.

———

Within this social structure stood the young couple of whose history we know almost nothing. But Jesus' followers wanted to know more of his origins. Without anything like our modern interest in a carefully produced scientific biography, they came instead to know him through religious reflection and through, as they believed, his continuing presence among them. The *meaning* of Jesus could be discovered, even in the absence of documents. And some of that meaning is given by the strange, haunting and complex story of the conception and birth of Jesus of Nazareth.

The Gospels attributed to Matthew and Luke tell their stories of the origins of Jesus in highly reflective, carefully composed imitation of other traditions, some biblical, some not. In Matthew, the beginning of Jesus is modeled on the religious traditions about the birth of Moses and the history of Israel; in Luke, the history of Jesus conforms to that of the teacher John the Baptist—of whom Jesus later became a disciple.

In a detailed, meticulously crafted genealogy, Matthew traces the ancestry of Jesus—"the Messiah, the son of David"—by beginning with the father of the Jewish people, Abraham, and then constructing three groups of fourteen names each, probably because fourteen is the sum of the numerical value of the three letters in the name David in Hebrew (DWD) until Matthew comes to Joseph. (As we shall see, Matthew apparently does not believe that Joseph was the biological father of Jesus, but this genealogy enables him to establish that Joseph was the *legal* and therefore proper father of Jesus.)

Luke, on the other hand, takes a somewhat different ancestral route from the point of King David backward, finally editing his list so that he arrives at Adam, the "son of God"—and this list he places, not coincidentally, immediately after the concluding revelation at the baptism of Jesus: "You are my Son, the beloved." For Luke, then, Jesus' kinship is thus not only with the Chosen People, but with the entire human race—with all of God's sons. The two genealogies present serious problems only if we require them to be like modern historical documents. But this was not the way of ancient writers, who set down the interpreted *significance* of a person's life and history, and for whom an epic past was the proper prelude to a great present.

In the first chapters of Matthew and Luke, as in the entirety of the four Gospels, the evangelists reflected on faith in the absolute uniqueness of the person of Jesus, who is described as God's ultimate self-disclosure. In him, according to the narratives of the infancy, God has forever entered and embraced the world. In this regard, Christian faith—rooted in God's action in history—does not in fact worship at the altar of the past, nor is faith dependent on this or that historical event. On the contrary, faith is always looking to what God is doing *in the present.*

As part of that process of discovery, Christians have always turned to the normative documents of the New Testament, for they constitute a clear guide to the earliest foundational faith. Their language, stretched and strained to express experiences unprecedented in human history, tried to exploit the whole range of metaphor. In this case, the allusive hints and guesses point to the unfathomable mystery of God and His definitive entrance into history.

But despite all the conundrums about crucial matters of background, and despite all the differences in the accounts of Matthew and Luke, they agree on one issue: during the interim time between the two stages of their marriage, Mary and Joseph are separately informed by an angel or angels that, although still physically a virgin, she is pregnant. Matthew's account tells this obliquely, by way of an announcement to Joseph in a dream: "the child conceived in her is from the Holy Spirit." Thus relieved of presuming her infidelity when he finds her pregnant (Matthew continues), Joseph subsequently marries Mary, "but had no marital relations with her until she had borne a son; and he named him Jesus."

Luke has different details of this early history, beginning with a sublime meditation in which he connects the origin of Jesus to that of John the Baptist; in fact, there is a carefully elaborated series of parallel proclamations and events in the announcement of the conception of the two in Luke. The angel Gabriel, he writes, visits John's father, an elderly member of the priestly class named Zechariah. Gabriel proclaims that the priest and his wife will have a child, but this Zechariah doubts because of his wife's sterility and the couple's advanced age. Temporarily struck mute until the promised child is born, Zechariah soon learns that his wife, Elizabeth, is indeed pregnant with this unexpected child, who grows up to be John the Baptist.

Sophisticated writer that he is, Luke constructs the two accounts of John and Jesus in terms of the Old Testament births of Ishmael (son of Abraham and Sarah), of Isaac (brother of Ishmael) and of Samson. What faith claims of John and presently even more wonderfully of Jesus is described according to the imagery and literary forms used by the Old Testament to express the faith of Israel; hence the infancy narratives provide a transition from the past to the present. Jesus is revealed to be at his conception what he was later revealed to be at his Resurrection— the Son of the Most High, the anointed Messiah whose name indicates his divine destiny.

Indeed, the story of the conception of Jesus is presented as even more astonishing.

"You will conceive in your womb," the angel Gabriel tells Mary, "and bear a son, and you will name him Jesus."

"How can this be," counters Mary, "since I am a virgin?"

The answer is immediate: "The Holy Spirit will come upon you and the power of the Most High will overshadow you . . ."

Mary replies humbly that she is the Lord's servant, ready to accept His word. The dialogue concluded, Gabriel departs—and is never again mentioned in the New Testament.

Mary soon goes to visit Elizabeth, whom Luke describes vaguely as her "kinswoman." Luke's point in creating the lovely scene of meeting between the two pregnant women becomes clear in light of a later development: by bringing John the Baptist within the sphere of Jesus' presence even in utero, the author attempts to rectify the late-first-century rivalry between their disciples. Once again, the metaphor of the language is striking, for the relationship between John and Jesus was not one of literal kinship but of spiritual brotherhood. (Nowhere else in the New Testament is there awareness of any such link between the families; in fact, John the Baptist insists, when he sees Jesus in adulthood, "I did not know him!")

The infancy narratives are notable, too, for the presence of angels—a nameless creature in Matthew, but specified as Gabriel in Luke. Like other spiritual beings in the Hebrew and Christian scriptures, Gabriel (who speaks in the tone of a Roman herald) is the dramatic representation of divine activity, a sign of God's personalized presence among His people. Bible texts dealing with an angel or angels are impressive precisely because they represent something much more than fantastic winged figures, and something much more potent than could be conveyed by philosophic discourse.

Angels are part of Semitic iconography, that kind of pictorial language that shatters the expected and the ordinary. Angels are a dramatic way of describing the unimaginable: the revelation of God to humanity. Such revelations occur in silence, stillness and invisibility; they may be expressed only through the kind of creative metaphors first established by the ancient Hebrew Scriptures and now brilliantly taken up by Matthew and Luke.

In this regard, the current obsession with angels may be one of the surest signs of the decadence of authentic religion, especially in American life. The cause is not helped by the kind of synthetic piety that offers angels as kindly policemen, wise uncles or earnest Boy or Girl Scouts in movie and television dramas. Note how the stories of angelic visitations in popular culture have virtually nothing to do with the things of God. For Hollywood, angels are not much different from friendly, cuddly aliens.

Biblical writers were after something richer, and "angel of the Lord" is a memorably metaphoric way of explicating divine revelation. The annunciation scenes to Zechariah and to Mary emphasize faith not in magic or side show events, but rather in the divine initiative in bringing John and Jesus into the world; the extraordinary circumstances of the conceptions proclaim God's direct intervention in history. "Nothing shall be impossible with God" is the message to Mary—just as, generations before, in the Book of Genesis, God overturned every expectation when the wife of the patriarch Abraham conceived in her advanced age: "Is anything too wonderful for the Lord? Sarah shall have a son."

———

We may indeed readily admit that nothing is impossible with God, Who is infinitely free to order reality according to His plan. Still, Matthew and Luke describe what is, for some people, one of the most difficult elements in the Christian proclamation: the assertion that Jesus was unnaturally conceived in the womb of his mother without the normal participation of a father. Only these two of the four Gospels posit a virginal conception of Jesus, without any help from Joseph. (This *virginal conception,* incidentally, has nothing at all to do with the Immaculate Conception—the later idea about the unique, sinless role of Mary, whom pious reflection subsequently believed to have been especially favored by grace from the moment of *her* conception. There is, contrary to what several generations have assumed, no biblical basis for belief in this doctrine.) Besides the matter of the Resurrection of Jesus, no issue so divides Christian groups—and Christians as a lot from others—as the literal understanding of the virginal conception of Jesus.

What, indeed, does this strange assertion *mean*—about Jesus, first of all, and then for Christians? Do we place our trust in an oddity of biology, a quirk of gynecology? What is the *result* of clinging to this idea? Is it possible that the institutional Church has at times made more of this teaching than do Matthew and Luke?

First, we have to investigate why a literal understanding of the virginal conception ought to be questioned at all. The most obvious answer is that when anyone reads carefully and seriously, there are almost insurmountable difficulties in adhering to such a reading of the opening chapters of Matthew and Luke.

During his ministry, as we shall see, Jesus did not speak of himself as the Messiah sent by God—this was an inadequate, political title to express his developing consciousness. Neither did he call himself the Son of God, for that, too, could be misunderstood by his hearers. This does not mean that, in light of his Resurrection and the developed post-Easter faith of Christians, Jesus was not finally understood to *be* God's anointed and God's Son in an unprecedented way in the core and center of his being. But Jesus did not, it seems, make any such claim of Messiahship or divine Sonship during his lifetime: he had to grapple with the limitations of his language (probably Aramaic) as well as with his own growing understanding of who he was and what the nature of his relationship to God was. If Christians deny these limitations as starting points, they deny a basic confession of their faith: that Jesus was a fully human being, "tested as we are, yet without sin." His existence as God's ultimate manifestation in history does not cancel his humanity.

The hesitation and silence of Jesus is essential to bear in mind, for it relates to the problem of how to understand the story of the virginal conception and of the birth of Jesus. Later Christian, and especially Roman Catholic, teaching has placed a great deal of emphasis on the circumstances of the betrothal and marriage of this couple, on the physical virginity of Mary, on the manner of the child Jesus' conception, and even on his parents' subsequent abstention from sexual activity after the child's arrival (which the New Testament, rightly, does not address). The rest of the Bible is, on the whole, surprisingly reticent. Only the Gospels attributed to writers called Matthew and Luke mention Jesus' conception at all, and while they certainly appear to take for granted the virginal conception of Jesus, they are more concerned with offering meditations on his significance for the present. Otherwise, the opening chapters of Matthew and Luke vary greatly, in their content and style, from every other kind of New Testament text.

According to Matthew 1 and 2, as we have seen, Mary and Joseph live in their home at Bethlehem. The visit of the magi from the East leads Herod to fear that Jesus is a threat to his primacy, and so he slaughters children two years old or under—an atrocity that precipitates the flight of Mary, Joseph and Jesus to safety in Egypt until Herod's death. The family then relocates to Nazareth. According to Luke 1 and 2, Mary and Joseph live in Nazareth and go to Bethlehem to register in a census. They then return peacefully from Bethlehem after a side trip to Jerusalem; there are no magi, no star, no slaughter, no flight into Egypt.

Except for the virginal conception, then, the material in Matthew 1 and 2, which focuses on Joseph, is entirely different from the material in Luke 1 and 2, which focuses on Mary. If we read the chapters as literally historical, therefore, we are left with the absurd impression that Mary and Joseph never got their stories straight, nor did they speak to each other about their very different experiences.

None of these preliminary narratives were known by other New Testament writers—not to Paul, who never mentions the conception and birth of Christ in his letters; nor to the Gospels according to Mark or John, the other evangelists; nor to those who said and sang the earliest creeds and hymns, fragments of which survive in the speeches of the Acts of the Apostles (also written by Luke) and in the New Testament letters.

Nor does anything in these writings have the slightest influence on what occurs in subsequent chapters. The miraculous virginal conception and the confusion and disturbance caused by the birth of Jesus are unknown to everyone in the accounts of Jesus' ministry—nor, indeed, have these events affected Jesus' own understanding of his nature and mission.

The silence of the biblical witness on this matter (except for the brief mention in Matthew and Luke) suggests either that this "fact" was not known and admitted in the first-century Church or that it was not regarded as essential for a profession of faith in Christ. In any case, it would be difficult to hold that belief in Jesus necessarily includes an affirmation of the literalness of his virginal conception and birth.

Furthermore, if we are going to retain a literal understanding of these stories—instead of seeking what their *meaning* is—then we must ask some hard questions.

Is it credible that so important a matter as the fact of the virginal conception (a) could have been unknown to so many or (b) would have been omitted in proclaiming Jesus' uniqueness in the world? In addition, how would it have been possible for Matthew and Luke (late-first-century evangelists writing in Greek outside of Palestine) to know such intimate details about the life of Mary and Joseph? And why is nothing in these early chapters ever mentioned by them again? Nowhere else in the same documents—when it would have been so helpful to their cause—do we read of a virginal conception, a birth at Bethlehem, a visit by Gentile astrologers, a slaughter of neighboring male children, a sojourn in Egypt. No one who meets or joins himself to Jesus seems to know anything about his special origins.

———

The problem is immediately evident: Is it reasonable that the mother of Jesus, at least, would not have told him of the dramatic circumstances of his conception and birth? And would not such knowledge have put him from the start on the road to a very different and lofty self-understanding? The man who lines up with others before John the Baptist at the Jordan to acknowledge his membership in a sinful people (to take just one instance) is not a man aware that he is much different from every other human being in history.

If such unique origins had been clarified for him from the start, how is it that he, his family and his followers never expressed any remote knowledge of his special nature during his ministry? How does Mary dare, then, in light of what was told to her at the annunciation, to scold her son when he stays behind in the Jerusalem temple at the age of twelve? "Child, why have you treated us like this?" she asks, in the reproachful tone of a good Jewish mother. "Look, your father and I have been searching for you in great anxiety!" When the boy Jesus replies that it is logical for him to be found in his Father's house, his parents "did not understand what he said to them."

Later, we are told that Mary and the siblings of Jesus come "to restrain him, for people were saying, 'He has gone out of his mind' . . . and not even his brothers believed in him." Why did they not believe, if indeed the circumstances of his entry into the world were so remarkable? Would Jesus' family have been in the dark, or would they not have told Jesus of his profound difference from other men? Very little in the rest of

Matthew and Luke (and everything in Mark and John) is difficult to read if the annunciation and conception scenes—composed in so radically different a style from the rest of the Gospels—are read as literal family history or modern news reporting.

The chapters are far richer if we read them as artistic, highly refined, dramatically structured and inspired religious meditations—declarations of Easter faith, lovingly and strategically placed at the head of the two Gospels to announce just who Jesus is, in opposition to those who understand very little of him, as the subsequent story of his ministry makes painfully clear.

He came to his hometown, we read of Jesus during his public life (which perhaps spanned from early A.D. 28 to the spring of A.D. 30), and people were astounded and said, "Where did this man get this wisdom and these deeds of power? Is not this the carpenter's son? Is not his mother called Mary? And are not his brothers James and Joseph and Simon and Judas? And are not all his sisters with us? Where, then, did this man get all this?" Notice that Jesus is "the carpenter's son" according to the speakers, and (more interesting still) later Luke calls Joseph and Mary "his parents."

To go further, though at the risk of indelicacy: How did anyone know about the virginal conception—about how and what actually happened—much less about the subsequent intimate life of Mary and Joseph, on which the New Testament has nothing to say, but which, nonetheless, has obsessed so many people in centuries since? Joseph, of whom almost nothing is known but his name and occupation, is mentioned in three Gospels only as the father of Jesus; since he never figures in the public life of Jesus, it is not unreasonable to suppose that he died before that began. This does not, however, justify a presumption that Joseph was an old man at the time of death, as later pious art is accustomed to depicting him, presumably to imply that he was more of a father to Mary than a husband. The image of an old man married to a young woman was obviously meant to imply a nonsexual union.

To put the matter briefly: Why do Jesus, his family and his followers never say of him what the angel is supposed to have proclaimed at his conception—that he was Son of the Most High, the one who would fulfill the literal meaning of his given name, Jesus (a shortened form of Joshua—"God saves")? The problem is obviated if we rightly understand that the angel's words reflect the fully developed faith of the Easter Church—a faith in Jesus, who, by virtue of his glorification after death, has taken his place as Lord of the universe and is now and forever the anointed Messiah for whom all creation has waited.

Later, postbiblical Christianity placed a very high value on consecrated virginity, and so it was thought appropriate to believe that Mary remained forever *intacta*, always a virgin. That is as it may be—or not. We have no way of knowing anything at all about her intimate life, and as a matter of fact (let us be very clear on this), the issue is really no one's business. The only sources for any reliable information about (what else can we call it?) the sex life of Mary and Joseph would have been Mary and Joseph themselves, and the Gospels not only reveal no evidence of their testimony, but clearly indicate that they were written without their influence or contribution.

———————

What, let us ask, is gained for the faith and salvation of believers by an insistence on a literal understanding of virginity? Nothing except the inference that we are all doomed to a far less exalted condition of birth and of birthing others. If we keep sounding the drum for the perpetual virginity of Mary and for the literally virginal conception of Jesus, it is difficult to avoid the impression that with Mary and Joseph, God second-guessed Himself—that He repented of the system He had created for the rest of humanity. In light of that, all sorts of problems and neuroses emerge: sexual congress and the ordinary means of procreation necessarily seem less appropriate, less *dignified*, if they are considered means inappropriate for the entrance of God into time.

There is no antisexual bias in the Scriptures; that was created centuries later, and to this day there is something faintly odious about the Western chagrin over sex. Directly connected to this is the quaint custom of a bride throwing her bouquet, after the wedding ceremony, to a crowd of squealing maidens. Traditionally, this is done just before her departure for the honeymoon—as she is on her way to you know where, to do you know what. The throwing of the flowers indicates that her virginity is about to be yielded (she is to be deflowered), and the pure state is "left behind" with her maiden friends.

This secular custom developed from an ancient one still frequently practiced by many pious and virginal brides, who, after the wedding ceremony, leave their bouquets in church, at the feet of a statue of Mary, before departing with the groom. In both cases, the meaning is clear whether the lady knows it or not: she gives up the totem of her virginity, either with a wistful toss, a dewy gaze, slightly reverent distaste or a cheerful glint, depending on the woman.

Perhaps these ritualistic practices have lost much of their meaning in a society in which men and women routinely consummate relationships long before the wedding day. Still, behind these secular customs is a strain of Puritan prejudice not found in the Gospels. Unfortunately, the idea of the virginal conception was later broadened to support a presumption that virginity is superior to marriage. That is going well beyond the text, and maybe beyond common sense, too.

Regarding the divinity of Jesus, that belief is not at all compromised by a fresh understanding of the virginal conception. That the fullness of God dwelt in Jesus of Nazareth is certainly the faith of the Gospels and an element constitutive of Christianity—that is, it is absolutely central to faith. God stands fully revealed in this man Jesus, and the only way to "know" this mystery is to experience it: one knows that one is redeemed for meaning by "knowing" the person of Jesus. But relative to this affirmation there is never any appeal to a virginal conception. And the Gospel of John, which contains the most developed Christology, has no awareness at all of a virginal conception.

In this same regard, it is interesting to cite the staunchly conservative Roman Catholic theologian Cardinal Josef Ratzinger, the prelate who presides over the Church's official teaching office: "According to the faith of the Church, the Sonship of Jesus does not rest on the fact that Jesus had no human father: *the doctrine of Jesus' divinity would not be affected if Jesus had been the product of a normal human marriage* [italics mine]. For the Sonship of which faith speaks is not a biological but an ontological fact, an event not in time but in God's eternity. The conception of Jesus does not mean that a new God-the-Son comes into being, but that God as Son in the man Jesus draws the mature man to Himself, so that He Himself 'is' man."

————

But the hallowed phrase from the Church's creed—"born of the Virgin Mary"—must be preserved, for it insists that Jesus was born in the flesh as a real man, of a real mother. The word "virgin" establishes Mary's status up to the time of the conception of Jesus; it states no more than does Matthew's citation of Jesus' conception as the fulfillment of the words of Isaiah: "A virgin shall conceive and bear a son, and they shall name him Emmanuel," which, Matthew adds, "means 'God is with us.'"

Isaiah was alluding to the imminent birth of a naturally conceived child who would, in his own time, seven hundred years before Jesus, help to preserve the House of David and thus the people of Israel. In any case, the Hebrew word for "virgin" in Isaiah is *'alma*—meaning simply a "young woman," with no reference to the fact of virginity; the Greek translation of *'alma* (*parthenos*, in both Isaiah and Matthew) simply means that a young woman who *has been* a virgin will soon conceive in the normal way and bear a child.

What is revealed for our faith is not, then, something anomalous about the mechanics of reproduction. Rather, the Scriptures proclaim that humanity cannot provide its own salvation, that God acts graciously and directly in sending His Christ into the world. Even the Roman Catholic Church, which more than any other tradition carefully articulates its belief in dogmas, has strongly warned Catholics against inappropriate considerations of the biological aspects of the virginity of Mary. Rome has also insisted that emphasis be placed on the religious—not the anatomical or gynecological—implications of the teaching. Still, it must be stressed that official Roman Catholicism continues to base the religious emphasis on a literal understanding of virginal conception, and many Catholic theologians continue to maintain that this understanding is basic to the faith of the Catholic Church. Some important scholars, however, disagree; the discussion continues.

What precisely is proclaimed by these chapters of the two Gospels? The reply can only be that the entrance of Jesus into history was the surprise of all time; that God offered more than any prophet or dreamer could ever have imagined; that He was once again overturning every expectation in the unexpected births of John the Baptist and of Jesus.

The perpetual virginity of Mary—a biological condition that, it is taught, endured miraculously despite childbirth and was preserved by her forever after—is something else again. Perhaps the goal of that belief (which is unsupported by any biblical statement) is simply to point out the singleness of heart that the Christian, like Mary, brings to commitment—alertness to and acceptance of the coming of Jesus into the world, just as Mary was faithful, just as she did not doubt, like Sarah and

Zechariah. "Here am I, the servant of the Lord," she replies to the angel. "Let it be with me according to your word." The believer can have no more perfect model in faith.

But to go any further—to postulate the literally perpetual virginity of Mary—is unwarranted in light of the fact that she seems to have had other children. "Look, your mother and your brothers and sisters are standing outside," someone tells Jesus while he is busy healing and teaching. The letters of Paul, as well as the Gospels and the writings of Flavius Josephus (who wrote independently of the evangelists), all refer to the siblings of Jesus.

This usually comes as a shock most of all to Roman Catholics, for whom the common understanding since the late fourth century—when the virginal conception began widely to be taken literally—is that the brothers and sisters of Jesus were really cousins or half siblings (children of Joseph by a previous marriage); and if Joseph was not indeed the father of Jesus, then these "brothers and sisters" of Jesus are not related to him at all!

But these explanations were retrojected (put back or imposed) from a later need to defend the nonbiblical idea of Mary's perpetual virginity. Contemporary scholars—even Catholics—who insist that "brothers and sisters" means just that, and that therefore Mary could hardly have been a perpetual virgin, have not, it should be noted, ever been officially denounced or condemned by Rome. More to the point, the New Testament has a Greek word for "cousin" (*anepsios*), but when the siblings of Jesus are mentioned (especially by him), the Greek words for "brothers" and "sisters" (*adelphoi, adelphai*) are calmly employed.

There is not one example in the New Testament of the word for "brother" meaning "cousin" or "stepbrother." That stretch of linguistic fancy did not occur until the fourth century, when it was thought unseemly for Mary ever to have had other children, much less sexual relations. The matter has been neatly summed up by Jerome Neyrey: "No linguistic evidence warrants our interpreting Gospel passages about Jesus' brothers and sisters as his cousins. 'Cousins' of Jesus, when noted, were called just that, 'cousins,' not 'brothers.' Therefore [New Testament] authors apparently understood Jesus' 'brothers' as blood brothers, not as 'cousins' or 'stepbrothers.' . . . The evidence for 'stepbrother' is merely legendary." Neyrey's position, quietly held by numerous other Catholic theologians and exegetes, has not deprived him of his status as a Jesuit priest or as a professor of New Testament at Notre Dame University, which is as about as Catholic an institution as one might find.

As for the intimate life of Mary and Joseph: that is no one's business but theirs, and of it we have no record. To presume that Mary took a vow of virginity, as if she were a nun, is to fantasize—and certainly to impose something very un-Semitic on a Jewish girl of that time.

In this regard, it is important to recall that when the Christian Church was legalized in the Roman Empire in the early fourth century, holiness was no longer expressed by martyrdom but by asceticism—by subordinating the life of the flesh to the life of the spirit. But this has unfortunately ballooned into an unhealthy attitude that simply degrades sex (and therefore scolds God for His technique of procreation); it also continues to support the un-Christian (indeed, the heretical) idea that Jesus was not, after all, really a complete human being. To deny Jesus a biological father raises the question of whether we can indeed call him a human being. As one Catholic biblical scholar has written, "One may ask whether the virgin birth is not part of an ancient worldview which is as much out of date as the clear biblical belief in a geocentric universe."

Matthew and Luke present the virginal conception as an emblem of divine initiative, which is something much richer than a statement of "what happened." The writers offer assertions that the God who raised Jesus from the dead brought about Jesus' conception. That does not mean that God thought it necessary to suspend the ordinary means of conception and birth decreed for all creation. The birth of Jesus, say Matthew and Luke—and those who come to believe in Jesus—begins a new creation. And the only way for the ancient writers to describe this new creation was by the inspired invention of new metaphors—not the fabrication of untruth, but an entirely fresh way of telling the truth. God's revelation, after all, need not be restricted to the form of literal history.

From the stunning account of Genesis to the promise of eternity in Revelation, the sacred writers were inspired with God-given stories to convey the truth. Stories—not the efforts of metaphysical speculation—have the power to alert and to alter us, for people may, after all, be instructed by forms other than history. Jesus, we must remember, told parables, and no one would dare say they are "untrue." Only the hyperrational modern man thinks (rather foolishly) that stories are not true. The first Christians, on the other hand, and their representatives who wrote the Gospels understood that of course the stories were true—in the sense that the authors meant them to be true, which was not always or even predominantly a literal sense.

We do not put our faith in either a traditional conception or a miraculous one. The object of faith is not words stating something about physical virginity: the object of faith is the confession that in Jesus God has once and for all disclosed Himself in human life and wedded Himself to its destiny—in every way, including darkness, suffering and death. And this He has done to save it for Himself for all eternity.

The story of the virginal conception thus represents the historicizing of a religious statement about Jesus—an origin that God certainly did not diminish by working through the "ordinary" means of conception with two parents (as if there were anything really "ordinary" about the birth of *any* human being). The Catholic Church has, notably, taught that "the Books of Scripture teach firmly, faithfully and without error that truth which God wanted put into the Sacred writings for the sake of our salvation." A loyal Roman Catholic must then ask whether the biological mode of Jesus' entrance into history is a truth that God put into the Bible "for the sake of our salvation."

The human nature and the divine sonship of Jesus are the elements that are constitutive of Christian faith—elements without which the Christian proclamation is gravely compromised. But is the bodily virginity of Mary equally constitutive of faith? If that is so, one must ask just how this odd fact adds to our quest for salvation. The story of the virgin birth is indeed true—in the sense the tradition appears to have meant it, which is *not* historical but theological: the presence of Jesus, truly God's Son in the world, demonstrates the prior divine activity.

————

The goal of this book is not to diminish the marvelous or the mysterious in God's revelation of Himself to us. But if a devout soul should raise the issue of Church dogma and papal infallibility on these matters, I can only respectfully reply that if the word of God must be read with respect for the richness of its language—if indeed our task is to determine what the sacred text means—then it is all the more important that we should also determine what the secular text means. Church pronouncements are, in other words, as capable of interpretation as biblical verses. If we deny that, then we deny that God still has something to say to us—in our particular circumstances, in the here and now.

In literary forms strikingly different from those that follow, the opening chapters of Matthew and Luke present two kinds of summaries of the meaning and importance of Jesus for communities steeped in Jewish history and folklore—just as the first eleven chapters of the Book of Genesis present an overture or curtain-raiser in light of everything that follows. The truth that God reveals is not, after all, always conveyed by historically literal "statements" to audiences, and every passage in Scripture must be judged according to its literary form. That is a basic axiom of Bible studies in every informed Jewish and Christian community of our time.

———

On the matter of Gospel truth, even the Roman Catholic Church's Pontifical Biblical Commission—a papal organization not known for seizing the fashionable viewpoint or for issuing wildly liberal statements—has for decades taught that the Gospels must be carefully studied according to the literary forms and norms of the time when the documents were created. The great encyclical letter of Pope Pius XII, *Divino Afflante Spiritu,* issued in 1943, first opened the door to Scripture scholarship even among Roman Catholics. One says "even" because as late as the first third of the current century, Rome viewed with suspicion and sometimes condemnation virtually any reading of Scripture that had taken into account the rich discoveries of language, archaeology, history and science in the last hundred years.

Even more important advances in Bible studies were made by the Catholic Church's Second Vatican Council, convened from 1962 to 1965, and again by the Pontifical Biblical Commission in its historic document "Instruction on the Historical Truth of the Gospels" in 1964. Alas, the scholarly, liberating effect of these official teachings of the Roman Catholic Church has not generally filtered down from Rome through seminaries to parish pulpits.

When good, churchgoing people or good churchmen seek to close off all discussion, rummaging through their pockets for three-by-five-inch index cards with the answers to all our questions about God, we should run screaming into the night. A prayerful, careful study of every element of the creeds, for example, does not "do away with" the meaning of the birth of Jesus "by the virgin Mary." Such a study may, however, show that sometimes we place our emphasis oddly, or at least (how could it be otherwise?) partially.

Jesus was really born; he was and is a real human being. He is also, once and forever, God's ultimate self-disclosure. How this can be defies comprehension. But the words of the angel are as good as anyone's: the struggling believer is promised, with Mary, that the power of the Most High will overshadow us, so that the one who is born in our lives may indeed be the Holy One of God.

———

"See—I am making all things new!" proclaims the glorified Lord at the end of the New Testament. The words are both a clue for what God does at every moment of time and a cue for those who wish to live in His presence, finding in every fresh hour God's approach to us in all our particularity. Evidently, He has not thought the past sufficient, for He has given us the present.

CHAPTER THREE

AT THE RIVER:
JESUS MEETS JOHN THE BAPTIST

P alestine, a small slice of the Roman Empire during the time of
Jesus, was just one hundred fifty miles long and fifty miles
wide; the entire country could have fit inside the state of Mas-
sachusetts. But the ancient land of the Jews was neither a common-
wealth, a sovereign state nor part of a federated republic. Strategically
located, it had for centuries known invasion and enemy tenure, destruction and oppression. Since 63 B.C., it had again been occupied territory,
and everywhere there were emblems of Rome—especially the ubiquitous
standard, a circular laurel wreath, the emblem *SPQR* (*Senatus Popu-
lusque Romanus:* The Roman Senate and People) and the eagle on top,
the symbol of watchful authority. Even the name of the country had
been altered by Rome—from Israel to Palestine, which recalled the ancient Philistines of the coastal area.

Early in the year 28, a man known to history as John the Baptist was
astonishing people with an unrelenting declaration—"Repent!"—and
inviting sinners to a ritual washing, in token of their need for a new life.
The scorching summer winds, regularly blowing up from the south,
forced people to take refuge where they could; often this meant huddling
together in makeshift tents in the Jordan valley or near the banks of the
Dead Sea—both of them John's customary stopping places: "The people
of Jerusalem and all Judea and all the region along the Jordan came to
John and they were baptized by him in the river Jordan, confessing their
sins."

Then in his mid-thirties, John had been born to a rural Jewish priest named Zechariah and his wife, Elizabeth. The boy's conception (announced by Gabriel in the Gospel according to Luke) was a surprise, for the parents were old and the mother was considered sterile. It is impossible to know whether John later also began the path to priesthood, which was expected of a priest's son. He may have prepared for this vocation in Jerusalem, the Holy City, where he learned about fasting and prayer, priestly practices he shared. And subsequent to that, he may have spent some time with the Essenes. Some of their characteristics (desert solitude and a longing for a purified life) and their practices (ritual washing as a sign of seeking forgiveness) resemble his own, and both John and the Essenes had a positive horror of religious—and especially priestly—hypocrisy and extravagance.

In any case, in that year 28, John was certainly not in any way connected to the Jewish priesthood, nor was he a member of any identifiable group within Judaism. He was, on the contrary, a loner and by any standard an eccentric—a fiercely austere man who denied himself ordinary food and drink, subsisting on wild honey and locusts (which were often a staple in the diet of the poor). He also wore a distinctive garb—a camel's-hair garment fastened with a leather belt—that recalled the ancient prophetic costume of the mysterious Elijah, who (it was believed by some) would return at a critical point in Jewish history.

So outfitted, John challenged the complacent, professionally religious people overconfident (as such people always are) of their own righteousness—pious souls who depend on the formalities of religion rather than on its enlivened spirit. Most of all, he excoriated those who ignored the plight of the poor. But for everyone, his message was one of protest and moral outrage: "You brood of vipers!" he cried. "Prove your repentance by the fruits you bear." John announced, in other words, an opportunity for radical conversion and change of heart, which is the meaning of the word "repentance."

This was only the beginning: he further shocked his listeners by proclaiming (against the conventional wisdom) that simply being a member of the Chosen People was not so much a guarantee of righteousness or salvation as it was a mandate to lead a godly, ethical, loving life: "Do not presume to say to yourselves, 'We have Abraham as our ancestor,'" he insisted, adding that if God wished, He could even transform common stones into a new generation of Chosen People. A judgment on sinfulness was imminent, according to John, and those who were planted in the vineyard of Israel would be lost forever if their faith was mere lip service, unconnected to a life of good works: "Even now the ax is lying at the root of the trees; every tree that does not bear good fruit is cut down and thrown onto the fire."

People must, therefore, renounce comfortable assumptions based on mere ethnic legacy. The same God Who summoned Israel out of Egypt and led them through the waters to safety was now re-creating them anew in the waters of a baptism of renewal. John was not founding a new religion: he was denouncing a piety that was evidently empty because its proponents oppressed others. His own garb, his fasting, his radically simple life and his self-denial identified him with the lowly.

But he had more to say. His proclamation and his baptism would eventually be superseded: "The one who is more powerful than I is coming after me. I have baptized you with water, but he will baptize you with the Holy Spirit." There is no indication that at this time John knew of whom he spoke. Hope and confidence encouraged his belief that a final great manifestation of God would soon occur in the world—the details of which he knew not.

Many devout Jews, aware of their individual and collective need for renewal and reform, responded to John. Flavius Josephus, the Jewish general and historian who wrote at the end of the first century, wrote approvingly of John the Baptist as "a good man who exhorted the Jews to lead righteous lives, to practice justice toward their fellows and piety toward God." John's invitation to sinners to submit to a baptism, to the religious rite of immersion in water, was (continued Josephus) "not to gain pardon for whatever sins they committed, but as a sign of consecration of the body, implying that the soul was already thoroughly cleansed by right behavior." Wandering among his fellows, John invited them to a ritual washing symbolizing a need to be transformed, to return to God in humility as His people. "I will sprinkle clean water upon you," the Lord had promised through the priest and prophet Ezekiel, indicating the end of captivity in Babylon six hundred years earlier, "and you shall be clean from all your uncleanness. A new heart I will give you, and a new spirit I will put within you." John, who knew his Scriptures, lived in that confidence.

Ritual washings were, of course, common gestures in many ancient religions, and they remain so to this day. From the ancient Jewish religious ablutions to the Egyptian rites of Isis, from the washings of the Qumran monks and the immersion of Jewish converts to the later Christian practice of baptism and the placing of water fonts near church entrances—few rites are more freighted with meaning than those that use the element necessary for all life.

Pouring water or immersing oneself in water is a universally recognized sign of the wish to be made new, to be born again (in a new cleansing, a new water of birth) and to have done with the old (in a washing away of the accretion of grime). Before entering the Jerusalem temple, the devout washed—trudging around the ancient world was, after all, a dusty and dirty business—and hosts offered their guests cleansing water when they arrived for a visit or a meal. This was an especially generous sign of hospitality, since water had to be laboriously transported in heavy jars from wells outside a city or village and then kept in a family's cistern for cooking or washing. Fresh, untainted water was precious among ancient peoples. Just so, on the brink of a new life in a new community, there were watery rites of passage or initiation.

But the meaning John gave to the rite of water was different: no ancient source, Jewish or Gentile, identified the sign of renewal with the offer of God's unconditional friendliness, for which another word is "grace." That was precisely the connection John made—water is a sign of God's extension of His own life to the world—investing an archetypal symbol with a profoundly religious significance. This baptismal washing was not to be repeated, like other pious or physical cleansings: it was, rather, to be performed only once in the lifetime of his disciples.

A radical change of life must follow, deepening the moment and reinforcing its meaning. Thus the baptism of John was the start of a process, of joining a new people with a common cause. Later, after Jesus' death, it was seen as the beginning of an intimate, mysterious connection to him—thus the later Christian tradition of being baptized "in the name of Jesus," by which is meant "by virtue of his presence and power."

Like the classical prophets of Israel who went before him centuries earlier (Isaiah, Jeremiah, Ezekiel, Amos), and like a few voices that have echoed through the corridors of history since John, he condemned the selfish luxury that existed alongside widespread impoverishment and economic oppression—the kind of sybaritic luxury that can lead to spiritual bankruptcy.

A true Jewish prophet—a spokesman for the things of God, not a fortune-teller—the Baptist had the prophet's sense of radical isolation. Jeremiah (in the seventh century before Jesus), preaching against religious indifference, felt that his calling was to be a thorn in the side of the smug. His vocation necessarily separated him from "merrymakers" and led him to a certain apartness. "I sat alone," Jeremiah said wistfully but without self-pity.

After he had listened to God in silence and apartness, he returned to the people with a message of warning about their infidelity—a proclamation always connected to the promise of God's counterbalancing faithfulness, and of His unimaginable forgiveness and the restoration of sinners to grace. "I am with you to deliver you. Only acknowledge your guilt and return, O faithless Israel, and I will not look on you in anger, for I am merciful." It is one of the glories of the Hebrew tradition that the prophetic literature is, from first stage to last, a reminder to God's people that He is faithful to His promise despite their pattern of infidelity. That is, in fact, a fair summary of the entire eight-hundred-year prophetic tradition, from Isaiah to John the Baptist.

Like Jeremiah, John had a stern announcement for the privileged and the powerful of his time, those who burdened the disenfranchised and the weak: they must change their ways or face divine judgment. Alienated from his own family's priestly roots, he had abandoned polite society for the desert wilderness—traditionally the locus for prayerful solitude. In the central event of the Exodus through the Sinai wilderness, in the journey from slavery to freedom, God had revealed Himself to be a loving, guiding Lord to a frightened, wandering people. Now John came, after his desert retreat, into the rest of Palestine, attacking society at its foundation. John spoke of a judgment of fire, just as the great apocalyptic prophets before him had warned of stars falling, the sun and moon going dark and the heavens collapsing—dramatic images that some may have understood literally, but that everyone took as emblematic of the announcement that God would utterly transform creation.

In any event, the good order of the world was certainly being upset by the kinds of injustice that bred deep social unrest: by the failure of a minority, the rich aristocracy, to recognize the needs of their disadvantaged fellows, and by the oppressive conduct of occupying Roman forces. In such an atmosphere, the hopes of some Jewish people were reawakened—hopes for a liberating king who, as God's Messiah (His "anointed one"), would lead them to victory over their enemies. In their scriptures and at their worship, the Jews heard constant reminders that God was faithful—that despite the lapses of His people and the failure of their kings, they were His people and would not be finally destroyed. This was the ground of their faith.

————

Then as now, the rich were not the majority of people. John's call was primarily to the powerful few who affected the lives of everyone—the aristocrats whose lives were bathed in luxury, who despised the common folk, kept slaves and believed they were sufficient unto themselves. The nearly one million inhabitants of first-century Palestine (about seventy percent of them Jews) were a heterodox aggregate with widely divergent creeds and practices. Mostly they were the anonymous masses: since the economic base of Palestine was agriculture, most workers were peasant farmers, eking out a livelihood from the recalcitrant soil, cultivating wheat and barley, vines and fruit trees, olives and honey. Between the multitudes of indigent poor and the few rich was a very small number of middle-class citizens, primarily tradesmen—stonecutters, masons, woodworkers, fishermen. But the typical citizen was not a wealthy or even a comfortable man; he was a day laborer. Women, of course, had no rights at all and careers were forbidden to them.

Everywhere could be seen the castaways of society—beggars, cripples, all sorts of diseased people, the blind and the insane wandering the streets and the poor elderly, which meant those over forty-five or so; most people did not survive to that age. Many pregnant women did not survive, either, and young people died in agony from appendicitis or fevers or paralysis; children suffocated with asthma; people were blinded by cataracts and sandstorms; the ravages of scurvy and beriberi were pandemic, and everyone was subject to serious vitamin deficiencies. Broken bones became deformed, useless limbs; serious blood diseases and death often resulted from infected wounds; and contagion was widespread, as were weakness, malnutrition, nervous diseases, and brain and neurological disorders. All sorts of skin problems, burns and eczema were classified with the dreaded leprosy, which was widespread and usually regarded as a sign of God's wrath (as was the illness of Miriam, sister of Moses and Aaron, in the Old Testament). Little could be done for most injuries except scraping or lancing wounds, preparing poultices made of crushed fruit, or applying herbs, roots or a mixture of oil and wine.

With no refrigeration for food, illness and poisoning were common; water was tainted, and dysentery, malaria and typhoid fever were common. Of course, plumbing was unknown, and raw sewage and human waste flowed in open gutters through streets and alleys. To guard against the pattern of nightly theft of livestock, animals were usually brought indoors and kept with the family, and the unavoidable filth and disease were impossible to control. Death was a brother in every household: most children were dead before their third birthday. There were very few pleasures to be had in life, and many needs to be met. A person of good will must have felt overwhelmed.

Yet there was no sense of life being "unfair," which is very much an attitude cultivated in a modern world accustomed to instant coffee and wonder drugs. Perhaps only in the twentieth century have great numbers of human beings expected life to be happy, healthy and virtually perfect—by which is meant easy and subject to our will and skill. Illness now offends; the deaths of children are read as signs of an indifferent God or a hostile universe. No such attitude characterized people two millennia ago. Life and death were not administered unfairly: they simply were what they were.

In precisely such a world—in which life was short, dull and brutish—the essentially compassionate message of John the Baptist struck very directly. Real godliness, he insisted, was not just a matter of attention to the inner life, but of its inevitable corollary: loving concern for those in need. "Whoever has two coats must share with anyone who has none, and whoever has food must do likewise." One must not only share one's surplus; the oppression of the powerless must cease. To that end, John had injunctions for specific groups.

Tax collectors (also called publicans), who had a special reputation for defrauding the poor, were summoned to mend their ways. "What should we do?" they asked John as they came to the Jordan to be baptized. His answer was swift: "Collect no more than the amount prescribed for you."

This was certainly a revolutionary demand to make of Jewish tax collectors, and it must have sounded impossibly harsh. After all, they acted as hired agents on behalf of Rome, of the priestly authorities in Jerusalem, and of Herod Antipas himself. Collectors commonly amassed considerable wealth, extorting from citizens more than the required amounts—and then turning over to the authorities much less than they collected. The entire system was little more than legally certified robbery. John's appeal, therefore, amounted almost to a definition of repentance—a concrete "change of heart" after sinful actions. To heed John, tax collectors had to consider a complete rejection of their careers.

The implication—lost on no one, including the highest civil and religious administrators—was that John struck at the foundation of the tax-farm system. In this regard, he could not have been unaware of the tax riots in the two decades before his mission: those had been bloody events, and the rebel leaders had come to a bad end. Preaching now to publicans and rousing the hopes of the beleaguered poor who were paying exorbitant revenue, John was infuriating everyone in power.

"All regarded John as truly a prophet"—such was an early claim for his authority, and as a result, crowds were going out to hear his radical message.

He did not stop with the country's money matters: there were soldiers and policemen to be corrected, too. "Do not extort money from anyone by threats or false accusation," he told them. Again, this was a bold challenge to the social order: extortion was as common as desert sand. And because soldiers' wages were already paid with the taxes of the poor—which went to subsidize vast royal palaces and the enormous Jerusalem temple—John forbade the usual request of soldiers and police for salary increments: "Be satisfied with your wages." A similar injunction centuries later might not win many followers.

And so those who abused the poor were summoned to mend their ways. Along with anyone who admitted the need for a new life in God, they were led into the river's waters by John. When they emerged, they were sent back to their homes and jobs. John's disciples were not, it must be noted, sent on to the Jerusalem temple to perform any acts of penance or for an official blessing, a ceremonial washing or any kind of conventional priestly reception. John himself had administered a new kind of ritual, which, accompanying the proclamation of imminent judgment and the concomitant necessity of repentance, implied the insufficiency of every previous religious formality.

This complex of word and gesture could hardly have gone down very well with the guardians of Jewish temple orthodoxy, especially since John was known to have come from a priestly family—and should, according to all traditional expectations, have become a priest himself. Not only did he fail to meet that prospect, he had also positioned himself outside polite society in every way. Indeed, everything about him—his look, his life, his words—was an embarrassment to the establishment; he was, in fact, a summary of impolite society.

But to anyone alert to the ways of God, the wholeness of John's benevolent proclamation and his method were radically consistent with the entire history of revelation. This was neither the first nor the last time that surprise was the essential element of God's compassionate attack against perversity and on behalf of humanity. One can say very little for certain about the ways of God, other than that they usually overturn every human perspective and prediction, which are severely limited in any case. We think we know what is best for us, but God in His mercy knows better. And in John the Baptist, God chose an unlikely hero to be the last of the great Israelite prophets.

———

Sometime during that same year 28, Jesus, now in his mid-thirties, made his way to the banks of the Jordan along with a crowd of people who had heard of the Baptist and were drawn to his powerful message about the dawn of a new age. "Jesus came from Nazareth of Galilee and was baptized by John in the Jordan." An ordinary carpenter with nothing in his life up to this time to suggest anything like a remarkable future, Jesus was meeting John for the first time. "I did not know him," admitted the Baptist.

Jesus had obviously heard about John and had deliberately headed south to meet him. Once there, he was deeply impressed and at once heeded this extraordinary messenger. And as a member of the nation of Israel—which for John meant a sinful people very much in need of a complete reformation of life—this new listener submitted to John's baptism in the river. The event says nothing about Jesus' individual spiritual state: confession of sin for the Jews of ancient Israel did not mean preparing a catalog of personal faults, but rather making a humble admission that one was, in solidarity with all people, needy of God.

Like great crowds that year, Jesus acknowledged that John the Baptist was a prophet at a critical time in the history of Israel, and clearly he saw himself as one who, just like his countrymen, needed to be transformed. Perhaps he was stung by John's castigation of the self-sufficiency felt by those who did not know the plight of the downtrodden—after all, Jesus had a recognizable and respectable training and trade that depended on the ordinary needs of even the very poor. Whatever Jesus' inner feeling about himself, we see in his acceptance of John's baptism (as certain a historical event as anything in Jesus' life) an acknowledgment of a need for conversion—for a change of heart and a radical purification in light of the coming judgment.

———

That day at the river probably seemed unremarkable to everyone present, and only in retrospect—like all great moments in history—did its significance become clear. That day at the river, there was a "happening"; only later was it seen as an "event." That day at the river, recorded by the New Testament writers decades later, was not meant as a kind of side show for those at the Jordan—after all, no one understood the identity of the hidden Jesus that day, nor did he make any impact on their lives until very much later. But a long oral tradition circulated later about the significance it had for Jesus and his connection with the Baptist; this tradition, then, stuck in the minds of those who came to believe that Jesus was the ultimate manifestation of God's will and presence in history.

In light of that developed faith, the Gospel writers included a kind of crystallized meditation on Jesus' meeting with John: "And just as Jesus was coming up out of the water, he saw the heavens torn apart and the Spirit descending like a dove on him. And a voice came from heaven, saying, 'You are my Son, the Beloved; with you I am well pleased.'"

In a rich use of familiar Hebrew texts, the account tells the reader who Jesus is. Entering history—not simply then but always, whenever he is welcomed into any life—Jesus arrives on the scene and "the heavens are torn apart" in fulfillment of the prophet Isaiah's prayer centuries earlier ("O, that you would tear open the heavens and come down"). And who is it that comes? Just as an ancient hymn celebrated the ritual anointing of the kings of Israel, calling them "sons" in a coronation-day anthem ("You are my Son, today I have begotten you"), so Jesus is once and for all the new leader of a new Israel, created, like the former Israel, in the desert. He is God's cherished servant, a representative personality who sums up in himself and fulfills the destiny of God's people—the "chosen, in whom [God] delights."

There is, finally, a clear literary sign of this: the presence of the dove, a traditional, affectionate biblical name for God's beloved people. The Gospel account of the baptism of Jesus, therefore, summons not to a nostalgic reverie about the past; rather, by exploiting all the richness of literary metaphor, it invites hearers to the present and the future. The Jesus who was, is; the one who was baptized remains forever God's chosen. And this was guaranteed by the "voice from heaven"—by which devout Jews, avoiding use of the divine name, meant the presence of God Himself.

John the Baptist was, as Jesus insisted, "more than a prophet"—he was like the promised Elijah, sent by God before the imminent final judgment. Hence after his baptism, Jesus in fact became one of John's most fervent disciples, helping to carry on John's proclamation, practicing the baptism of repentance he offered to all who would accept it. Israel, he believed with John (and with the great prophets of Jewish history), was to be renewed after generations of spiritual infidelity.

But within the space of several months, there was a complete change, for Jesus was committed to a new life. He did not return to his home and to his previous career as a woodworker; instead, he completely abandoned his past in favor of a new preaching mission. And his presence and personality, his single-minded dedication and his charismatic manner, must have been remarkably effective, for soon some of John's adherents decided to leave him and to go with Jesus. "Jesus and his disciples went into the Judean countryside, and he spent some time there with them and baptized. John also was baptizing at Aenon near Salim, because water was abundant there."

As the popularity of Jesus grew, John's most ardent partisans, annoyed by this upstart they now considered a rival, complained to the Baptist: "The one who was with you across the Jordan—here he is baptizing, and all are going over to him!" John, however, felt no threat. Time was short: for his proclamation to reach the widest possible audience, he needed all the help he could get. Entirely focused on his mission, John was unaware that he was facilitating the developing mission of Jesus, which would soon reach far beyond anything John ever envisioned.

The language of the baptism of Jesus was concerned not with on-the-spot reporting but with the religious significance of an event that continued to affect believers a half-century later, when the Gospels were written. Jesus' time of discipleship with John was seen as a time of training but also as his anointing at the head of God's new Israel, just as, later, Christian baptism was seen as an initiation.

That idea of initiation is important. While John's baptism, practiced by him and by Jesus, signified a change of heart and action because of the imminent end of something, Christians after the death and Resurrection of Jesus continued the ritual of pouring water as the beginning of something.

But none of it has to do with a magic act. People do not experience transcendent, invisible realities in the sphere of God by the simple performance of words and gestures, nor does anyone but God have "power" to establish our friendship with Him. No priest can effect it, nor can we bring it on ourselves. We count on water and words, now as then, to externalize—to represent an inner transformation we ask God to achieve. In this regard, the ancient practice of baptizing unaware infants speaks loudly: it is God who acts first, even before we have the wits to respond.

Just as the Jewish people dedicated male infants to God by way of the initiation rite of circumcision, so baptism places the Christian newborn among the community of the new Israel that was continuous with the old. Plunged into the waters of baptism as Christ was plunged into death, the newly born, once and forever, emerges "in Christ," who now fills the universe, not merely the limited space of fleshly existence on earth. In our complete incapacity as helpless children—itself a metaphor of our condition before God throughout our lifetime—it is He who acts first, coming to embrace us even in our infantile sleep, our wailing and complaining. God claims for His own what He has made. He loves it and saves it. Can any other idea about God make sense?

Just so, the process of the journey toward God is entirely His doing: the act of longing for Him as we progress from infancy, of reaching out in conscious trust, which is the ground of faith, merely tills the soil within us; only God can plant, water and bring to full flower.

Christian baptism, practiced uninterruptedly in history from the late first century, is not, therefore, the conclusion of something, the sealing and finale of salvation, but the emergence of a lifelong process in which, over and over, we are transformed from sleeping children to alert adults. Salvation—being saved for meaning—is entirely a divine prerogative, but it asks for a response, and that is our task. Salvation—being saved for eternity—is God's promise that the love for which we so long will not, at the end, elude us.

————

These first considerations of the multiple meanings of "the hidden Jesus" and "a new life" have brought us up against a series of astonishing phrases, all of them richly symbolic, all of them kinds of metaphors that are unavoidable: getting on in years . . . bearing fruits of repentance . . . brood of vipers . . . raising up stones . . . ax at the root . . . washing as a sign of new life . . . God meets those who come to Him . . .

Every time we write and speak, we are engaging in a symbolic activity; it is useless, therefore, to pretend that when we discuss the ultimately important things in human life and destiny, we can speak literally about what is exactly true, or that one word or phrase or sentence accurately represents the full truth of what cannot be finally and forever expressed. Everything in our expression of human experience is, in one way or another, a metaphor (literally, a transfer, a carrying over by signs): writing and speech, like painting and music, stand in for another reality.

When Romeo speaks of his love—

What light through yonder window breaks?
It is the east, and Juliet is the sun!

—we do not rise up in fury from our seats and race down the theater aisle, protesting that indeed Juliet is not the sun, that he means she is *like* the sun, and so on. We accept the truth of the poet's meaning, which is something like "Juliet brightens everything," her presence bestows light and warmth and growth—and those words are not nearly so good as saying "Juliet is the sun." Romeo's words are absolutely, unqualifiedly true—Juliet *is* the sun—in the sense in which he means the words to be true.

Which brings us to a point crucial for this book.

We communicate an understanding of our reality by constructing narratives—not just large stories, epics, extended biographies, but the small sharings of every day. "Last year, when I was working . . . This morning I read the newspaper . . . Yesterday, police reported that . . . Tonight, snow is expected in the mountains . . . Next year, I hope to take a vacation . . ." Events and experiences, real or hypothetical, actual or fictionalized, are conveyed in little stories, to which we bring the embellishments necessary for supporting the meaning of what happens. These embellishments do not falsify, they interpret an event—that is to say, they give to a happening its meaning for us. But while we construct and comprehend our identity by narrative, metaphor is the way we think—especially when we are trying to relate what we do not know to what we already know. Aristotle was right: language is itself a system of symbols running parallel to reality—but it never meets reality.

The deepest realities known and unknown to us force us into metaphor. Lovers know this: "I love you with all my heart" is pure metaphor, as is "I send you all my love." Metaphor is not the least we can do to express our deepest feelings: it is the best kind of expression to share those deepest feelings. Metaphor, which is our greatest tool, only becomes our greatest problem when we forget that all language is metaphor. In this regard, each era of human history has, it should be noted, its own metaphors. One of ours, at the end of the twentieth century, is something called "historical accuracy," which is, in a way, a very deceptive and dangerous illusion. "What actually happened?" has not as much significance as "What did it mean for me?"—or for us or for others.

Every utterance in human speech, and every word on a page, is always symbolic. When I converse with someone, something astonishing happens—and it is all with symbols. In a moment of immeasurable time, I have a concept in my mind. I force air up through my diaphragm. I position my lips, tongue and teeth in such and such a way. I utter words that create sound waves that fall against the tiny bones and nerves of another's ear, and—again in a moment of immeasurable time—because I and another have agreed on the meaning of certain noises and grunts in an established language, I communicate an idea. In a sense, the only concrete things are the air waves, the sound waves, the tiny motions of brain waves. Everything else, when you stop to think about it, is in the broadest sense a spiritual reality: the communication of ideas.

It is the same thing with the words you are reading on this page. Lines of ink are arranged this way and that—vertical strokes, horizontal swatches, half-circles and dots and so on—and your eye scans them. You and I have agreed on a common understanding about all these scribbles: they are but symbols—like linear semaphores, if you will—to facilitate the communication of realities that are fundamentally invisible, spiritual.

But no less real for all their invisibility and spirituality, and maybe more real.

———————

Every written human text, from ancient poetry in a half-forgotten language to next year's tax forms, is a symbolic rendering of experience, just as speech is a symbolic rendering of experience. The only way for us to understand and to communicate those experiences is by available cultural symbols. Sounds, lines on a page, "meanings" and referents—everything is metaphor, which is the closest we can get to the reality whenever we break the silence, which is where understanding precedes communication.

It is tempting to read as if language were not metaphor, as if words expressed anything fully enough. Words, we might say, are fine as far as they go, but they cannot go far enough—at least not when we are discussing more than the weather or the stock market or the amounts of ingredients in a recipe. If we want to communicate something more profound, we break into metaphor. We throw words together illogically, we smash the rational and burst into poetic discourse. "God came down," we say, but we know that God, being pure spirit, does not move from place to place, nor is His dwelling place (also a metaphor) someplace "up there" from which He can "come down."

Yet we understand the truth of the words, even though our paraphrase, too, is metaphor. "God came down," we might add by way of nuance, is a way of saying "God approaches us, embraces us, accepts us." These are metaphors, drawn from anthropomorphisms—those wonderfully helpful forms by which we try to fit the things of God into human clothing: He walks, reaches, listens, touches. Even as we say this, we realize it to be true in a way other than language can ever express—just as we know that our expression of love for another is beyond the reach of human expression. Which is why we have poets and composers, who may be the most real of realists.

We know that there are always fresher, better, newer ways of bending language to serve the most important things in human life. "Unhappy that I am," laments King Lear's devoted daughter Cordelia when asked for a protestation of love, "I cannot heave my heart into my mouth." Which lover or poet does not nod in agreement? The greater the conviction, the more we fall back on metaphor. All human language is provisional.

We never seem to find enough to express our ongoing discovery. Someone we love, for example, is never completely "gotten" or understood or grasped entirely by us. We stay with some relationships because we experience them as constantly revelatory: in the presence of this other, we always go deeper, receive more—and see accepted what we have to bring.

But God is not less than a person, and so we are ever in a condition of being filled even further by this infinite giving. Hence we are in the presence of the ultimately rewarding relationship when we face God in silence and adoration, when we stand inwardly naked before Him, needy and poor and unfazed to admit our condition of absolute poverty. The good news, then, is that we always have more to say of the mystery, more to receive of it—of Him—not less.

———

Every word pertaining to God in the history of the human race—whether expressed in ancient Hebrew or Greek or modern English—is necessarily conditioned by the circumstances of its time and the possibilities and limitations of human language. When we say that God or Jesus has "spoken words," therefore, it does not mean that those words escape the provisional nature of all human language. Some people think this means there is no eternal, absolute truth. There is—God Himself is the truth—but every human perception and expression of God is necessarily partial and incomplete. Only visible human beings speak words and grapple toward clarity. God—invisible, silent, changeless, hidden yet present—*is* that clarity.

The four Gospel "accounts" about Jesus in the New Testament (years after their composition called traditions "according to" Matthew, Mark, Luke and John) are not free of this partiality, nor, it seems, would God have them be so. Even the last and most mystical of them, the one traditionally written "according to John," has a warning: "There are also many other things that Jesus did," concludes the Gospel. "If every one of them were written down, I suppose that the world itself could not contain the books that would be written." The meaning is incomplete on the page: it needs to be fulfilled in the reality of the believer, in the order and realm of grace, the free, lavish gift of His friendship, which God bestows.

Not only that: the Bible contains various traditions about the same event or saying in the life of Jesus—each of them, as the original authors and audiences understood, conditioned by time, locale, language. Those provisional forms, believed the third generation of Christians, have been taken up by God and are guides for His self-disclosure in Jesus in every age. Like all human words, however, the words of the Bible conceal and reveal, even when they are the normative words of Scripture. In the New Testament, Jesus is called the "Word of God," and that is an interesting corollary: he, too, in his life on earth and thereafter, conceals and reveals. What you see is not all you get: God is greater than perceptions suggest.

And is that not, after all, the very condition of everything? All is metaphor, all points forward, all draws us further. Insecure, frightened and faithless, believing yet full of doubts, wondering, longing—we want all human words to be absolute, which is another way of saying that we want to be God. But He does not conform to our small ideas of Him. He will be God, not a fantasy of what we think God should be.

Related to this and in fact dependent on it is the sublime faculty of the imagination, by which we form images or concepts of realities (not unrealities or fantasies) that are not present to our senses. In reading traditional biography, we often presume that the author has suppressed his imagination. But that is not so: in order to see and feel the texture of another's life even as he adheres to his sources, the biographer must somehow have feelings and intuitions—all of them derived from imagination.

The problem derives from our rationalist, post-Enlightenment mentality, for today we think of imagination as fabrication or fantasy, contrary to "the truth." "Oh, that's just your imagination," we tell someone as we attempt to dispel a groundless fear; or "Stop imagining things!" The word has taken a decidedly negative cast. When Joan of Arc stood before the bishops, they asked, "Do you not believe that what you call your voices from God are really nothing but your imagination?" To which the illiterate nineteen-year-old peasant replied with a wisdom worthy of the mystics: "Of course it is my imagination! How else does God speak to us except through our imagination?" That silenced the bishops for a while.

The young woman was right, of course. There is no other way to consider our experience except in images, in inner concepts that utilize the high faculty of imagination—the emergence of images. We do not fabricate, we literally invent—that is, we come upon, we discover what is already there.

———

The account of the baptism of Jesus is a splendid example of how the experience of early believers expressed something beyond human understanding—the choice of Jesus by the eternal God, a choice that can be traced back to the first emergence of Jesus in society, when he met the Baptist at the river. The verses describing the baptism utilized texts that preceded generations earlier, and so the communities turned to poetic images of their Jewish forebears and put them in the setting of a new experience.

Something happened to the carpenter from Nazareth, something occurred in his life when he met John. His future was altered, his destiny shifted and, in light of what happened later, believers could say confidently that God was "well pleased with Jesus." Open to the summons of God, he was ready to have his life radically altered. If we deny him that, if we say that he was not surprised by grace, we deny his humanity and conveniently omit the insistence of the New Testament that he "increased in wisdom, and in divine and human favor."

———

God may have been well pleased with John and Jesus that year, but the highest civil authority in the land, Herod Antipas, was not. As Rome's legate and the petty ruler of Galilee and Perea (a fourth of Palestine, hence his title "tetrarch"), Antipas was disturbed by reports of the Baptist's critiques of social injustice. Egotistical, hedonistic and crafty, Antipas (then forty-nine) came from an Idumean family that had been forcibly converted to Judaism when their territory was subsumed into Judea. The House of Herod was in any case considered only nominally Jewish, since the female ancestors were of mixed Arabian descent.

In any case, the subjects of Antipas knew that he was spiritually a Gentile with little more than contempt for Jews. A consummate politician who knew how to court Rome and yet prevent outright Palestinian rebellion against the Empire, Antipas had once been married to the daughter of Aretas of Nabatea, a neighboring Arabian chieftain-king, but he had divorced her and (in violation of Jewish law) married his half brother's sister, Herodias. To John the Baptist this was flagrantly immoral conduct that set a shameful example to Jews and roused his fiery eloquence.

John, who would hardly have waited five years to denounce the conduct of his sovereign, must have issued his first salvo against Antipas in 23, when the marriage to Herodias took place. At that time, the tetrarch and his court could perhaps afford to ignore the ravings of a wandering eccentric. But now, in 28, John was a serious force to reckon with: his critique of the social order, his injunction against the tax system and the oppression of the poor might bring the Jews dangerously close to rebellion, for they were already offended by everything about Antipas—his forgotten Jewish roots, his collusion with Gentile Rome, his luxuriant immorality, his corrupt disregard for the masses.

At precisely this time, Antipas's former father-in-law, Aretas, who had been seeking revenge for the rejection of his daughter, found a pretext to begin saber-rattling—a dispute with Antipas over territories on the border separating Perea from Nabatea. Facing the possibility of war just when John was protesting the policies of Antipas and arousing the social conscience of the Jews, Antipas took preemptive action and decided that the best solution was to shut the Baptist up—in prison. "Because the crowds were aroused to the highest degree by his sermons," comments Josephus, "[Antipas] became alarmed. Eloquence that had so great an effect on mankind might lead to some form of sedition, for it looked as if they would be guided by John in everything that they did."

Hence Antipas had John arrested and brought in chains to the fortress at Machaerus in Perea, a splendid Herodian palace to which was attached a frightful prison—the entire complex less than ten miles from both the Dead Sea and the Nabatean frontier. Herod had come here not only to forestall a border war but also to excite public appreciation by throwing himself a lavish birthday party, proclaiming a short holiday season and doling out favors to a few influential Jewish leaders; evidently he knew the value of the Roman tradition of bread and circuses. John in prison, Antipas hoped, would end this unwelcome and menacing influence, and for the moment no more serious action against him was planned.

———

The Baptist's most effective disciple, meanwhile, had been preaching on his own in Judea, to the west. "When Jesus heard that John had been arrested, he withdrew to Galilee"—about a hundred miles north. "He left Nazareth and made his home in Capernaum by the sea." Here Jesus centered his Galilean ministry—in a small village on the northwest shore of the Lake of Galilee.

John's imprisonment clearly altered whatever plans Jesus had that year. In another dramatic development in his life, Jesus now decided to continue the proclamation in Galilee, a territory not yet entirely evangelized by his mentor. This was not, as might be rashly presumed, a flight by Jesus to avoid any conflict with the court of Antipas. Quite the contrary: the tetrarch's principal residence was at Tiberias, about twelve miles to the south, on the western shore of the lake. John's message had not yet penetrated the whole region, and so Jesus saw his future there. As John's faithful disciple, in other words, he was about to take up where the mentor had left off—no matter what the signs of the times indicated, no matter what peril Jesus himself might encounter, not only from his association with the Baptist but from the effect of his own mission, too.

By the end of the year 28, all that was known of Jesus was that he had been a disciple of John the Baptist and that he had attracted at least a few of John's disciples to himself. But soon after, he had something to say quite on his own. He was one who "went about doing good and healing all who were oppressed by the devil, for God was with him." Thus was the character of Jesus of Nazareth summed up once and for all in the earliest Christian proclamation.

———

For Jesus, the arrest of John clearly indicated that a final crisis was at hand. "The time is fulfilled," he told his people, "and the kingdom of God has come near. Repent"—thus far, the words certainly echoed John, but now there was a radical shift—"and believe in the good news." Herein lies the difference, obvious almost at once.

John preached in the spirit of classical, prophetic Judaism, with its sense of menace and of impending doom haunting everyone. Last of the great Jewish prophets, John announced the imminent kingdom or rule of God: the just will be vindicated, the unjust chastened. As eternal King, God was about to enter finally into human history—and this, according to some, would mean the defeat of the occupying Roman armies.

Jesus, on the other hand, proclaimed that God's approach was "good news"—that the kingdom, the activity of God in the world, meant not condemnation but grace for all and, in fact, what might be called a new world order. The kingship of God means a new life and access for all to the mercy of God—already introduced, his words and actions imply, in his own ministry.

God's kingdom is certainly not a fixed order; much less it is a political or social entity. On the contrary, it comes into our experience as what we call grace. The kingdom of God is at work in us: what does this mean?

There are, of course, many "kingdoms" or powers that try to claim our allegiance: people whose influence we covet; people to whom we are bound by obligation or by love; those who give or withhold, who help or trouble us. Just so, many kingdoms battle for primacy in our life: the desire for more and more comfort, perhaps, or for greater and more luxurious possessions, or for mere pleasure and diversion rather than for real recreation; and the desire for the subtleties of power over others, the sorts of manipulation that grant the spurious sense that one is in control.

As for the kingdom of God within us: "God rules only in spite of people," wrote the great philosopher Romano Guardini. "He reigns only inasmuch as consciousness of His presence is able to force itself upon me, to coexist with the people in my life." God does not, Guardini mourned, dominate our lives. "Any tree in my path seems to have more power than He, if only because it forces me to walk around it!"

But what would life be like if God did rule within me?

For one thing, I would recognize at once that my real life consists of nothing outside God. All that mattered would be the relationship between, on the one hand, the people, issues and things in my life and, on the other, my life in God. "My life shall be a real life, being wholly full of Thee," was the prayerful hope of Saint Augustine. That may be the deepest meaning of the kingdom of God—the gradual awareness of every human being of attachment to a loving Creator.

But the kingdom of people effectively controls us, and to the extent that we will it so, there is sin in our lives: the kingdom of goods and services, of earthly powers, of business, the kingdom of fear, the kingdom of things. In themselves, these are not wicked, but how easy it is to allow them to suffocate the presence of God right out of our lives. "How is this possible," Guardini asked, "that the tree in the road is more real to me than He? that God remains but a word to me? that He does not stream overpoweringly into my heart and consciousness?"

———

John was an ascetic, while fasting and abstaining from wine were not customs of Jesus: "Why do we and the Pharisees [zealous and influential observers and devout interpreters of the law] fast often, but your disciples do not fast?" ask the Baptist's disciples of Jesus, who replies with a question: "The wedding guests cannot mourn as long as the bridegroom is with them, can they?"

John awaited a future event, while Jesus announced a tension of partial fulfillment in the present moment—in fact, in his own preaching and ministry, God's reign was breaking through once and forever. Like John, Jesus was celibate; unlike John, Jesus did not observe ritual fasting. Both practices marked Jesus as a marginal Jew. An apparently ordinary Galilean, he never studied under a significant rabbi. Nevertheless, he was often radical in his teaching, challenging authorities and announcing a completely new way of considering God.

What was the reason for this urgent and positive action, so different from the tone of the Baptist's message and typical Jewish reasoning? The answer was clear from what Jesus began to say and to do almost immediately. He not only taught, he healed; he not only preached, he blessed, consoled and transformed lives. Not only was there good news for the poor, but for everyone. He was "a friend of tax collectors and sinners," and of the sick and the possessed, the smug and the sedate, the demented and the lonely, the impolite and the unattractive—everyone who was unacceptable and every kind of outcast came within the reach of his saving embrace.

It was no longer a matter of people repenting of their oppression of the poor, receiving a baptism of water as a sign of that repentance and a desire for newness of heart. Now—in everything that Jesus was saying and doing—God's mercy was washing over the world for everyone, like the sweep of a cool spring rain over the hot, parched wilderness.

CHAPTER FOUR

OF THINGS HIDDEN:
THE EARLY LIFE AND TIMES
OF JESUS

I f we did not consider the complex literary and religious history of
the infancy narratives, the enterprise of setting forth a conventional
biography of Jesus might look like a fairly straightforward business—
especially in comparison to the hopeless muddle presented when we
consider the lives of other great religious figures.

Buddha, who died about 480 B.C., is presented—in writings not set
down until at least five hundred years after his death—as an ideal wisdom type rather than as a recognizable man. The personality of his
contemporary, Confucius, is completely unrecoverable from either the
Chinese ideology that interpreted him or from the first documents about
him, which date from four hundred years later. And as for Lao-tse: he
may have lived at any point between the fourteenth and the sixth centuries B.C., and a formulation of teachings about the Taoist Way was
not attempted until the first century B.C.

But the writings that witness to Jesus of Nazareth, and of the communities that believed in him—the twenty-seven books that constitute
the New Testament—come from a period of only twenty to seventy
years after his death, and we have accurate and complete manuscript
copies of those writings dating from the third and fourth centuries.
These documents place us much closer to the primal events of Christianity than any other religious scriptures do regarding their origins.

The earliest New Testament writings (the letters of Paul, written from
about 50 to 65) make only one or two allusions to the life of Jesus, but
that is understandable: neither Paul nor his contemporaries were much

interested in establishing the details of the past, for Jesus was, to them, entirely of the present. The only interest the New Testament has in a "past" is the Hebrew Scriptures (the Old Testament), for the first Christians saw them as fulfilled—brought to full realization—in Jesus. Risen and among them, ever present in their life of faith, Jesus did not invite any nostalgia for what *had* happened—he only evoked a determination to discover what was then happening and what the future challenged and promised.

In any case, the later attempt to recover a precise set of details about the life of Jesus—in other words, the construction of a biography in the modern sense of the word—invariably fails, precisely because the Gospels were not written with that modern sense of history in mind. As we shall see, that does not mean we can know nothing about Jesus. The silence of the Gospels in failing to respond to our twentieth-century obsession to know exactly what happened, and to pin down just who said what to whom, is not a silence of negation: it is a silence full of meaning.

My point is that the Gospels are silent about the past because they shout loudly about the present—their own and, more to the point, ours. We inquire, with them, not into the facts of Jesus' life in the flesh, but into the meaning of his existence forever. The Jesus to whom they witness is of an eternal now, ever discoverable; he is not of the unrecoverable past. The man who came as God's anointed and was executed by crucifixion is, say the Gospels, more alive than in his former life in the flesh— and he continues to be encountered and experienced. In this regard, the voices of the evangelists must be allowed to converse with our own; and in a way, such a conversation is the goal of this book. The entire task of trying to determine "what happened" is avoided if we understand that the evangelists also describe "what happens" when faith enlivens life.

Jesus himself did not leave any written words, nor did he charge anyone else with that task; hence no transcription of his words and deeds was made as they occurred. He lived, preached, performed wonderful deeds and was executed as a Galilean Jew in the first third of the first century.

After his death and the unprecedented event of his Resurrection, Jesus' disciples began to preach; thus began, in the second third of the century, a second stage, the oral transmission of his words and deeds. Preaching, of course, takes into account the style of the speaker and the needs of the audience, and as it draws on recollections, it tends to group items synthetically. Sayings are classified according to topic and altered

to suit new situations of contemporary communities; deeds are interpreted and extended to fit new life contexts; and collections of those
sayings and deeds circulate widely and differently.

The emphasis during this first-century preaching was still very much
on the present moment: Jesus was proclaimed alive and active in the
community and, although hidden and invisible, he was disclosing himself in faith to those who drew near to him. Now, God's unconditional
love and His offer of Himself was proclaimed to Gentiles as well as to
Jews, and in Greek as well as Hebrew or Aramaic. And now, too, the
meaning of this good news was enriched by translating—not just into
another language, but into new situations. This partly oral and partly
written second stage in the development of the Gospel tradition is mostly
impossible to recover, although there have survived fragments of apostolic preaching, of sermons, early hymns and remembered sayings in the
final written documents.

The subsequent formulation of the four Gospels, in the last third of
the first century (from about 65 to 100), occurred only because of several
clear factors in the ongoing life of the communities. For one thing, it
was evident (contrary to the widely held assumption of the first Christians) that the world was not soon going to end. Then, as the original
eyewitnesses died, it was necessary to have something that reflected Resurrection faith for the ongoing life of what was becoming an extraordinary new movement. Furthermore, this movement was spreading
beyond Judaism and beyond the borders of Palestine, and so reference
had to be made to non-Jewish believers. In fact, the four Gospels were
all written in Greek, for that was the universal common language. The
Gospel according to Mark was probably completed a little before 70,
Matthew and Luke between about 80 and 90, and John in the mid-90s.

None of the evangelists was an eyewitness to the original events, but
each had access to rich oral traditions, each arranged the material according to his own plan and genius, and each presented a unique understanding of the meaning of Jesus for his own community—an
understanding that interpreted and presented his deeds and words in
light of his risen, new life. The Gospels, as the scholar Donald Senior
has remarked, "proclaim Jesus as risen Lord, as the fulfillment of God's
promise, as the supreme moment of creation and history where the very
life of God is revealed. All incidents recorded about his life are seen in
this light; every word attributed to him has been etched by this faith."

That Jesus is proclaimed as God's "supreme moment" is clear from the vivid examples in the infancy narratives. There was no attempt to reconstruct the past life of Jesus in literal or chronological detail; rather, the writers' aim was to demonstrate the eternal importance of the Risen Jesus by conveying the truth of his preaching, the importance of his deeds and the impact he once had and continued to have. Hence the authors were exactly that—creative developers of the tradition of faith, organizers, shapers, interpreters and directors of that tradition toward particular goals relevant to their communities. That their faith was not anomalous, that it was emblematic and representative, is demonstrated by the fact that the earliest Churches affirmed these four and rejected others as representative of their faith in Jesus.

————————

The Bible may indeed be, for the believer, the word of God. But however sacred they are held, these writings do not escape the limitations of knowledge and of history and the metaphoric nature of human discourse. Naturally, the Gospels reflect the views of the periods from which they derive, and the historical context must always be taken into account in interpreting the weight and significance of their religious message.

It would be foolish, therefore, to pore over the Bible in search of a moral or ethical tract on biology or anthropology, or on evolution or mass production: these were not issues during biblical times. It is odd, in this regard, that even when Christians understand and accept the historical limitations of the language of the Bible, they are so often unable to accept that Church proclamations labor under the same limitations. Doctrines and Church teachings may certainly express an aspect of revealed religious truth, but the linguistic forms of those teachings do not exhaust the truth.

"The substance of the deposit of faith is one thing, and the way in which it is presented is another," Pope John XXIII sagely reminded. In this regard, the official teaching of the Roman Catholic Church is remarkably open and provocative, for it has been acknowledged that change is the constant. All the teachings and dogmas of the Church have, of course, been expressed in human words by human beings: so much was proclaimed by Rome itself as recently as 1973. Doctrines must, therefore, be interpreted in light of the expressions, concepts and circumstances of the time when they were expressed.

The way in which faith is presented in the Gospels, then, tells us much about the belief of the first Christians but very little about the actual chronology and day-to-day facts in the life of Jesus. The inability to construct a modern biography is not at all a hindrance toward knowing Jesus, however; as both the Bible and faith disclose, that is a matter of the present in any case. This point deserves some elaboration.

History, we often wrongly think, can be set down by scholars and writers without bias, prejudice or viewpoint—as an enterprise in which we have no agenda and are in search of "just the facts, please." But this is impossible to achieve, for the sum of the facts is irretrievable; hence it is absolutely impossible for any historian, however brilliant, and however thorough the research, to know every actual detail of the circumstances under which anything in history occurred.

What can be retrieved through study, research, interviews—all the resources of scholarly digging—comprises only some of the facts, and they are at once selected, edited, arranged, given context. In other words, the material is judged, assessed, evaluated. Some aspects of the event are considered less important than others and are omitted, some are marked as more significant and they are developed, some details are connected to these causes, others to those effects.

In other words, interpretation occurs at once—and this act of interpretation does not falsify the past: on the contrary, it discloses its meaning, or at least some of its meanings. The historian can describe an event meticulously, but from the evidence alone one cannot say what the event signifies. The meaning derives precisely from the interpretation of the facts, not from the facts themselves. And interpretation depends on the creation of a narrative. This is why the historian (and the biographer, who writes a specific kind of history) has to have a very modest attitude. The complete truth of something always eludes: he offers only a "take."

Every human life—and for the Christian, the life of Jesus especially— is all nuance, paradox, ambiguity, mystery. We shall never have done with it. Something is always yet to be revealed; something always remains wonderfully hidden. Thus we can speak of the life of Jesus as always and ever a new life—precisely because something of it is always ahead of us, always waiting to be discovered—not the facts, but the living person who discloses himself to us. "Truly, you are a hidden God," writes Isaiah.

All of this is as true for daily events in our lives as it is for understanding the meaning of history and the impact of the past on the present. We are constantly interpreting reality: that is the only way we can process it, make sense of it, use it constructively.

When we tell friends what happened yesterday, for example, we focus on one or two moments that were interesting for us, or perhaps we think of what might be interesting for the friends. In sharing the news, whether or not it is life-changing news, we tell little stories to one another, we arrange narratives, we categorize and classify and evaluate and assess—thus the accounts that convey our experiences require, in the telling, interpretation. Something is meaningful in light of our past, for example; or something touches us in light of our present or our hopes for the future. We omit the humdrum, we arrange, and yes, we dramatize—but that does not mean we falsify or fabricate.

————

The key to interpreting the reality of our experience is reflection, in two senses of that word. I reflect—I contemplate, I think and allow myself to feel—and then reflection occurs: the other re-flects (bends back toward) me. The event or person peers out at me, in a way "speaks" to me, shows me myself, and so I enter into a situation of dialogue. I see a greater reality than the one on which I focus, and a greater reality than myself. Connective threads suggest themselves, points of confluence begin to emerge—links between myself and others, between myself and the past. And in this realization, I have the capacity to escape from the chill prison of self.

I discover, for example, something that resonates in an event of the past or in the life of another, and I nod, I affirm, I understand. That is why historians and biographers, at their best, become empathetic partners with their readers, linking past and present. They do not merely drag facts out of the past and into the present: they suggest why and how the arc of time and the mystery of human life go deeper than any individual moment or lifetime. Like all good creative writers, the evangelists were not mere reporters; they reflected sublimely, and they make it possible for us to do the same.

This is why we can speak of two senses of history: history as a narration of an event or a life, or as a process through which the world goes and my life evolves—and through which its significance is perceived. You may speak of Gibbon's written history of Rome, and you may speak of your own history. It is the same with biography. In addition to a merely written account of facts and details (which is never more than the stuff of an almanac entry in any case), a biography at its best offers the sense and significance of a life. That is the achievement of the Gospels: they set down the meaning of Jesus for present faith, not for mere historical consideration.

The modern kind of biography, based on an array of detailed facts, sources and resources, was an unrecognized category in the ancient world. The danger for us is that we think the modern biography is superior; it is not—it is just different. And because some modern biographies so often seem to strive for a patently impossible neutrality (or worse, approach the subject with a negative agenda), they are frequently less. Striving to be valueless, they lack interpretation, and so the reader has no frame of reference, nothing with which to work as he finds his own meaning. Footnotes documenting every fact, and interviews supporting every opinion, are, in any case, very recent adjuncts to the craft of history or biography—not much more than forty or fifty years old. For centuries before that, it was taken for granted that the viewpoint and the experience of the writer gave as much meaning as the bare facts the writer presented. And if the writer had been touched, moved, even inspired by the subject, that gave the work more value. In a modern narrative, facts can too easily substitute for reality: they are not reality—interpretation leads us to the reality.

A life only becomes real for us when it is interiorized, only when we find those connective threads of meaning and make the link to ourselves. But this does not reduce the life and meaning of a person to a mythic shell. For the believer, the facts of Jesus' past are not nearly so important as the reality of Jesus' present—and presence—to, in and among us. Hence the Gospels describe and summon us not to the past but to the present, and they point us to the future. The Risen One they proclaim is not of mere historical interest: he is alive and at work now, and he invites us to the future.

This is why we attend to a deeper truth than can be found in mere facts. This, too, is why we attend the great stories of art in epics, novels, poetry, music, drama. The Bible, perhaps preeminently, offers not an attempt at mere historical truth, but a deeper truth—the truth that is relevant for our discovery of meaning and purpose, in this life and the next: that is what we mean by "the truth of salvation."

———————

A person's life continues to disclose itself after the person's death, for the meaning of that life is more deeply perceived and understood as it is received by others. Biography at its best tries to capture the meaning beneath and within the process that lasted from birth to death—a meaning that can only be discerned and communicated by reflection after the fact.

When we read the life of a famous person in history, we are gripped not by the facts but by someone's spirit, mediated by the author. The text conveys, first of all, a sense of the subject's primal experience. Then the text must somehow communicate the writer's passion—lively prose is the first result, and then the kind of insight that can only come from understanding (which presumes compassion). From there, if we are attentive readers, we make the final link: the text of the life addresses our own experience. It is not, we must note, that our own experience mediates the text and the understanding: that would not lift us out of self. Instead, we allow the text to grasp us: we allow ourselves not to be drawn into the past; rather, we allow the past to demonstrate its vitality in our present. It is we who are changed by the text. We do not change it to suit our fashions and fantasies.

Under no circumstances is this truer than when we allow ourselves to be perceived by the transcendent—in other words, when we allow ourselves to be beheld by God. This is an awesome thing. It is also unavoidable, for it is the condition of our very existence. We need only acknowledge the ultimacy of this truth for it to transform us.

One way to begin this is by allowing the texts of the Bible access into our lives, the way we allow any person or influence or art or achievement access into our lives. The words have altered lives and changed human consciousness for centuries: clearly they have an inherent power to mediate an experience that transforms human destiny, that raises human potential. Much is cloudy, to be sure; much is not well understood by us because of the wide gaps separating our culture and language from those of the authors. But this, too, is part of the good news, for the understanding is part of a process still unfolding. We do not worship the Bible or its individual texts: we worship, we fall silent, in the presence of the God Who stands behind them, Who sanctions and ratifies them. The words that point to Him are not dead and final—they live, they open us to ourselves, for the act of interpretation interprets the interpreter to himself. And as I dig deeper toward an understanding of the words, I simultaneously dig deeper toward an understanding of myself.

————

For the reader in search of a full-scale modern biography, one of the most astonishing things about the Gospels is their silence about everything up to the time Jesus began his public ministry. The simple truth is that by the time the evangelists began their task, there was virtually no recollection about the first thirty-odd years of Jesus' life. His closest friends and followers did not meet him until he was an adult, and then—for what was perhaps only about two years—Jesus and his disciples were, to understate the matter, busy. And none of the original eyewitnesses to his life and death wrote a single word about him, as he himself did not. The traditions about him preserved nothing about his past, nothing about his early years—precisely because by the time those traditions were reshaped, it was only the living, Risen Jesus in his new but hidden life that concerned them. As we have seen, everything that circulated about his teaching and his deeds was passed through the prism of that faith.

The entire earthly life of Jesus up to the time of his ministry has always been called, in popular piety, the hidden life—and on it the New Testament is quite succinct: "They went back to Galilee, to their own town of Nazareth," writes Luke about the family after his birth, "and Jesus increased in wisdom, in stature and in favour with God and with people." And that is the digest of more than thirty years. Still, it is possible to say something about the contours of life at the time, and to have at least some general idea of the kind of man Jesus was becoming during this long hidden period.

Galilee is a small region—not more than forty miles from north to south and twenty-five miles east to west. It was apparently outside the mainstream of Jewish life in biblical times, and by the time of Jesus it was held in some contempt by the Jews of Judea.

The dwellings of Nazareth (whose population was between fifteen hundred and two thousand) were unexceptional, as we have seen: one or two rooms around a central courtyard; stone and mud-brick were the basic ingredients of the walls, and the flat roof was constructed of wooden rafters on which were placed planks covered with sticks and branches and a layer of lime marl. Fire was a constant danger.

At home, Jesus was certainly taught the traditions and rituals of ancient Judaism. Each morning and evening, faithful Jews recited the *Shema,* the ancient creed of Israel: "Hear, O Israel: The Lord is our God, the Lord alone. You shall love the Lord your God with all your heart, and with all your soul, and with all your might." Devout Jews prayed three times daily—hymns of praise and blessings, with personal prayers added to the formal words. Prayer was thus part of the fabric of everyday life.

In addition, Jesus' familiarity with the Old Testament and with liturgy suggests that he had a religious education at the local synagogue in Nazareth. Indeed, when he begins his public life, we are told that he does so by entering the synagogue of Nazareth "on the Sabbath day, as was his custom." The synagogue was the local gathering place for prayer, rabbinical instruction and study, for the Jerusalem temple was of course inaccessible for most Jews. Ordinarily, unless they were wealthy enough to afford both the journey and time off from labor, Jews went to the Holy City for Passover only, when the great deliverance from slavery in Egypt and the amalgamation of God's people were solemnly commemorated.

The journey from Nazareth to Jerusalem would have taken at least four or five days. Women were not required to make this annual trip, but according to Luke, Mary and Joseph went to Jerusalem with Jesus when he was twelve, and this provides the only incident in the life of Jesus between his presentation in the temple when just forty days old, and the man of more than thirty years.

The Talmud mentions thirteen as the maximum age for beginning the observation of Jewish ritual and law, and twelve-year-olds were routinely brought to Jerusalem for Passover, to accustom them to the event that, the following year, would become a solemn obligation. Luke recounts a tradition that had circulated orally:

"When the festival was ended and they started to return, the boy Jesus stayed behind in Jerusalem, but his parents did not know it. Assuming that he was in the group of travelers, they went a day's journey. Then they started to look for him among their relatives and friends.

When they did not find him, they returned to Jerusalem to search for him."

Searching and finding are major motifs in Luke's Gospel, and they recur with such frequency and urgency that it is impossible to read them as accidental repetitions. The shepherd, in a Lukan parable, loses and then finds his lost sheep; in another parable, a woman loses and then finds her lost coin; in a third, the Prodigal Son is lost and then found; and Jesus speaks of losing and finding one's whole life. The key to Luke's meaning may lie in the words immediately following: "After three days they found him, sitting among teachers, listening to them and asking them questions." For the first hearers of this episode, this may have recalled Easter Sunday, when the Jesus who had been "lost" in death for two days was "found" on the third day.

Now the narration continues with a curious dialogue:

"His mother said to him, 'Child, why have you treated us like this? Look, your father and I have been searching for you in great anxiety.' He said to them, 'Why were you searching for me? Did you not know that I must be about my father's business [literally, "in the things of my father"]?' But they did not understand what he said to them."

And with that, Jesus goes back to Nazareth with Mary and Joseph and becomes an obedient teenager, and Luke adds (in exactly the words used to describe Samuel in the Old Testament), "he continued to grow both in stature and in favour with the Lord and with the people."

The story is a bridge from the Lukan infancy narratives to the beginning of Jesus' adult ministry, which follows at once. Here, he is identified as a child with an extraordinary destiny (known in light of what later occurred) as God's son in a unique way. The fundamental claim on Jesus' life is made by God, who is his Father analogously and metaphorically; this is one of the terms the New Testament uses in its struggle to express the growing post-Resurrection awareness that Jesus was the fullness of God in the world. At his presentation in the temple a few verses earlier, Jesus was unable to speak on his own behalf: now he does, stating the purpose of the mission that will begin a few verses later— "to be about the things of God."

———

As for Jesus' constant reference to God as Father, it is of course critical to keep in mind that this designation, too, was a metaphor. Neither

Jesus nor Jews before or during his time considered God masculine. But because in Semitic culture the role of the father was both authoritative and venerated, it was natural for Jesus to speak of God this way. It was not masculinity that was at stake, but an intimate, living bond between Creator and created.

It is astonishing, in this regard, to encounter those in modern times who are offended by the designation "He" for God—as if Jews or Christians have ever ascribed gender to God. But here they are, the small minds with an agenda: everyone has been on the wrong track these thousands of years, claim these verbal politicians. Surprise: God, they insist, is not "He." But are they not creating false problems? Only a misguided, literalist mind fails to understand that all speech about God is necessarily limited, allusive, metaphorical; alas, when that misguided mind forms a club, what you get is rewritten Scriptures: God must not be spoken of as "He," and so you hear and read (in the crudest politically correct translations) about God "the Parent." Or worse, God as "She," which is neither any better nor worse than God as "He."

Occasionally, I have to admit, the sudden and unexpected use of "She" may be healthily jarring—may upset us just for a moment, reminding us that our talk about God should always be provisional, always rethought, reconsidered, felt anew. The great thirteenth-century English mystic Julian of Norwich was right to refer to "Jesus our Mother." Julian knew, in the vivid and instant insight of one who lived close to God, that language indeed had sometimes to be reshaped. Jesus nurtures, embraces, envelops, holds tenderly: Julian herself would not have resorted to psychological jargon, but these are qualities we associate as feminine. No harm, then, as long as we do not literally attempt to desexualize him, in calling Jesus our Mother.

————

At home in Nazareth, Jesus' parents would certainly have seen to it that their boy learned enough Hebrew to read the Scriptures. (Jesus most likely spoke a Galilean version of Western Aramaic, a Semitic dialect closely related to Hebrew that was the common language of Israelites in the first century.) Since the fourth century B.C., however, Greek had been the worldwide language of commerce, politics and culture. Palestinian Judaism was not isolated from the wider Greco-Roman world, and every Jew knew at least enough Greek to recognize official proclamations and basic business documents. As for Latin, it was used mostly by Roman officials.

It is critical to keep in mind that there was not a monolithic reality known as Judaism: there were in fact many Judaisms. At the core of the tradition, of course, were the Torah (the Law of Moses in the first five books of the Hebrew Bible), the Jerusalem temple and the sacred character of the country itself. But research has made it abundantly clear in the last forty years that in fact we know very little about Jewish life and religious practices at the time of Jesus, and it is extremely difficult, as one scholar has observed, "to put together what we already know in a coherent package, [for] Palestinian Judaism . . . appears to have been quite diverse and multifaceted. Our increased understanding of its diversity has made it even more difficult to be sure precisely what kind of Jew Jesus was."

Nevertheless, he was certainly a Jewish boy, and it would be contradictory to two millennia of Christian faith to deny that in his childhood and adolescence he knew ordinary physical, sexual and intellectual maturation. The New Testament is very clear on this: "The child grew . . . He had to become like his fellow human beings in every way . . . In every respect, he has been tested as we are." To put the matter succinctly: Jesus experienced everything in the normal physical and psychological development of a human male. To reject this is to repudiate his humanity.

But we must be wary of going further. It is one thing to say he matured intellectually, psychologically, sexually, emotionally. But what specific shape and outlook his inner life took is hidden from us, and what normal sexual curiosity and development meant to him we have no way of knowing. Certainly the fact of his humanity requires us to assert that he strove to discover himself and develop his perspective on life and society, but again, the steps and stages of his inner growth must not be fantasized.

A full appreciation of his humanity also obliges us to take very seriously the limitations of Jesus' human knowledge: despite the flights of pious fancy, the babe in the manger did not gaze upward and think about the theory of relativity, nor could the adult Jesus hum a few bars of Mozart. "If Jesus' knowledge was limited, as indicated in [the Gospels]," writes Brown, "then one understands that God loved us to the point of self-subjection to our most agonizing infirmities." Indeed, to believe in a Jesus who glided through life able to distract himself from the frailty of ordinary people by inner recitations of English poetry and a calm, clear awareness of his own ultimate meaning for the ages is not to have much more than a figure for mute admiration.

But for us who must sometimes wonder and worry, for us who feel dread in the face of final suffering, death and the possibility of annihilation, then belief in a fully human Jesus who, like us, trembles with fear, who is uncertain of the outcome, who experiences an agonizing sense of failure—this is one who is fully on our side, who completely takes the part of humanity. And that is the Jesus whom the Gospels present—one who was not spared anything that is our lot in this world, and whose final destiny transforms the destiny of all creation.

Eventually, those who came and come to believe in him also assert that Jesus is more than the best creature who ever lived: he is also truly of God. We see in him a clear and final declaration of God's love for us—a love that did not shun complete self-abasement. It is, I think, not a tenable position that these complex, singular and incomprehensible mysteries were concocted by a group of semiliterate first-century Palestinians, or by a quartet of community writers a half-century later. Hoaxes, much less literary frauds, do not change the course of world history.

———

Of the physical appearance of Jesus, which countless painters and sculptors have imagined, we know nothing for certain. As a practicing Jew of the time, he very likely had long hair, not necessarily a beard, and perhaps curling locks at his temples. A short undergarment covered with a single flowing cloak completed the basic wardrobe; everyone except Roman slaves wore sandals or soft shoes made of camel skin. His food was the staples of ordinary Palestinian life: fruits and fish, olives and nuts, the dark, thick country wine that had to be diluted with water, and various breads. The Greek custom of reclining on simple divans or couches at mealtime was widespread in the first century: diners leaned on one elbow and reached toward a table, taking from common bowls and plates with their fingers. People were dedicated to cleanliness, and the frequent washing of hands, head and feet took on religious and legal significance.

"He who does not teach his son a craft teaches him robbery" went a familiar maxim at the time of Jesus. According to Matthew and Mark, Joseph's trade was carpentry or woodworking and, as the firstborn son (who traditionally followed his father's profession), Jesus practiced the same craft. Jews considered these artisans honorable craftsmen and, when they could afford their skills, paid them good wages. Steady income would have been necessary to sustain Joseph's household in any case, for there were a wife, five sons and an indeterminate number of daughters. Jesus and his family, then, would have been no more or less poor than the average family in Nazareth; neither as distressed as a country slave nor as deprived as an itinerant laborer, they could perhaps be vaguely compared to today's middle-class workers and artisans.

As for the precise nature of the labor, it should be noted that the Greek word translated as "carpenter" is a generic term that includes more than just woodworking: such a man was proficient at house-building as well as furniture construction, and he had to master a wide range of skills. He made and repaired doors and locks, frames and furniture, windows and roofs, plows and yokes; and the raw materials of his work were (among other trees) sycamores and figs, cedars, firs and junipers, olives and palms. The tools of the trade were remarkably similar to those used by woodworkers today: hammers, mallets, chisels, saws, hatchets, rulers, levels, plumb lines. Nails, which were very expensive, were used only rarely.

Until he was in his mid-thirties, Jesus lived quietly in the somewhat obscure village of Nazareth in southern Galilee, engaged in a profession that required training, intelligence, concentration, dexterity and physical energy. Sometime during these uneventful years, his father died, for once the ministry of Jesus begins, there is no mention of Joseph—only of Jesus' mother and his siblings. Other explanations for the silence about Joseph are of course possible, but they are also without foundation (that is, that Joseph left his family or was not at all interested in his eldest son after Jesus left the trade). If Joseph was in his late teens when he married Mary, he would have reached his early fifties—and hence would have been a venerable senior citizen, subject to the ravages of advanced age at that time—when Jesus abandoned woodworking for preaching.

Two aspects of Jesus' life at this time deserve consideration, however.

First, it is critical to keep in mind that he was a pious layman but not a member of the priestly or aristocratic lay castes. Therefore, he later encountered opposition from them, and was marked and mocked as an inconsequential rural peasant when he dared to contradict and correct the politically entrenched Jerusalem establishment.

Second, it is significant that apparently Jesus remained celibate throughout his life. His parents and siblings are mentioned—and even his brothers' wives—but there is no indication of a wife. Whereas celibacy was rare among devout Jews, who took very seriously the obligation to propagate the children of Abraham, it was not unusual for an occasional prophetic figure to remain single. In the seventh century B.C., Jeremiah had seen his own celibacy as a divine mandate, a sign of the destruction attending the punishment of a faithless people. John the Baptist, a contemporary of Jesus, was also evidently celibate, like a small percentage of Jews who voluntarily chose not to marry. The Essenes, for example, were radical retreatants who lived in communes of quasi-monastic life—many of them as celibates—at Qumran, on the shores of the Dead Sea.

There seems to have been no simple explanation for this irregular state among Jews, but fundamental to celibacy in every case was a radical choice that expressed a conviction about urgent times and total dedication. The single life, then, was not unknown, but it was uncommon enough to mark Jesus of Nazareth as atypical—something of a marginal character. His vocation to summon Israel to God's embrace completely consumed his life.

To remain celibate throughout his teens and twenties certainly would have marked Jesus as anomalous but not completely odd. In fact, in light of the lack of any evidence for marriage or concubinage, we are left with the impression—especially in light of the strangely provocative incident of the finding in the temple at the age of twelve—that this Jesus of Nazareth had, from his earliest years, a sense of calling or mission. It may have been vague, it may have been unformed and it may have had no clear direction. But as he plied his craft as a master woodworker, contributing to his father's business and, we may presume, helping to support his mother and siblings, we are left with an image of Jesus as one who is awaiting the clarification of his destiny—waiting, in other words, for God's clear summons. In this regard, all of us who endure periods of watchful waiting in our lives, who wonder precisely what it is to which we are called, what our work is to be, what our future means—yes, all who wait—have as our model God's son, watchful, wondering, waiting to learn what is the fullest meaning of his life.

The reward of that waiting came when Jesus met John the Baptist, a man of uncommon features and unlikely fashion. And in that meeting, Jesus changed. The ordinary confusions of youth began to fade in the astonishing light of conversion.

CHAPTER FIVE

THE LURE:
THE TEMPTATIONS OF JESUS

I t is impossible for us to discover what the Gospels did not intend: a firm chronology for the order of events in the life and ministry of Jesus. Fixing such a timetable was not part of the evangelists' goal. Their aim was instead the reflection and radiating of faith, and to that end the oral and fragmentary written traditions that carried the sayings and deeds of Jesus were reworked by the writers and arranged synthetically—often according to categories (sayings, parables, exorcisms, healings and so forth).

But it is certainly possible to suggest a probable general time framework, and this we can do thanks to recent scholarship. Jesus was born about the year 6 B.C. and probably began his ministry, as we have seen, at the age of thirty-three or thirty-four, early in the year 28. He was very likely executed on Friday, April 7, of the year 30. His public ministry, in other words, lasted for two years and a few months, and he was dead at about the age of thirty-six. During that brief and busy ministry, Jesus often moved from Galilee to Judea and back again, in a constant rhythm of preaching and healing.

The focal point of his life was one of the loveliest spots in Palestine—the area around the freshwater Lake of Galilee, also called Gennesaret or Gennesareth. Twelve miles long and eight miles wide at its broadest, the cool, blue waters are (now as then) bordered by striking cliffs and verdant plains. The population counted many fishermen, for the lake was densely stocked, and some of these men Jesus called to be his disciples.

The area was also a favorite spot for his prayer and reflection: "In the morning, while it was still very dark, he got up and went out to a deserted place, and there he prayed . . . He made his disciples get into the boat and go on ahead to the other side [of the lake], to Bethsaida, while he dismissed the crowd. After saying farewell to them, he went up on the mountain to pray." Also along the border of the lake dwelt merchants, craftsmen and government officials—many of them among Jesus' audience and some of them particular recipients of his concrete acts of mercy and regeneration.

On the northwest shore lay Jesus' primary headquarters, Capernaum, and in its synagogue he often taught and prayed. Four miles away, across the Jordan (which flows into the lake), was Bethsaida, originally the home of some of his followers. Exquisite as it is, the Lake of Galilee and nearby areas experience sudden temperature changes, and (because of the height of the surrounding hills) violent storms can occur at any time.

Other kinds of storms troubled Jesus during his ministry, for he had to deal continually with a singular risky result of his activity. He spoke with such authority and dealt with people so directly and compassionately that often people hailed him as a specific kind of messiah—indeed, a king. They wanted him to be the deliverer whom popular sentiment longed for, one who would lift up Israel from political subordination and establish its prominence among the nations. But such earthly aspirations were never his—hence his persistent and determined rejection of the celebrity, the pomp and the temporal supremacy that public zeal might have secured for him.

Woven into the Gospel tradition is a poignant theme in the life of Jesus: the constant temptation to take the easy way out, to give in to the cry of the crowd, to accept adulation as a king. As Jesus saw it, this would have been infidelity to his mission, which was something more spiritual: the proclamation and inauguration of the kingdom of God— the good news that God is indeed at work in the human sphere, drawing to Himself and saving what He has made. Of this deliverance and salvation, the liberating message of Jesus and the wonderful deeds God performed through him were the establishing signs. God's domain has nothing to do with any kind of temporal power or supremacy. Jesus, therefore, was not to be an earthly potentate. The prophets ever since Samuel had constantly warned that kings coveted, usurped or infringed on God's sovereignty. Then as now, power corrupted. In any kind of authority, a good man was hard to find.

Jesus must have been particularly tempted to yield to popular flattery when he met opposition from religious leaders and interference from his enemies, and in this regard the tradition behind the Gospels has preserved—in a single, brilliantly concise episode—this motif of the perilous lure of renown and of power. The so-called temptation narrative is nothing like reportage; rather, an essentially interior struggle has been artfully rendered in a classic rabbinic dialogue.

From the start of his ministry, Jesus was called to be God's true, faithful son—the new leader of a renewed Israel. Hence the Matthean infancy narrative (in which the genealogy, conception, birth and childhood of Jesus were elaborated) established him as the one who lived out the destiny of God's people, the collective Son delivered from slavery to freedom ("Out of Egypt I called my son"); so, too, the meaning of the baptismal scene ("This is my son, the beloved, with whom I am well pleased"). Thus at the outset of his ministry, there is set before us the tradition of a "temptation," an account that represents not a single, strange occurrence but a danger that attended Jesus throughout his ministry.

"Then Jesus was led up by the Spirit into the wilderness to be tempted by the devil. He fasted forty days and forty nights, and afterwards he was famished. The tempter came and said to him, 'If you are the Son of God, command these stones to become loaves of bread.' But he answered, 'It is written, "One does not live by bread alone, but by every word that comes from the mouth of God."'"

In the wilderness forty days and nights: the allusion to Israel's forty-year trek through the desert (and Moses' forty-day fast on Mount Sinai) would have been clear to the Jewish Christian audience of the Gospel. Proclaimed God's son a few verses earlier in the baptism account—the fulfillment of Israel's hopes—Jesus begins to consummate the destiny of the people.

Now comes the enticement: Make it easy on yourself—stop fasting and praying, and turn stones into bread. Behind this is the popular notion that the Messiah-King would wondrously provide food in abundance for everyone. But no: on the lips of Jesus is placed a verse from the Torah: "One does not live by bread alone"—a line that follows the remembrance of Israel's desert hunger during the Exodus, and of the promise that God's living word satisfies all human longing. Ultimately, life is nourished by the Spirit, not only by a good meal.

"Then the devil took him to the holy city and placed him on the pinnacle of the temple, saying to him, 'If you are the son of God, throw yourself down, for it is written, "He will command his angels concerning you," and "On their hands they will bear you up, so that you will not dash your foot against a stone." ' Jesus said to him, 'Again it is written, "Do not put the Lord your God to the test." ' "

Once again, the last sentence refers to God's complaint against Israel, in the desert experience of the first Passover. According to the Book of Exodus, the Hebrews "put God to the test"—that is, they challenged and doubted His care for them by "threatening God" with apostasy and idolatry. Whereas the Old Testament indicted the Jews of old for their lack of faith, the evangelists claim that failure to be reversed by Jesus.

Finally comes the great offer of secular messianism, the temptation to use worldly power to accomplish a political goal:

"Again, the devil took him to a very high mountain and showed him all the kingdoms of the world and their splendor, and he said to him, 'All these I will give you, if you will fall down and worship me.' Jesus said to him, 'Away with you, Satan, for it is written, "Worship the Lord your God, and serve only Him." ' "

With a touch that may have sounded comical to the original audience—Satan making the offer of earthly kingdoms as if they were his to give—the classically structured, tripartite dialogue draws to a close. Citing for the third time verses from the Exodus experience he fulfills, Jesus announces that he will not yield. He succeeds where others failed; he will not seek the earthly authority that is one of those false gods Israel worshiped in the desert in place of God. And so that we do not think that this artistically constructed account actually ended the lifelong temptation set before Jesus, Luke adds a coda: "the devil departed from him until [another] opportune time."

The Gospels reiterate that the entire ministry of Jesus was hedged round with inducements to ease instead of sacrifice, to power instead of poverty of spirit. As late as his last meal, Jesus spoke with weary gratitude to his closest disciples: "You are those who have stood by me in my trials." Those trials and temptations virtually defined the entire arc of his life—not only the lure of social-political power, but also the occasional efforts even by his friends to deter Jesus from his difficult but destined road, to encourage him to seek comfort above commitment.

Behind the primitive narrative lies the tradition that Jesus drew his growing self-understanding from constant reflection on God's word. He would be the faithful son and servant. As for ultimate supremacy: constituted the reigning Messiah of the universe in his Resurrection by virtue of his fidelity and obedience even to death, Jesus can claim (at the end of Matthew's Gospel) what Satan had so presumptuously offered: "All authority in heaven and on earth has been given to me." This was conferred on him only after a bitter but finally victorious struggle to be the faithful fulfillment of the vocation offered to Israel. Evil had suggested that Jesus subscribe to a brand of false, political messianism that, he knew, was contrary to the will of God. But Jesus did not falter.

One thing remains to be considered in this rich and strange account. What are we to do with the ancient language about Satan? The short answer might be that the devil and his minions are perhaps best understood the way we read about angels. The concept of God as an oriental potentate, surrounded by a court of messengers, includes the Near Eastern idea of the adversaries of the King—those always causing trouble and inciting to rebellion.

The devil is not an important figure in the Old Testament: he occurs in only five books out of almost fifty, and he is mentioned only once in four of those five. He is certainly not depicted as the incarnation of evil. Instead, he is what his name means, "the Accuser." He is an angel in the heavenly court who accuses humans of wrongdoing—a kind of prosecuting attorney. In the intertestamental literature (apocryphal books such as Enoch, which come from a period between the Old and New Testaments), the devil appears more frequently, doubtless because of the late dualist belief in the cosmic fight between eternal good and eternal evil. The serpent that tricked Eve in the Book of Genesis, it should be noted, is not anything like the devil or a demon. Snakes were used in pagan worship, and so the incitement to sin is depicted as having a godless, pagan source.

In the New Testament, it is difficult to distinguish the corruption that results from the devil and that which comes from human sin. When the disciple Peter says that Jesus must never, under any circumstances, suffer anything, a loud rebuke is deserved: "Get behind me, Satan!" is Jesus' response. The language is, of course, as metaphoric as when we refer to a child as "a little devil." But Jesus is in earnest: any suggestion that he ought to avoid inconvenience (much less suffering) is a terrible temptation to infidelity. In the early centuries of Christian life, "the devils" meant heresies or pagan cults. And in these same critical centuries, when Christianity expressed its faith in formulas, it is significant that the devil is not mentioned in any creed.

Of course there is evil. You need go no further back than Hitler and Hiroshima to see concrete examples of it. Even today, examples abound: the lunacy of terrorism; all kinds of violence, especially against children, women, minorities and dissenters; political torture; exploitation of the poor. All around us is the reality of evil in its stark and effective horror, gnawing away at everything that is good and noble and decent in the world. Every day we see very clearly the awful toll that humanity is capable of exacting against itself. But it is too easy to blame it all on Satan; we cannot excuse ourselves by protesting, "The devil made me do it!" We have met the enemy, and he is us. The denial that we are incapable of any evil in us may be one of the surest signs of its existence.

But as for a personal being, a devil who is the incarnation of immortal evil . . . ? How is it possible to believe in God, who is eternal love and mercy, and at the same time to believe that this good God could create a being capable of evil to the point of eternal—eternal!—damnation? If one posits unrestrained personalized evil in a being or beings, then anything can happen and God's hands seem tied. Wicked spirits can take over the bodies of innocent little girls and put them through hell before a ritual dispels the demon. But while books and movies like *The Exorcist* might impress us as horror stories, they fail miserably as meditations on evil. We can read the book or see the movie and say to ourselves, "If this is evil, then evil is not present in my world—nothing in my experience is like *that!*" And then we can go on our merry way, content that everything is just fine with us, that we may have bad manners sometimes, or we may unintentionally offend, but as for evil—no, none of that has any place in my life.

All creation is subject to infinite, unconquerable goodness. We either believe in the mystery of the eternal love of God or we believe in a creator who, at least once, miscalculated badly and could do nothing to correct it. And this makes the event of Jesus incomprehensible, for in Jesus we see the human face of God. Unimaginable compassion breaks in upon a world so needy of it precisely because we are so miserly in offering it to one another.

———

"He went about doing good." This description of Jesus does not always evoke admiration.

Preaching the gracious coming of God, healing the sick and bringing the imprint of his transforming person and personality, Jesus had to cope with the lure—the temptation to give it all up.

The bait could come from home. The crowds pressed in on Jesus, and suddenly there was his family. Those close enough to Jesus to get a message through to him relayed the news: his mother, brothers and sisters were outside. He was causing some embarrassment to them with all this preaching and healing, and so they had come "to restrain him," for some people were saying, "He has gone out of his mind!" To make matters worse, "not even his brothers believed in him."

Jesus apparently expected this kind of incomprehension, for his reply was to ignore the family tension—he simply had no time for it. "Who are my mother and my brothers?" he asked rhetorically. And with that he looked around at all the needy, the ill, the poor and the scoundrels sitting around him, captivated by his presence and his teaching. "Here are my mother and my brothers! Whoever does the will of God is my brother and sister and mother!" Neighbors around Nazareth, familiar with Jesus and his family since his boyhood, sometimes narrowed their gaze and asked who he thought he was. And Jesus sensed the smug distrust. "Prophets are not without honor," he said, "except in their hometown, and among their own kin, and in their own house"—and, amazed at their unbelief, he withdrew from his own native territory. If charity can begin at home, so, it seems, can hostility.

———

John the Baptist, meanwhile, was languishing in the hellish prison at Machaerus. His disciples, naturally, told him of the notoriety attending his former pupil. And John, losing confidence in himself and others, sent a message to Jesus, asking if he was the true Messiah for whom they had all been waiting, and if so, what kind of Messiah? Or ought they to look elsewhere for the fulfillment of their hopes?

Jesus' answer was to point to what he was doing as a sign that a new age had indeed dawned. "Go and tell John what you hear and see," he told the messengers—and then he listed the effects of his own preaching and healing: the blind received their sight, the lame walked, the lepers were cleansed, the deaf heard, and the poor received good news. Even John's expectations were being surpassed; healings and marvelous cures had not been part of his mission. But John had to draw his own conclusions, Jesus seemed to imply, for it was not up to the pupil to instruct his teacher.

This is the last we know from or about John the Baptist, chained a few miles away. There is no indication of whether he came to believe that Jesus was indeed the one who would in some still unknown, mysterious way fulfill the longing of God's people once and for all. There is only silence about John, no hopeful word to report—only more suffering.

There was no neat, sweet ending to this episode. There was not even, for John, the comfort of a newfound faith, in whose security he could face execution. Nor was there the satisfaction of knowing that his tutelage had been even more decisive for universal salvation than he could have dreamed.

John remained in prison. To himself, he seemed a failure: his mission aborted, he was bereft of the comfort of his disciples, snatched from the world whose destiny he sought to alter. Imprisoned by a nominally Jewish king who was a disgrace to his people, John faced the possibility that his life added up to very little. All the self-denial, all the fasting and prayer and hardship—all of it seemed worthless, for God had apparently abandoned him.

The end came with ugly suddenness. Antipas decided that it would have been foolish to wait for the twofold upheaval, caused by the social rebellion John was inciting and by the saber-rattling of Aretas at the borders. It was better to strike against John and be rid of him once and for all. And so, perhaps using the old complaint that John had insulted him and his wife, Antipas ordered John beheaded. This was a grisly, dreadful execution, for death by the sword was rarely accomplished with one clean swipe.

The news was brought to Jesus, who retreated into solitude for prayer and mourning, and perhaps because he now had to consider himself, too.

This habit of retreat was a motif in the life of Jesus: he constantly withdrew from the press of the crowds, the circle of his friends and the attention of his followers in order to hear more clearly the voice of God. Hence Jesus paradoxically revealed something crucial about himself by parting from others, by becoming, in still another sense, the hidden one—linked in the core of his being to the hidden God.

John's execution only put Jesus' own future in doubt, for Jesus, too, was beginning to stir up controversy. Having continued his ministry after the imprisonment of John meant he risked imprisonment, too; to continue his ministry was to court the Baptist's fate. "Get away from here," some people warned Jesus, "for Herod [Antipas] wants to kill you!"

For one thing, he was putting himself in a situation of Jewish ritual impurity. John warned of imminent judgment. Jesus, however, announced that God is not a fearful, distant, terrifying judge but rather a loving parent who longs to regain His lost children. In witness of that, Jesus freely and gladly associated with all those considered untouchable according to Jewish laws. He dined with tax collectors, adulterers, those outside polite life, and all the impious, poor souls sunk in depressed and forlorn situations that made them pariahs.

Religious people and their authorities, who worked hard to keep the faithful in line and struggled to set an example, were appalled. "Why does your teacher eat with tax collectors and sinners?" someone asked his friends. Jesus overheard and replied, "Those who are well have no need of a physician." And then he sent the questioner back to the Hebrew Scriptures: "Go and learn what this means, 'I desire mercy, not sacrifice.'" In the same spirit, Jesus was becoming a fierce nonconformist, for he did not insist that offenders practice the usual religious rituals of repentance and sacrifice in order to be readmitted to official religious life.

At once, there was trouble over the unprecedented table fellowship that Jesus exercised. He accepted invitations from every quarter, he welcomed all those who were rejected and unwelcome elsewhere—and he neither fasted nor abstained from wine. "Look, a glutton and a drunkard—a friend of tax collectors and sinners!" John was not yet cold in his grave, and already the hostility had shifted its focus. Nothing is more outrageous to popular sentiment than that outcasts should be friends of God.

You can almost hear the devout: We have worked so hard, we fast, we contribute to the synagogue, we go to the Jerusalem temple for feasts, we observe every letter of the law. And here is this layman—a fellow no better than anybody else around here—and he is proclaiming God's unconditional love for . . . for all these *sinners*. No one could remember anyone like him. This indiscriminate mingling of the pious and the outcasts at the table of one who professes to be a Jew—well, *really,* something ought to be done! Eventually, something will.

Against all objections, Jesus proclaimed the presence of the kingdom of God—not only God's unconditional acceptance of humanity but also His real, hidden activity in human affairs as He draws the world to Himself. Although a great fulfillment lay in the future, Jesus insisted that he did not know when that final consummation would be: he trusted it to God's hands—and God's hands were active in the present, reaching right into time and history, healing in the very touch of Jesus himself. Extraordinary things were occurring wherever he went—signs of the inner, invisible transformation God was effecting for the benefit of all the world.

There must have been something enormously attractive and powerful about the personality and character of Jesus of Nazareth, for he changed the lives of those who met him. Not long after he began his ministry, he drew together a cadre of followers, some of whom left everything and followed wherever he went, while others kept their ordinary jobs, lived with their families and put into effect the message of Jesus in their daily lives.

Among them—and this is opposed to rabbinic custom—were a number of women "who had been cured of evil spirits and infirmities." There were, for example, Mary of Magdala, whom Jesus had healed of a terrible illness ("seven devils") perhaps due to a wild or irresponsible life; Joanna, whose husband worked at the court of Antipas; Susanna and Salome, of whom nothing is known but their names; several other women with the name Mary, "and many others," some of whom (probably like Joanna) supported Jesus by monetary contributions and by raising funds from others to pay for food and lodging.

————

His association with women was as revolutionary and unprecedented as his sharing meals with outcasts, and it put him in direct and immediate confrontation with prevailing Jewish convention. For him, all people were to come within God's saving embrace. Women, slaves and children constituted the trio of the disenfranchised in Israel, hence they were among those (like tax men and public sinners) who received the special loving attention of Jesus. He did not say that these people were more deserving or more pious or better than others. He simply insisted that they receive their human rights, and he championed them because no one else did. Jesus did not, however, endorse the romantic notion of the virtuous sinner; much less was he concerned with the empty cliché about "heart over head" or with fomenting a class struggle.

It is not going too far to say that his was perhaps the first mission in history that had no gender bias. It may also not be going too far to suggest that, in our own time, some of Jesus' most outspoken partisans may not be faithful to his vision. In some Christian churches, for example, women are still very much second-class citizens, denied—only because of their gender—the ministerial functions to which men can aspire and that women themselves evidently held in the early days of the Christian community.

To put the matter succinctly, Jesus departed from virtually everything in the spirit of the Jewish law concerning the status and dignity of women. Women were entirely without civil and legal rights in Israel, and they could not bear witness at trials. They were expected to submit to their husbands in all things; they were separated from men in synagogues; they could neither teach in public nor read prayers aloud at home; and even at the Jerusalem temple, they were forbidden to go beyond an outer courtyard.

"Do not speak much with a woman on the street" was a common rabbinic admonition; the custom referred even to a man's wife, who had to remain several paces behind her husband. A man was forbidden by Jewish law to be alone with a woman not his wife, nor could he even greet a woman, much less look at her, and a woman who spoke with strangers could be immediately divorced by her husband. Since they aroused lust, women had to be kept out of public view: hence their faces were veiled in public, and their entire forms were swathed in layers of cloth from head to foot. The best thing for everyone, said the rabbis, was for women not to go out at all.

Jesus offered a startlingly different perspective.

First of all, many of those he healed were women he encountered in public, and his healing invariably involved touching them and speaking with them. The mother-in-law of one of his disciples was among the first: she suffered from a serious fever, but when Jesus visited, he took her by the hand. She was cured at once, happily left her sickbed and prepared a hearty meal for her visitors.

And there are close friends like the sisters Martha and Mary and their brother Lazarus, who lived in Bethany—two miles outside Jerusalem— and who provided lodging for Jesus when he visited the Holy City.

A stranger, an unnamed woman with a blood disease, was similarly affected by the touch of Jesus: "She had been suffering for twelve years, and though she had spent all she had on physicians, no one could cure her." Just being close to Jesus did that, and when she was near enough, she touched the fringe of his garment. Instead of rebuking her, Jesus turned around and praised the woman: "Your faith has made you well— go in peace!"

This open contact and conversation with women was pernicious enough, but there were more shocking examples of Jesus' conduct: his dialogue with the much-divorced and remarried woman he met at a well, for example. When a few of his male disciples turned up on the scene, they were bewildered by his behavior: not only was he speaking with a woman in public, but she was a Samaritan, from a despised subgroup regarded by the Jews as heretics.

Women tirelessly and generously supported the mission of Jesus by their friendship, their practical assistance and their fidelity. Their loyalty was taken very seriously by the earliest Christian communities, who seemed to have had no difficulty including women among the ministers. Interestingly, at least one of them, named Junias, is called an apostle—a broad term meaning those sent out on a mission proclaiming the Resurrection of Jesus.

Not long after he began his public ministry, in early 28, Jesus was walking near the Lake of Galilee. There he saw two fishermen casting nets; they were brothers named Simon and Andrew, and until very recently they had been, like Jesus, disciples of John the Baptist. Something in their manner—perhaps their energy and intensity, maybe their simplicity and their optimism about a good day's catch—stopped Jesus in his tracks. "Follow me," he said during the course of their conversation, adding (possibly with a smile), "and I will make you fish for people." He may have had in mind the image of the prophets: Habakkuk, for example, had described the Jewish people at the time of the Babylonian Captivity as comparable to "the fish of the sea, like crawling things that have no ruler." And Jeremiah had looked forward to the restoration of God's people: "I am now sending for many fishermen," promised the Lord, "and they shall catch them."

Something in Jesus' manner mightily impressed them, too, for in short order, they either dropped their nets or did their jobs in a radically transformed way. In either case, they became part of Jesus' entourage. Their lives were at once altered—virtually turned upside down as all security was taken away in light of their decision. We can only imagine what Simon's wife and family, and the relatives of the others who were called, thought of this sudden career change. This much we can know for sure: it could not have been easy for anyone. There was too much that was unknown, there was too much insecurity in throwing in your lot with this fellow Jesus. Much that he said seemed elliptical, mysterious, unclear. In addition, he was dramatically changing the lives of all those he met—reversing terrible ailments and diseases, freeing them from all kinds of constraints, announcing eternal and boundless mercy and calling for a complete change of heart. What did all this mean?

Of these first two men who were specifically called—as distinct from the women and men who voluntarily attached themselves to Jesus and followed on his rounds—Simon was a major presence in the New Testament. First of all, Jesus quickly understood his personality and so changed his name. For Jews, this is always a significant moment marking a shift in someone's destiny: God changed Abram's name to Abraham, for example, and Jacob's to Israel, and Mattaniah's to Zedekiah. Just so, Jesus saw that Simon was a strong, confident man and thus he changed his name: Simon (Shimon or Simeon) became Cephas—from the Aramaic *kêpa,* "rock." From there, it was only a short distance, in the Gospels, to the Greek word for rock, *petros*—Peter.

But when Jesus extolled Peter—"on this rock," he said, he would build his new community—he also sensed that the rock-bold Peter, despite his evident leadership qualities, could cause trouble, too. Hence "the rock" was also "a stumbling block," as Jesus said. The master was ever a realist and knew, perhaps, not to expect too much even from the most outspoken of the lot. As for Peter's brother Andrew, memories about him (as of all the other company of disciples) had dimmed by the time the Gospels were written.

And so, over the course of several months, Jesus summoned a crew out of the larger group of his followers—twelve men he sent out to preach and heal as he was doing. The number of them deliberately reminded everyone that Jesus was announcing the spiritual restoration of God's people, founded on the twelve ancient tribes of Israel. He was certainly not founding a new sect or religion with lieutenants under his sovereignty. His mission was to summon Israel to renewal, to accept the reign of God in their midst.

Peter and Andrew were among the twelve, and so were two more fishermen: James and John, also brothers, were apparently a quick-tempered pair, for Jesus nicknamed them Boanerges—"the hot-head brothers." Of them we know practically nothing, as we do not of the others: Philip (a close friend of Andrew), Bartholomew, Matthew (perhaps a tax collector), Thomas, Thaddeus, another James and another Simon, and one more.

In fact, the list varies from Gospel to Gospel, for by the time each was written, the faces and personalities of most of the twelve had faded from memory: only what was important survived them, and that was their work and their witness in faith. The mission of the twelve was literally unique—a one-time charge that could never be repeated. Hence the descriptions and characteristics of most of the original group are lost to us. It is as if I were asked, about a friend, "Who were his closest companions when he was in college?" Based on my knowledge of him, I might offer some names, but it might be a somewhat different list from that given by another. We apprehend the relationships of others by way of our own limited perspective.

And so, within a few years after the deaths of Jesus and his disciples, the collective memory of who among the followers belonged to the inner circle of special companions was already blurry. But the name of the twelfth has survived with all its chilling indications: "Judas Iscariot, who became a traitor," is mentioned quietly and almost apologetically by the Gospel writers.

The group of twelve, usually mingling with the larger number of followers, surrounded Jesus throughout his ministry. They watched, they tried to learn, they usually missed his point and hankered for earthly supremacy (for themselves and for Israel), they bickered among themselves, they jockeyed for position and they tried to overprotect Jesus—until the end, when they simply abandoned him to his enemies. In general, they were an exasperating lot, and the Gospels neither glamorize nor mythicize them. The twelve were altogether unremarkable men—until after the death of Jesus, and then a remarkable transformation in their lives enabled them to proclaim good news to all the world.

As he continued to go about, to preach and to heal, people were becoming aware of the radical aspects of Jesus' behavior—that his preaching and healing were paralleled by his free association with women, his refusal to fast, his consorting with outcasts. Just so, they saw his great kindness and gentleness, and because of his reputation for welcoming children, they often brought their young sons and daughters for a blessing. The disciples spoke curtly to these parents: the master's time should not be taken up with trivial introductions like this. Although children were the visible emblem that the people of Israel would survive, they also held the lowest status in Mediterranean societies and had no legal rights whatsoever.

They were, then, the "least of all." As Jesus reminded his friends and listeners, one who desires God's favor must be the "servant of all"—in witness of which, he embraced a small child. "Whoever welcomes one such child"—that is, the lowliest member of society—"welcomes me . . . and the One who sent me." This was an astonishing remark: those who welcomed the message of Jesus, he said, are those receptive to the will of God Himself.

Who was this who spoke "with such authority," as the crowds so often remarked during his ministry? It was impossible to ignore the words and works of Jesus: he overturned expectations, invited decisions, roused the heart, dared to promise what only God Himself could

achieve. As his public life progressed and his urgent proclamation gradually alienated anyone with vested interests and dearly held power, it
was increasingly necessary to take a stand—not only for or against what
Jesus was saying and doing, but for or against him.

How could he be so certain that behind his proclamation was the
endorsement of the Almighty Himself? This is one of the elements in
the life of Jesus enabling us to glimpse the boldness of his self-awareness,
and of his confidence that he offered the good news of God. Conscious
of a call to proclaim the kingdom—the presence and activity of God in
human affairs—Jesus was single-mindedly committed to responding to
that call. Nor did he waver, even in the face of death, when God seemed
to abandon him.

Children were as welcome as women and slaves, and Jesus pointed to
their natural confidence as signs of faith: "Whoever does not receive the
kingdom of God as a little child"—that is, with absolute trust—"will
never enter it." When he spoke of the kingdom, Jesus was not talking
about the next life—God would see to that. He indicated instead both
the welcome that God finds in the hearts of His beloved, and the influence God is permitted by them in their lives. And with that, Jesus picked
up the children in his arms, embraced them, blessed them.

The twelve, in a circle of special amity around Jesus, were often sent
out on missions "to the lost sheep of the house of Israel." But they always
returned to the wise and gentle tutelage of their master. Jesus shared with
them his power to heal, his mandate to proclaim the arrival of God's
mercy. Like Jesus, the disciples did not proclaim a new law; instead, an
entirely new ethic was promulgated. The law is love—not easy, poetic
love, much less romantic-erotic love—but love as radical and pervasive as
God's undiluted love for all people. This meant, essentially, attentive
concern for the needs of others. Forgiveness of grievances. Abandonment
of the desire for power, for revenge, for control over others. A love that
seeks to give, and that in giving finds its recompense.

Jesus knew that this proclamation is easy neither to offer nor to receive—it is all a matter of interior renewal, a revolution in heart and
conduct, not in political achievement. "I am sending you out like sheep
into the midst of wolves; so be wise as serpents and innocent as doves,"
he counseled, and added that they must travel lightly and simply, with
no more baggage than the bare necessities.

But the closer his disciples came to him, the more often they fell into
the old trap of petty jealousy and of a desire for pride of place. Which

one of them was closer to the master? Who was primary in his affections? "What are you arguing about?" Jesus asked one day in Capernaum. Their embarrassment and perhaps a few murmurs and glances gave them away. Who are acting like children *now?* And so Jesus sat down—that was always a sign that a rabbi was about to say something important— and he beckoned to the twelve. "Whoever wants to be first must be last of all, and servant of all—not like the rulers of nations, who act like tyrants," he told them gently, correcting but not scolding. When they approached others, it must be to serve them, to show them what God is like as they have seen Him act through Jesus.

Jesus was no autocrat; rather, he was an endlessly patient listener, the healer, the one whose heart was full of benevolence, who was always on the alert for any kind of human misery and moved forward to correct it.

"When he saw the crowds, he had compassion on them, because they were harassed and helpless, like sheep without a shepherd . . . When he went ashore, he saw a great crowd, and he had compassion for them and cured their sick . . . 'I have compassion for the crowd, because they have been with me now for three days and have nothing to eat, and I do not want to send them away hungry, for they might faint on the way.' "

How often we say that people behave like sheep without a shepherd— lost, unthinking, wandering about, separated from inner moorings, needy of a guide to bring them back home and (perhaps most poignantly) blindly unaware that there is even need for a shepherd. There was in the time of Jesus (and is there not now, two thousand years later?) a profound sense of desertion, an awful sense of feeling forsaken despite our own best instincts. Something is askew in us, something does not fit, somehow we fail ourselves all too often. That is as good a definition of sin as one could require.

To all who have felt or feel or fear feeling lost, Jesus came with the announcement of God's limitless compassion. In Jesus' words and actions, God was drawing near to everyone without exception.

The commission given to those who follow Jesus of Nazareth was to announce that compassion, to proclaim God's infinite attention to human need.

But just as he did, the disciples of Jesus—and all those who later so identify themselves—had to renounce, wherever it appears and however one is tempted to it, the precarious lure of power.

CHAPTER SIX

NEW BEGINNINGS:
JESUS THE JEW

The center of community life in Capernaum and Nazareth, as elsewhere, was the synagogue—an assembly of people and, by extension, the gathering-place itself. It had originated when the Jerusalem temple was destroyed in 587 B.C. and a great number of Jews were exiled outside Palestine, mostly in Babylon. To maintain their faith and cult in such circumstances, the people set up (usually in a room of a private dwelling) locations for prayer, education, study and debate. By the time of Jesus, the synagogue had become a distinct place wherever there was a Jewish community. Here the Scriptures were read, here the people prayed in common, children were taught and visitors welcomed.

An essential part of Jewish life and cult, the synagogue was a lay establishment, not a priestly organization: services were conducted by members of the congregation or guests. (Sacrifice, on the other hand, was offered only by priests and only in the Jerusalem temple.) The place itself was usually very modest, and there was no universally prescribed design or layout other than separate sections for men and women.

At the time of Jesus, the Sabbath service began when someone was invited by the synagogue attendant to intone the great proclamation of Jewish faith—the *Shema* (from its first word in Hebrew), the proclamation of Moses as recorded in the Book of Deuteronomy:

Hear, O Israel: the Lord is our God, the Lord alone. You shall love the Lord your God with all your heart, and with all your soul, and with all your might. Keep these words which I am commanding you today in your hearts. Recite them to your children and talk about them when you are at home and when you are away, when you lie down and when you rise. Bind them as a sign on your hand, fix them as an emblem on your forehead, and write them on the door posts of your house and on your gates.

Following this, a long prayer (sometimes improvised) was recited, a section of the law was read in Hebrew and then translated or paraphrased in Aramaic. A homily or sermon was offered, psalms and other prayers were often sung and (if a priest happened to be present) there was a final blessing.

The Gospels reiterate that, as an observant Jew, Jesus regularly attended synagogue, where he actively participated, read the Scriptures and offered commentaries that gave him the opportunity to proclaim the good news of unconditional acceptance and divine benevolence. Often, amid precisely this kind of setting and format in the synagogues of Nazareth and Capernaum, Jesus opened the scroll of the sacred text, read a portion aloud and offered commentary. But where the tendency of the time was to lengthy exposition and even debate, he spoke very much to the point.

———

When he visited Nazareth one day, for example, the scroll of Isaiah was handed to him one Sabbath morning by the *chazzan* (the synagogue assistant). Jesus unrolled it carefully, reverently, until he found exactly the place he had in mind. As was the custom, he then stood up to read the text: "The Spirit of the Lord is upon me, because He has anointed me to bring good news to the poor. He has sent me to proclaim release to the captives and recovery of sight to the blind, to let the oppressed go free, to proclaim the year of the Lord's favor."

Then he rolled up the scroll, handed it back to the attendant and sat down to instruct, as teachers did. His commentary was dramatically brief: "Today, this scripture has been fulfilled in your hearing," he said as a hush fell over the crowd and everyone gazed at him.

———

The moment was critical, both for Jesus and for everyone who saw and heard him. In the account of his baptism, it was announced that the

Spirit of God was upon him. Now we learn why: "to bring good news" to all.

The centuries of waiting were over, but the fulfillment of God's promise had nothing to do with political power. Jesus defined that fulfillment—which was synonymous with his own mission—as liberation for the poor, for the sick of heart, for all the needy. This was a message not only for the materially deprived, let it be noted, but for all those who rightly regarded themselves as spiritually impoverished, too—which meant everyone, for all (aware of it or not) are needy of God. Grace comes to all those held captive by economic, political, physical or moral obstacles.

God, Jesus insisted, embraces all who desire Him, and even, in a mysterious way, those who do not. Regardless of nationality, race, gender, impolite or socially unacceptable subgroup or physical or moral wholeness, everyone is the target of God's favor. Grace (that which binds us, at the core of our being, to God Eternal) is radically inclusive and entirely gratuitous: it cannot be subjected to the narrow parochialism of a country, a religious institution, a pious contingent.

In an important way, the verses of Isaiah sum up the entire activity of Jesus' life and death: he not only preached divine benevolence, he acted in such dramatically different ways that the preaching was clearly underwritten, endorsed by God Himself. The blind were literally given sight; those held captive by illness, sin and death were delivered; in his time of ministry, the year of God's favor (the traditional Jubilee Year) had arrived once and for all.

It is comforting for many people to think of themselves as religiously proper and acceptable, as pious, pleasing to God and worthy of blessings and salvation because they have been faithful to laws or rituals. Conversely, the righteous consider outsiders as pathetic, if not downright contemptible. But in excluding others, they exclude themselves from the flow of eternal mercy. God's lovingkindness embraces everyone. No individual or group can market it or control the breadth of it.

To the smug and the unforgiving, to those who become angry at the thought that mercy embraces all, it is self-evident that some people do not deserve to be the object of God's goodness. They refuse to believe that a sinner can repent, that a criminal can turn to God. The self-righteous cannot endure the idea that God desires the conversion of *everyone*—hence, that Sabbath day in the Nazareth synagogue, one group in the room was ready to do away with Jesus, to take him off and kill him on the spot. But there was not yet enough support for such a violent reaction. With great dignity, Jesus simply departed the synagogue, quietly enduring the waves of resistance.

———

It was early in the ministry—perhaps just after the imprisonment of John the Baptist. Jesus continued on his way, leaving the hostility of Nazareth for the relative calm of Capernaum. Now the words of Isaiah were incarnated in action, and the Gospels are unanimous in summarizing and outlining, by category and location, Jesus' extraordinary deeds. He saw the sick, the lame, those paralyzed and deranged and, in a shocking gesture unknown in the Old Testament and in later rabbinic literature, Jesus reached out and touched them. Walking through the endless tide of human misery, pain and confusion, of appalling physical ailment and emotional suffering, Jesus was more than adequate for all the misery. He found nothing repellent, no one repugnant. In and through him (and he became gradually aware of it), God embraced the world as never before.

The gesture of touch, in this regard, had everything to do with human intimacy. The tubercular, the leprous (a designation that included sufferers from all kinds of skin diseases), the blind and the lame (whether deformed from birth, illness or accident): such people, it was commonly believed in the time of Jesus, were sinners, suffering for transgressions and consigned to separation from God. The contagion of many diseases was often taken as a sign of that. Pariahs, they were shunned in public and unwelcome everywhere except among those more unfortunate.

Those facially disfigured and those suffering from severe psychological illness (often, perhaps, designated in the Gospels as possession by demons) were especially to be avoided and were excluded from synagogue and community. Unlike the rabbis of his time, however, Jesus did not avoid them. Moved to pity, he touched them, to bring them under his protection. This, of course, was a major departure from Jewish custom. In human experience, Jesus knew, illness isolates people from one another; lonely and frightened, the sick and suffering highlight the tendency of every human society to mark the acceptable from the unacceptable, the polite from the embarrassing, the insider from the outsider.

But here was Jesus, a healthy young man, stopping when he saw suffering—drawing close to outcasts living in darkness, frailty and pain, comforting them with perhaps the first touch of another in so long that they had almost forgotten the feeling. But their astonishment at his compassion was followed by an even stronger reaction—awe, shock, consternation. The sick were healed.

The Gospels are full of such incidents, and they derive from the earliest stages of the oral tradition about Jesus:

A man with a dreadful skin condition approached Jesus and, aware of his reputation, the man begged, "If you choose, you can make me clean." Leaning over and touching him, Jesus said gently, "I do choose. Be made clean." And he was.

On another occasion, Jesus spotted a man paralyzed—perhaps because of stroke, muscular dystrophy or multiple sclerosis. Dependent on others to cart him about on a mat, the man was brought to Jesus, who surprised everyone by saying quietly to him, "Your sins are forgiven." This statement was a typical Semitic circumlocution to avoid uttering the holy name of God: the meaning was "God forgives your sins."

Did Jesus, in the spirit of his time, equate the man's frail condition with a condition of personal sin?

Two things must be said about this. First, although Jesus occasionally contradicted the prevalent view that sin caused physical suffering, in general he did not contradict the popular view of his own time. But, second, this connection was never the point of the healings: instead, Jesus (in this case) indicated the man's pathetic condition as a sign that the world itself was caught in the grip of failure and imperfection, and God was coming to reverse this unhappy situation. Healing of the body restored one to active concern for the things of God, and that is the meaning of conversion, of forgiveness of sins.

But before Jesus could say or do anything further, he was interrupted—not by the lame man or his friends, but by the scribes, who were the intellectual experts and interpreters of Jewish law and lore, respected for their piety and their learning.

Most of these laymen were Pharisees; the designation probably means "separate ones," for they believed that their interpretation of the Mosaic law gave them a special relationship with God. Strict adherents to the tradition of the Mosaic code, Pharisees were not priests but laymen who prayed and studied in private homes and eventually helped prepare for the rise of the rabbinic movement in the second century A.D.

First of all, they rejected any compromise with foreign Gentile influence. But Pharisees, often the targets of wholesale defamation in the Gospels, were not rigid and unfeeling legalists: their vocation was to meditate on the law and then to demonstrate how it was livable in each generation, alive and powerful to enliven Jewish faith. How might one know, for example, if one were faithful to the command of Sabbath rest? How far could one walk on the Sabbath, or how much could one eat? Pharisaic commentaries by scribes were designed to give the precise guidelines for every possibility in life.

"Why does this fellow speak in this way?" asked a few scribes after the healing. "It is blasphemy! Who can forgive sins but God alone?" Throughout the Gospels, Jesus was a threat to their influence among Jews.

Jesus turned to them. "Why do you raise such questions?" Now he has one for them: "Which is easier: to say to the paralytic, 'Your sins are forgiven'—or to say, 'Stand up and take your mat and walk'?" The answer was obvious: it was much easier to say "Your sins are forgiven," for it was impossible to tell from external evidence whether the invisible spiritual effect was achieved. On the contrary, it would have been much harder to say "Stand up and walk," for the result of that command could be immediately judged as occurring or not. One simply had, in this case, to deliver the goods.

And with no further delay and no need for an answer, Jesus turned back to the lame man: "I say to you, stand up, take your mat and go to your home." The man leaped up, and the crowd was duly amazed. But lingering in the air was Jesus' remark just before he touched and healed the paralytic: he did this, he announced, as a sign of the forgiveness of sins. The man was not merely healed of lameness: he was invited to set aside everything that was weak, frail and jaded and to enter into the kingdom of grace. His restored health was the sign of that transformation. The grip of pain and imperfection was being loosened from the world: God claimed creation as His own, He was working anew to heal and to save, and His way, His means, was the action of Jesus.

From the earliest Christian communities after the Resurrection of Jesus to the present, this healing continued in the forgiveness of sin that was always available to the penitent—hence the phrase in Matthew,

Mark and Luke is that Jesus "*has authority on earth* to forgive sin" precisely because God was acting through him. The words were quite deliberate, for they envisioned Jesus as present, risen and continuing his work on earth through the faithful at the time of the Gospels' composition. Where forgiveness was offered, the redeeming work went on, the healing continued.

But even as Jesus announced a new beginning in humanity's relationship with God, harassment attended him.

One Sabbath in the synagogue, he saw a man with a crippled hand. Jesus' adversaries were at once on the alert to see (as they knew he had done before) whether he would heal the man—an action in flagrant violation of prescribed Sabbath rest. As one scholar has summarized the regulations, the holy day meant "no secular everyday work, no buying and selling, no lengthy journeys, no lighting or extinguishing of a fire, no cooking, no medical treatment of illnesses outside of life-and-death situations, and no military activity except in cases of self-defense." Healing could mean trouble.

Nevertheless: "Come forward," Jesus said to the disabled man. And then, instead of violating the letter of the law and falling headlong into the trap of religious fundamentalism, he turned to the silent objectors. "Is it lawful to do good or to do harm on the Sabbath, to save life or to kill it?"

Silence. The bystanders had no reply. Jesus confronted them: "If one of you has a child or an ox that has fallen into a well, will you not immediately pull it out?" Critical situations, in other words, call for critical response; real piety does not conflict with common sense. "Stretch out your hand," Jesus said, and everyone watched as the man regained full use of the limb.

Jesus' merciful gesture did not endear him to those "religious men" of the establishment with their rigid self-interests. But for the moment he foiled them—as he did when he and his disciples walked through a field on the Sabbath and plucked edible heads of grain to eat. "Look," said some of the most pious Jewish observers, scandalized, "why are they doing what is not lawful on the Sabbath?"

Jesus turned to them. "Have you never read," he asked these experts, who certainly *had* read the account, "what David did when he and his companions were hungry and in need of food? He entered the house of God . . . and ate the bread [reserved for religious services], which it is not lawful for any but the priests to eat, and he gave some to his companions. The Sabbath was made for humankind, and not humankind for the Sabbath." The laws about Sabbath rest, in other words, serve man's need; man was not made by God to serve human laws. God wishes to satisfy human need—on the Sabbath as at other times.

Sometimes the healed persons helped in foiling adversaries. Nowhere is this clearer than when Jesus healed the blind.

In Jerusalem, Jesus saw a man sightless from birth. Some of his disciples asked if this tragedy was a result of sin. No, Jesus replied enigmatically, the situation existed so that God's work might be revealed in the man.

Then, instead of offering a verbal explanation, Jesus acted. He spat on the ground and made a muddy paste from the dust. This was a powerful image to Mediterraneans of the time, who believed saliva had medicinal powers; to Jews, it may also have recalled God's creation of man "from the dust of the earth."

Jesus spread the little paste on the blind man's eyes and sent him to wash in a nearby pool of fresh water—and shortly thereafter, the man returned, seeing clearly. His neighbors, accustomed to seeing the poor fellow begging, were astounded; some even said it had to be someone else. "I am the man," he said cheerfully, looking around, fascinated by his first view of the world.

People who knew the man kept asking him, "How were your eyes opened?"

"The man called Jesus made mud," he replied over and over to repeated questions from friends and strangers. "He spread it on my eyes and said to me, 'Go to the pool of Siloam and wash.' I went and washed and received my sight!"

"Where is the man who did this to you?" they asked.

"I do not know."

Before long, some people brought a few religious authorities to the healed man, for Jesus—would this problem never stop?—had healed on the Sabbath yet again.

"How did you get your sight?" they asked.

Again, the man replied; he was not annoyed with the repeated questioning—it was a marvel to him most of all. "He put mud on my eyes. Then I washed—and now I see!"

"This man Jesus is not from God," some insisted, "for he does not observe the Sabbath."

Some bystanders, eager to associate with religious leaders, agreed: "How can a man who is a sinner, who breaks Sabbath laws, perform such signs?" Never mind the wonderful deed itself—people were taking sides already for or against Jesus. He worked—he made mud—on the Sabbath. Who did he think he was? Well might they ask.

The guardians of orthodoxy turned again to the fortunate man. "What do *you* say about him? It was *your* eyes he opened."

What could the man say? He summed it up in one reverent phrase that gathered the meaning of every marvelous word and deed in the history of Israel. For an answer about Jesus, this man quietly replied, "He is a prophet"—one who speaks and acts on behalf of God Himself.

Well, said some observers, clearly this man was not blind before: this must be a hoax. To prove their point, they found his parents. "Is this your son, who you say was born blind? How, then, can he now see?"

"We know that this is our son," the parents said, a little alarmed at finding themselves the objects of public attention. "And we know that he was born blind. But we do *not* know how it is that now he sees, nor do we know who opened his eyes. Ask him—he is of age, he will speak for himself." And they returned to their tasks.

Back went the questioners to the man once blind. "Come now, tell us the truth! We know that the man who claims to have healed you is a sinner!"

Now the man, who wanted only to get on with his new life, to see everything he had imagined all these years, was becoming a bit perturbed. "I do not know whether he is a sinner," he said with some exasperation. "One thing I *do* know—that though I was blind, now I see!"

Like lawyers in court, the adversaries pressed forward again. "What did he do to you?"

The man stopped and stared at them long and hard—doubtless he saw their stubbornness as well as their faces and the color of their cloaks. "I have told you already," he said deliberately, "and you would not listen. Why do you want to hear it again?" And then perhaps a smile flickered across his face: "Do you also want to become his disciples?"

Now the objectors were hot with resentment: "*You* are now his disciple, but *we* are disciples of Moses. We know that God has spoken to Moses—but as for this man, we do not know where he comes from!"

"Here is an astonishing thing!" replied the man. "You do not know where he comes from, and yet he opened my eyes!" We know, the man continued to argue, that God does not listen to sinners who refuse to convert, who insistently turn their backs on God—"but God does listen to one who worships him and obeys his will. Never, since the world began, has it been heard that anyone opened the eyes of a person born blind. If this man were not from God, he could do nothing!"

This was too much for the adversaries, who then admitted that perhaps the man had been blind after all. "You were born entirely in sin," they said, insisting (despite the teaching of the Book of Job) that a physical affliction like blindness was a sign of individual wickedness. "Are you trying to teach *us?*" With that, the man was tossed out of the community of polite religious people fixed in their self-confidence.

Soon after, Jesus heard that the man had become an outcast, and he sought him out. Face to face with his healer, with the man who had brought light where there was only darkness, the man knelt at the feet of Jesus and, in a tentative, grateful voice, professed his belief that Jesus was indeed sent by God.

He was in the world, said Jesus, helping the man to his feet, so that the blind might see—but these troublemakers were deliberately unseeing. "Surely we are *not* blind, are we?" asked some of the righteous who had caught up with Jesus and the seeing man. Jesus corrected their presumption: their spiritual blindness remained. Rightly could the author of the Gospel place on the lips of Jesus the assertion "I am the light of the world," for as the evangelist wrote decades later, Jesus remained, ever hidden but alive and present, to all who came to him. He still gave sight to the blind and insight where there was confusion, hope where there was only despair and light where obscurity reigned. This superb Gospel account shows how one who sat begging in darkness was brought to the literal and spiritual light. But it also reveals how those who think they see can blind themselves to the light invisible and plunge deliberately into spiritual night.

———

Just as the blind were given sight, so the deaf heard and the mute spoke.

Jesus continued on his way during that brief ministry from 28 to 30. He proceeded north over the Galilean border to towns in Phoenicia— to the port cities of Tyre (the modern town of Sur, fifty miles south of

Beirut) and, twenty-five miles north of Tyre, to Sidon. Everywhere, he and his disciples were met with crowds influenced by word of mouth about Jesus. Some wanted to know if the end of the world was at hand or if they might soon expect political vindication of Israel. But Jesus had nothing to say about such matters. Earthly power did not interest him, and he was not impressed with the desire for worldly supremacy. As for the end of the world, "no one knows," he told them—"not even the Son, but only the Father." Meanwhile, they were to take on a new attitude about everything and to prepare for the final embrace of God in history.

Southeast of Galilee, on the eastern shore of the lake, was the border of Decapolis, and on Jesus' arrival a deaf man who could barely speak was brought to him. He took the confused man away from the crowd, and when they were alone, he gazed into his eyes and placed his fingers gently in the man's ears. Then Jesus spat onto his fingers and touched the man's tongue. Gazing heavenward, he took a deep breath—as if shutting out every distraction and becoming wholly aware of God's presence—and then Jesus said to the man (in Aramaic, their own language), *"Ephphatha,"* which meant "Be opened."

And with that, the man spoke clearly and heard perfectly. It was not lost on the crowd that, as the reports of Jesus' deeds were spread around the countryside, the messianic hopes of Isaiah were being fulfilled: "Then the eyes of the blind shall be opened, and the ears of the deaf unstopped; then the lame shall leap like a deer, and the tongue of the speechless sing for joy."

In these remarkable healing miracles, the point was never the miraculous manner of the change, much less any guarantee that believers somehow would avoid illness or always be cured of it. God's power was the issue, working in the world on behalf of humanity. That renewed world, Jesus implied, had something to do with breaking down every barrier that existed—whether pride of race, primacy of religion or presumptions about gender supremacy.

In this regard, just as he welcomed the friendship and discipleship of women, so was Jesus unafraid to ignore the hallowed codes of conduct regarding them. One Sabbath, while he was again teaching in a synagogue, Jesus saw a woman entirely bent over with scoliosis. Moved to pity for the woman, he called her over and gently placed his hands on her. As if she had only been bending over for a moment to pick up something, the woman then stood straight for the first time in eighteen years. The synagogue attendant was at once indignant: Jesus had interrupted the service and had broken the Sabbath again! And some in the crowd agreed, despite the beatific smile on the face of this woman before them.

"What hypocrites!" Jesus said to them. "Does not each one of you, on the Sabbath, untie his ox or his donkey from the manger and lead it away to give it water? And ought not this woman, a daughter of Abraham whom Satan bound for eighteen long years, be set free from this bondage on the Sabbath day?" Once again, he stressed not that the ailment was the result of sin, nor that evil spirits caused deformity; rather, Jesus emphasized that God was at work countering the worst evils people could endure.

Of equal significance: the relief of human suffering took precedence over regulations about Sabbath worship. Why, this woman was certainly worth more than a farm animal; she was a daughter of Abraham. The kingdom—and what a shock this was to traditional religionists!—was offered to and effective among women, who were systematically denied their proper status and "bent low" by pious restrictions.

The story of the stooped woman is the story of women everywhere, and the point was clear. Jesus was releasing those oppressed and therefore raising up the children of Abraham. We can only imagine the reaction of the woman's family and friends when she returned home that day. Indeed, Jesus was continuing to go about "doing good and healing all who were oppressed, for God was with him."

———

In almost every account of the healings, there is a curious element. It certainly seemed possible for those hostile as well as those merely curious to remain unimpressed by what happened. Were such events commonplace? Or was this merely a literary device?

Is it not impossible to accept these accounts at face value? Just how are we to read these miracle stories? As pious legends designed to arouse faith in Jesus? As symbolic of spiritual realities but not to be taken as literal accounts of what happened?

How can people of the late twentieth century accept the possibility of miracles? Have not the scientific revolution, the discovery of natural laws and the collapse of magic and superstition done away with belief in miracles?

To put the question bluntly: Did such things happen? *Can* they happen?

We must face these hard questions without flinching, for miraculous events form an important part of the narratives of the ministry of Jesus. To that task we now turn.

CHAPTER SEVEN

SIGNS AND WONDERS: THE MIRACLES OF JESUS

J airus, a synagogue leader, came to Jesus one day and begged him to come to his house, for his daughter was dying. Jesus at once responded to the man's need, and as he proceeded, the crowds, as usual, pressed in on him. Among them was a woman who had been suffering for twelve years from a distressing problem: no physician could cure her tendency to violent hemorrhages. Believing that she would be healed if she so much as grazed the fringe on Jesus' garment, the woman did that.

"Who touched me?" Jesus asked, turning around.

Peter, never at a loss for words, was partly amused, partly surprised at the question. "Master, the crowds surround you and press in on you. How can you ask, 'Who touched me?'"

At that moment, the woman feared she would be pointed out by someone else, and so she came forward, trembling, and declared why she had done the deed—and that she knew she had been healed. "Your faith has made you well," Jesus said—as usual, deflecting the astonishing event away from himself and toward the woman's faith in God's power. "Go in peace."

Just then, someone arrived from Jairus's household. "Your daughter is dead," Jairus was told. "Do not trouble the teacher any longer."

"Do not fear," Jesus said quietly, and then took his cue from the woman just healed. "Only believe, and she will be saved."

Arriving at the house, Jesus left the crowd outside and took only the child's parents and three disciples with him. "Do not weep," he told the mourners gathered round the body, "for she is not dead but sleeping." That changed their mourning into mocking merriment, for everyone knew very well that the girl was dead and cold.

Ignoring the laughter, Jesus stepped to the bedside. "Child, get up!" he said. She did so, and Jesus told her parents to give the girl something to eat.

————

The word "miracle" occurs nowhere in the Scriptures. There are multiple references to "acts of power," to "signs" and "works" that clearly indicate God's action in the world, but the Scriptures know nothing of a philosophy of science, of nature or of natural laws that neatly divide the "natural" from the "supernatural." Our ordinary understanding of the word "miracle" contains a notion that would have been incomprehensible to the world of the Bible.

No term corresponds to the rather misleading English word "miracle" (from the Latin verb *mirari*, "to wonder at"). The word in modern usage commonly refers to something astounding, occurring above or beyond the natural sphere—an event in time or a change in natural circumstances that defies rational explanation and dramatically proves the fact of divine intervention. But for the Jewish and Christian people of biblical times, God was trusted as the Lord of everything created; nothing was outside the range of His power.

There is a certain integrity to this mode of thinking, for belief in God makes belief in miracles reasonable. It is an interesting paradox to hear professed believers denying the likelihood, or even the possibility, of miracles, thus limiting the divine freedom by insisting they know what is appropriate or inappropriate for Him to do. But cannot God enter into His creation? Can He not alter the usual order of reality? Is God not God precisely because He astonishes? At the root of the matter is one simple question—for ourselves: Can we not allow God to be God?

————

More to the point, it is no longer possible, in light of modern physics, to regard the universe as it has been described since the end of the eighteenth century—as a quantifiable reality that operates according to a fixed system of "natural laws." Twentieth-century science has seen the passing of a neat, mechanistic view of the world, and now it is difficult to find physicists and astronomers insisting that the movement of the universe and the activity of substances within it *invariably* produce specific effects. Although a certain consistency may be observed in nature (the rhythm of the seasons, for example, and the patterns of biological reproduction), modern science postulates randomness within events. The world is shot through with uncertainty and obscurity, and individual occurrences in it often contradict what are called the ordinary capacities of nature.

But randomness does not necessarily imply purposelessness; what we call chaos may not be disorder at all, but rather a clear sign of the limitations of our comprehension. Our sense of what is proper pattern and order may, in other words, not be the only sense of pattern. A random moment—an exception in the expected order of things—then becomes the carrier of an even greater significance than the pattern itself.

Ordinary human experience validates this approach.

In our own individual histories, is not a moment of apparent accident or chance often later seen as the bearer of great significance and even as the beginning of a new stage of life? If I did not attend this school at such a time, for example, I would not have had this inspiring teacher, taken this important course of study or gained this lifelong friendship. If your parents had not met at such and such a moment, they would not have become your parents. If you had not attended this or that meeting, you would not have met the love of your life or begun an important career. It is no exaggeration to assert that the most important elements of human life and love are as dependent on what we might be called purposeful accident as on deliberation, intent and goal-directed action. The French novelist and playwright Georges Bernanos put it well: *"Ce que nous appelons hasard, c'est peut-être la logique de Dieu"*— What we call chance may be the logic of God.

In our time, we are often tempted to think that we have achieved the summit of human genius, but future generations may regard us with the same bemused condescension that we bring to a discussion of those who once believed the world was flat. How *could* they have been so wrong? But for what will our descendants regard *us* as wrong? Perhaps for nothing so much as the presumption that we know it all, that we have understood everything perfectly and ironed out all the mysteries.

————

Physical science and psychology have opened up for us so much of the visible and invisible worlds: perhaps it is unfortunate that we do not see that these fields of knowledge, too, are part of our metaphorical and mythical language.

Not so long ago, some astronomers and astrophysicists spoke of the "big bang" theory, according to which they could discuss the origins of the material universe. But like the theory of electricity, it is just that: a theory, a workable, practical way of discussing something that is essentially mysterious and, in important aspects, unverifiable. Some astronomers, in fact, have recently jettisoned the big bang entirely, in favor of approaches that sound remarkably like old-fashioned philosophical theology. That the material universe had a beginning from nothingness (activated by whom or by what, science is unable to say) is no longer a statement limited to believers; many respectable scientists believe this is the only way to discuss physical etiology.

Our inner world is similarly elusive and defies univocal explanation; each era finds its own way to discuss the mysterious. Once upon a time we described the mentally ill as possessed by demons. Later they were considered victims of disordered humors. In both cases the poor victims were ostracized, chained in dungeons, submitted to various tortures, regarded as sinners or simply allowed to expire. Now we often say that such and such a pathetic soul is, for example, a homicidal, paranoid schizophrenic with an Oedipus complex, or we study their genetic history and constitution, or we seek to know the chemical or emotional sources for such disorder.

But do fancy labels enable us to understand the situation of madness? How is it that a healthy personality can be entirely swallowed up in lunacy and death? The problem of full understanding remains, even as we attach terms that give us a way of dealing with the full horror. Science and psychology enable us to cope; they rarely make the world or the human psyche less mysterious. For everything in the universe that comes under our control, we see almost at once how much more is beyond us.

Few topics in a conversation are as certain to divide people as belief in the possibility of miracles and the existence of an afterlife. Discussions tend to become extreme in both cases, and this is often understandable, for these matters are outside ordinary experience. All sorts of presumptions attend the talk about them, which often quickly becomes a debate.

Some people insist that all the miracle stories of the Bible happened in exactly the way they are described; others will deny from the start that such things can ever happen, because they contradict invariable laws of nature. Still others find ingenious (if sometimes illogical) ways to approach the issue. Whether or not miracles can or did occur is unimportant, they maintain: what matters is the *significance* of the accounts. This is a curious approach, for it is hard to understand how something can have significance if it never happened.

Another argument, often misunderstood but containing the seeds of some very important ideas, takes as its starting point the conviction that God is of course not confined in space and time. He is everywhere as the first principle of existence—as the ground of being—and so whatever happens, happens contingently upon Him, through His mysterious benevolence and, ultimately, for the good of creation and hence of all humanity. According to this line of thinking, everything that *is* is a miracle, the operation of divine activity in the world. But taken to this bald conclusion, the argument (however comforting) begs the question. "Well, then," one can hear an objector reply, "if *everything* is a miracle, then *nothing* is a miracle. Do not miracles by definition indicate something exceptional?"

———

Our ancestors would have found all this arguing tedious. The codifiers of the Hebrew Scriptures wrote of wonders, portents and works of power—acts by which God delivered His people from slavery and guided them to their inheritance. The marvelous element in these gestures was their timing and their effects on the people. Faith, inspired by the events and articulated after the fact, disclosed to the people of Israel that God had indeed been at work on their behalf. In the event of the Exodus, for example, He safely led them, as fugitive slaves, across an isthmus at low tide and prevented their enemies from recapturing them by the fortuitous return of the waters—that is, by high tide, just when they needed it to make a getaway from the Egyptian pharaoh's pursuing chariots. Then, during a long trek in the wilderness, the people were sustained by desert edibles timely provided in sufficient quantity.

Only after the experience, when the motley crew of wanderers was amalgamated in Israel as the Chosen People, did the provident guidance of their God become clear. Natural phenomena were thus seen as the obvious results of divine activity on their behalf, and the tradition demonstrated not so much a faith in the unusual, as in God—the Lord of history who bends the created order to His purpose. Language found forms appropriate to express the grandeur of the experience.

Neither the Old nor the New Testament emphasizes the marvelous deed itself, but the power of God that was *behind* the marvelous deed. Unlike the absolutist who seeks for a new set of explanations when confronted with something wholly inexplicable, the original Jewish and Christian traditions saw even the ordinary workings of nature as directly attributable to God. The world, in other words, is the forum wherein God acts on humanity's behalf. The world and all that is in it belongs to Him, and He claims it for Himself.

————

As for the Gospels, miracle narratives are central to the activity of Jesus and occur at every level of the oral and written traditions. Of him it may be confidently said that he was viewed by those both during and after his lifetime as an exorcist and a healer. Whoever he was, Jesus was not merely a teacher of ethical maxims or a preacher of religious truths. The primitive proclamation is that he was (as Luke wrote in the Acts of the Apostles) "a man whom God sent to you with miracles, wonders and signs as his credentials"; so much is everywhere borne out by the four Gospels. The first half of Mark's account, for example, is virtually a catalog of miracles; several chapters of Matthew describe an array of miracles; Luke intersperses teachings with miracle narratives; and John offers seven great "signs" that are the carriers of Jesus' meaning.

Even Jesus' enemies never denied that he performed astonishing deeds; their resentment had to do with his timing (on the Sabbath) or with the effect these had on people: he gained a following that threatened their primacy. Nor did later Jewish literature contest the record that Jesus was a wonder-worker: rather, it was said that he was guilty of sorcery or that he acted through the intercession of the devil and thus led astray devout Jewish people (so said, for example, the Babylonian Talmud).

In attempting to adduce Jewish and pagan parallels to Jesus, historians must confront the problem of sources. First of all, the notion that wonder-workers like Jesus were common in his time is simply not supported by historical research. If we consider Onias and Hanina, famous Jewish wonder-workers of the two centuries immediately before and after Jesus, it is clear that virtually everything known about them came from later Jewish sources eager to counter early Christian accounts about Jesus; they hardly influenced the New Testament accounts—the situation was the reverse.

Among Gentiles contemporaneous with Jesus, the Cappadocian philosopher Apollonius of Tyana is frequently mentioned as a parallel to (or even a literary inspiration for) Jesus, but for our knowledge of Apollonius' activity we are dependent on writings that come from the third century. Sometime after A.D. 202, the Roman empress Julia Domna (a Syrian), eager to offset the growing Christian influence on Roman civilization, engaged the Greek writer Flavius Philostratus to write a life of Apollonius. Philostratus, allowing his imagination full rein and probably relying on the Gospels for a guide, spun the tale of a wonder-worker even more powerful than Jesus. His work had the desired effect, and shrines to Apollonius soon dotted the Empire. As with Onias and Hanina, it was the accounts about Jesus that influenced Philostratus' life of Apollonius.

In any case, the differences between the miracles of Jesus and the side show atmosphere of the pagan magicians of legend are everywhere evident. The deeds of Jesus are soberly, austerely and simply described: he acts with quiet dignity, deflecting attention from himself and to both the recipient and to God. Nowhere are there the trances and trickery, the phantoms and avarice of the traditional sorcerers. Nothing in the Gospels is trivial, nothing capricious; nothing inflicts punishment on anyone or merely arouses awe.

All to the contrary. The great deeds were signs of the saving presence of God, who was at work in history to reverse the reign of sin and darkness in the world, and to embrace humanity in its deepest needs. The acts were never merely kindnesses performed to help people: they announced God's definitive claim on creation and the radical change His presence made in history. They were, in fact, the beginning of the transformation of the world that was accomplished in the event of Jesus.

Miracles are not to be separated from what faith accepts as the totality of God's action in Christ; they are not, in other words, a proof of anything. Rather, they are signs that illness, pain and death do not ultimately conquer; they all point forward to (and take their meaning from) the Resurrection of Jesus.

But it is important to read miracle stories carefully, and to differentiate certain of the wonders from others. Calming a storm, controlling dangerous waters and "walking" on the waves: these are qualities ascribed to God alone in the Old Testament, for the Israelites were not a seafaring people but a nomadic one, and the ocean terrified them. "You divided the sea by your might," proclaimed the psalmist, referring to the Genesis account of creation, in which God subdued the sea-monster of chaos before beginning his work of creation. "You broke the heads of the dragons in the waters . . . You rule the raging of the sea; when its waves rise, you still them."

No wonder, then, that the Gospels described Jesus and some of his followers beset by a sudden squall on the lake. Their little boat was swamped, waves washed over the sides, and Jesus stood up and rebuked the wind and the sea: "Peace! Be still!"—literally, "Keep quiet! Shut up!" And with that the winds ceased and there was dead calm on the lake. The disciples were awestruck and asked one another, "Who is this, that even the wind and the sea obey him?" Another time, the disciples were fishing, but Jesus was not with them. A gale blew and they were in danger, but Jesus came to them—walking on the sea. "Take heart, it is I; do not be afraid." He climbed into the boat with them, and the wind and sea became calm.

Exceptional moments like these in the Gospels perhaps ought not to be considered in the same way that we read the numerous healings and cures. The distinct "nature miracles" affirm something of Easter faith about Jesus, his relationship to God and his lordship over the universe by virtue of his Resurrection. The marvelous healings, on the other hand—events far more numerous, more frequently attested and almost certainly more historical—convey something about the recipients, about what God does for those who draw near to Him.

The exorcisms require careful reading, too. "There was, in their synagogue, a man with an unclean spirit . . . and Jesus rebuked him, saying, 'Be silent, and come out of him!' " The people were astonished: "He commands even the unclean spirits, and they obey him!" Similar moments occur in the New Testament: people howled and swore, foamed at the mouth, cursed and generally made themselves terrifying—until Jesus arrived, and at once they were restored to health. What are we to do with stories that make Jesus seem like a magician or a character in a horror story?

Psychology, one of our recent helpful guides and a fascinating form of mythic language, has rendered it almost impossible for us to read the Gospel accounts of unclean spirits and of demonic possession. When we come to descriptions of Jesus casting devils out of people and returning them to normalcy, we instinctively recoil; reading or hearing these episodes, people often simply turn away, disgusted or feeling somewhat superior. The people were not "possessed by devils," runs a typical response: modern medicine and psychology tells us they were simply (simply?) mentally unstable, or perhaps epileptic.

But even if we grant that emotional or physical illness (deriving from what is called either a psychogenic or organogenic cause) may indeed have been at the root of these situations, we lose nothing of the Gospel's power. As a man of his time, Jesus shared the anthropology as well as the religious language of that day—in other words, he was limited by all the myths and metaphors that then expressed perceptions of reality. Hence, when Jesus commanded an evil spirit to quit someone's body, he addressed what was *behind* the symptoms—the situation of a disordered personality. This was what he confronted, what he embraced, what God healed through him.

Just as with the brilliant religious meditations couched in terms of a virginal conception, so here. The genius of the New Testament is that, like all documents of faith, religious truth is greater than precise historical facticity. Fundamentalists tend to forget that the biblical accounts are neither eyewitness reports nor medical-psychological records. They are, on the contrary, popular narratives written to proclaim faith in the Lordship of Jesus. And in these narratives we read a wide variety of episodes—some, indeed, based on a kernel of actual history; others modeled on hallowed Old Testament accounts; and still others based on stories familiar in current or recent Jewish or Hellenistic cultures.

————

Just as in the time of Jesus, all too many mad people roam the streets of our cities today—some of them harmless, some on the verge of violence, and some the victims of drug-induced dementia. What misery, what genetic predisposition, what illness or what pattern of life once deliberately adopted might have effected this unfortunate condition of mental derangement is really secondary to the fact of its awfulness.

We may choose to say that the ancient talk about a "possessed person" was really naïve, and that the poor soul was actually suffering from brain fever or malnutrition, from an inherited mental illness or from chemical psychosis. But does the patient today not, after all, represent a disordered world or a disconnected life every bit as much as those called "possessed" two thousand years ago? At stake in the Gospels is the embrace of God— of all the sick, all the socially unacceptable, the drugged, poisoned and demented. Jesus recoils from nothing. Nor ought his followers to do so.

———

To be sure, the New Testament and modern science have different views of the world. The way to understand the accounts of demonic possession and of Jesus' healing exorcism may not, therefore, be to force a choice (in the explanation of either wicked spirits or of medicine). Jesus beholds this terrible form of suffering, sees it as a manifestation of the power of evil in the world, and reaches out to heal it. Can any modern person object to this reading? We speak of the tragedy of mental illness just as we do of cancer or of a hurricane or other disaster—fully aware that these things disturb the good order of our world, that the very existence of pain and suffering indicates the radical incompleteness of creation.

To this day, our language sees this connection: disasters are called "acts of God," although it is perhaps not entirely clear why God is blamed for catastrophes and not credited for blessings. Just so, if a young person receives a diagnosis of terminal cancer, or if a tornado destroys a man's home and family, we hear dour complaints: "Why has God done this?" For every misery in human experience, from the Holocaust to a devastating flood, people speak of good and evil more than of social or scientific causes, and (like Job) they ponder how God could cause or allow things so horrific.

If anything can be said about the Jesus whom experience and faith affirm as hidden in the Gospels and in the world, it is this: that it is he who continues to make possible the *process* by which the world is brought to God. In his earthly ministry, he proclaimed that the definitive coming of God into the world meant an eventual end to sickness, catastrophe and death. That was the promise. Our task is not to repeat the Jewish worldview that Jesus shared so long ago, which we can hardly recapture in any case (and would probably misinterpret). Rather, we need to see just what Jesus announced—a world claimed and saved by God—and find appropriate words to make that announcement sensible in our own time.

———

Something significant and important occurred in the ministry and person of Jesus of Nazareth, and the earliest oral and written traditions about him are laced through and through with accounts of extraordinary deeds that define that significance and importance. Something must have been responsible for the incredible reaction of people to Jesus—not just to his teachings, but to what he did. If miracle stories are later embellishments (the argument adduced even by some modern Christians), then what did the original preaching emphasize? Jesus was unprecedented in history; why should unprecedented signs not accompany him?

The believer finds all this tautological. God is the Lord of all creation, and He is at work in Jesus. And there you have it . . .

The miracles, therefore, complement and implement Jesus' proclamation about the reign of God, his teaching about the inner transformation of all people and the primacy of other-centered love that characterizes the arrival of God's kingdom on earth. Acts of power by which he once healed the sick, gave sight to the blind and temporarily restored the dead to life in this world were the signs by which he proclaimed the inauguration of God's new relationship with the world.

That Jesus aroused hostility from religious and civil leaders indicates that he did not merely announce some vague program of religious renewal or a comforting philosophy of life. His person and his actions, as well as his proclamation, were simply unacceptable to many who coveted dominance. Jesus did not, in other words, come to his hideous execution because he was merely impolite. Everything about him upset the dearly held convictions of powerful, polite and political groups.

The kingdom arrived and its power began in and through Jesus. Precisely at this point, we can see that Jesus believed he had a fundamental and unique position as God was establishing the final destiny of the world as His own. And clearly his presence affected countless people: in the way he treated the ill, the anxious and those bowed down with grief, Jesus accomplished startling things.

As his ministry continued, that presence and its startling effects were felt far and wide.

About twenty-five miles southwest of his home base at Capernaum was the village of Nain. As Jesus approached, he saw a funeral procession and was told that the ceremony was for a young man, the only son of a poor widow. Moved to compassion for her, Jesus drew near and said to her, "Do not weep." Then he touched the bier, and the pallbearers stopped. "Young man," Jesus said to the corpse, "I say to you, rise!" The dead man sat up and began to speak, and Jesus gave him back to his mother.

On another occasion, two good friends of Jesus, the sisters Martha and Mary, who welcomed him to their cottage in Bethany when he visited nearby Jerusalem, sent a distress call. Their brother Lazarus was gravely ill—in fact, by the time Jesus arrived from Galilee, Lazarus had been buried four days.

Martha went out to meet Jesus. "If you had been here," she said to him ruefully, "my brother would not have died." Her sister echoed this sentiment when she arrived soon after.

Seeing how the sisters and their friends were grief-stricken, Jesus was deeply moved, and he wept with Martha and Mary. "See how he loved him," said some observers of Jesus' affection for the dead Lazarus.

The little group arrived at Lazarus's tomb—in the tradition of the time, a cave with a stone sealing the entrance of the burial place.

"Take away the stone," Jesus commanded.

"But he has been dead four days," Martha told Jesus. "There will be a stench!"

But the command was carried out. The heavy stone was rolled away. Silence everywhere. And then Jesus shouted: "Lazarus, come out!"

A moment later, Lazarus emerged from the darkness of the tomb, his hands and feet still bound with the traditional burial bands and his face wrapped in the cloth of death.

"Unbind him, and let him go," Jesus said quietly.

"What are we to do?" muttered some of Jesus' enemies, among them certain jealous religious authorities. "This man is performing many signs. If we let him go on like this, everyone will believe in him." Well, perhaps not everyone, but surely numbers significant enough to give the authorities pause.

The high priest of the Jerusalem temple that year shook his head. "You know nothing at all! You do not understand that it is better for you to have one man die for the people than to have the whole nation destroyed." A few self-righteous, jealous administrators began to conspire with the Roman occupiers against Jesus.

———

Very many good people presume that the New Testament miracles could not have happened because such things do not ordinarily happen—or, more to the point, that these things could not have happened because they defy the laws of nature. Anyone who expresses belief in miracles is then condescendingly regarded as a child who believes in ghosts, witches or goblins. Disbelief in miracles, one hears, is demanded by reason: Jesus did not work miracles, because miracles are impossible. But this may be a kind of circular non-reasoning that even serious scientists and historians would question.

Since the dawn of what is still called the Age of Enlightenment—the period of seventeenth- and eighteenth-century rationalism that swept across Europe and quickly caught on in the New World—there has been an assumption that the primacy of reason makes belief in miracles impossible because they contradict laws that govern the physical world. Locke, Hobbes and Bentham in England and Rousseau, Montesquieu and Voltaire in France brought reason to bear on fresh thinking not only about religion but also about social change. Hence, discussions about the rights of man and political democracy prepared for revolution in France, England, Germany and America. Much of this had beneficial influences on the social order, as tyrannies were swept away and many absolute monarchies toppled.

But the Enlightenment was finally a victim of its own excesses. The more academically precise and rarefied the rationalists became, the less they had to offer an increasingly complex and mysterious world. The French Revolution, with its horrific Reign of Terror and blood literally flowing in streams through the streets of Paris, called into question the new confidence that people could always govern themselves very well.

Soon thereafter, questions about the (recently denied) world of the spirit, of imagination and speculation about unseen reality, reemerged in the new nineteenth-century cultures known as Transcendentalism and Romanticism. Ghost stories and Gothic horror tales, with their supernatural, awe-inspiring surprises, were nothing so much as rejections of rationalist ideology.

———

But the rationalists prevailed even as the Age of Enlightenment dimmed. Thomas Jefferson, for example, was one of the authentically brilliant men influenced by the Enlightenment, at least when it came to a philosophy of government and a perspective on statesmanship. But to be consistent with the supreme function of what was then considered scientific reason, Jefferson produced, in 1820, a "Life and Morals of Jesus" that would be acceptable to a rationalist age. In his edition, Jefferson blithely excised all Gospel miracles, which he considered embarrassing for a really enlightened person. Jesus according to Jefferson was, on the page, a pale moralist.

To this day, some well-meaning but misguided people attempt to make Jesus acceptable to sophisticated, "enlightened" readers and modern churchgoers who, paradoxically, cannot deal with the possibility of the numinous—with what is mysterious and still poorly grasped, with what arouses awe. One wonders precisely what are the components of faith in the beyond if there *is* nothing that is beyond or above—by which, of course, is not meant spatial or geographic dimension but a certain stratum or sphere of reality.

Hence the first activity of rationalists is to explain away miracles as literary symbols or pious fables. The Jesus who then emerges is a pleasant, unchallenging fellow who does nothing very remarkable but who says vaguely comforting things about kindness and gentleness, and who conforms to all of our minimalist expectations of what we claim is possible or acceptable. In effect, Jesus of Nazareth becomes Jesus of Nashville, a nice, unthreatening bumpkin who brings a simple little country message about love to slick urbanites and—in one of the worst clichés of our time—makes us feel good about ourselves. To some of us, such a man sounds suspiciously like those singers on "light" radio stations. He is not someone to excite my imagination and arouse my devotion (much less can he help me get through what is dreadful in life); almost anyone else would do. If Jesus is remade in the image of the rationalists, I say that image is spinach and I say to hell with it.

―――――

Rationalists, in other words, have certain muddy presumptions about both science and history that no serious scholar can endorse. If today's rationalists had been around in the middle of the eighteenth century and someone had been able to tell them about air travel, anesthesia and lasers, they would have said, "Impossible—those things you are describing are impossible—they would be miracles, and miracles don't happen." Surprise!

But this may seem to imply that the wondrous is only what has not yet been explicable in scientific terms. For what appears miraculous, continue the rationalists, we have only to discover underlying explanations: individual or mass hypnosis or hysteria, facile and superstitious credulity, or conditions that have unknown but eventually detectable medical or scientific bases. Since Bayle and Spinoza in the seventeenth century and Hume in the eighteenth, miracles are considered impossible contradictions to the laws of nature. The world is immutable, fixed. "How do I know? Science told me so." This kind of thinking implies that everything marvelous eventually has a scientific explanation.

But something marvelous may have a *linguistic mode* according to which a new experience can be described—and that is different. Physicists in the late twentieth century have found fresh terms to describe matter in the world, but it would be dangerous to think that the terms used in the Middle Ages were *wrong:* they expressed what they could in their time—with all their limitations. Just so today: we must be very careful indeed that we do not cling to the conviction that our words (or physicists' words) describing the world are the last word. Linguistic modes shift and change as our understanding of reality shifts and changes.

Just so, human language shifts and changes—and ideational imagery alters with each time and culture. Language is allusive, metaphorical: it points beyond itself. It is a sign, an emblem or symbol of something greater than words. One wonders if the big bang theory would have been developed or so named if there had not been nuclear fission and atomic explosions: does not the mode of thinking and naming the mysterious depend entirely on our recent, limited experience?

It has been clear for more than a century that the poetic narrators of the first two chapters of Genesis, for example, had neither knowledge nor interest in the "how" or the "when" of the world's origins: they were interested in the "why" of the world and its relationship to a benevolent God. Their concerns, in other words, were religious, not scientific or historical. We ought to allow the Hebrew poets to be Hebrew poets and not insist that they be television reporters.

But fundamentalists insist that the seven "days" of creation were just that—seven periods of twenty-four hours each. On reading, of course, this insistence becomes an embarrassment even to them, for although there are seven "days" of creation in the first chapter of Genesis and mankind is created last, there is only one day of creation in the second chapter and mankind is created first. Which account is true? Both: each contains a religious truth about the world and man's relation to God; there is no concern for scientific history, for that was unknown to ancient people.

To insist on a literal reading of Genesis is not an act of faith but an egregious lack of it. The literalist believes he has all the answers right here on index cards; and sometimes the scientist makes the same mistake. Neither one has anything more to learn, ever. God (or Einstein) has spoken, and one knows what God (or Einstein) has said. God, of course, thus speaks the fundamentalist's own language; presumably God is limited by it. God, therefore, is not God at all.

This, of course, is rank atheism, for the only kind of God Who makes any sense is a God Who constantly exceeds all expectations, Who gradually and continually discloses Himself. "If God wanted to speak to me, why did He speak to Abraham?" asks the skeptic. Well might he complain, for God is not God unless, indeed, He continues to speak, to disclose Himself, to reveal the profound limitations of our understanding in any era. Rightly do the Scriptures speak of "the *living* God." Curiously, this is bad news for the fundamentalist, who, when you stop to think about it, does not want God to be God. He wants God to be as severely limited as he himself is.

In this precise regard, one has to ask a hard question of the devout doubter of miracles. As fresh discoveries like jet propulsion, painkillers and laser beams are found and refined, does the universe become *less* mysterious? Or does not every unfolding or disclosure about *possibility* disclose a more complex set of (shall we say) *wonders* at the heart of the world? Without any reference at all to faith, we must ask whether we have ever really understood everything there is to understand. Is there nothing more, nothing new to find? No scientist or historian would say so.

The arguments of these rational, reasonable folks reveal, at the root, a poor sense of both history and of science, which must always be very suspicious of any philosophical talk about "laws of nature." Are these "laws" engraved in stone? When were they invented or discovered? By whom? Do they not in fact make certain presumptions about the physical and chemical composition of the universe? Do these "laws" allow for the astonishing discoveries of each generation as time passes? Can we, in the final analysis, speak of laws of nature the way we speak of laws of the land? If we do, we fool ourselves into thinking that we are above them, at least potentially.

Neither history nor science approaches an event with the judgment that it *could not have occurred* because such things *do not occur*. Quite the contrary: the historian and the scientist constantly encounter events that are exceptional—even anomalous—and neither of them, if faithful to methodological principles, makes a priori judgments on what is possible in every imaginable situation. Furthermore, responding to the objection that such things "do not happen," one might counter, "*To whom* do they not happen—to absolutely no one in the history of the world?"

It is not tangential, in this discussion, to offer a negative comparison. It is axiomatic of modern medicine that some people who are severely ill with certain diseases respond to protocols of powerful medications; others die, despite applications of the same treatment. Most of the time, human fetuses gestate according to a recognizable pattern—but sometimes they do not. In fact, since we now have the models of DNA and genetic encodement, perhaps we cannot really speak of a "pattern" at all if we acknowledge the absolute uniqueness of every individual being. People can hardly be considered less important than snowflakes, of which, so far as we know, no two are exactly alike.

How, then, have the so-called laws of nature operated? Discussing illness and medication, we have to admit that the constitution of some people is receptive to a particular compound; for others, that same compound provides no cure at all. Any doctor worth his sheepskin will tell you that sometimes things work, sometimes they do not. The art of medicine is often best practiced by including the art of listening, of acting on a hunch, of trying this and rejecting that. How can we discuss "laws of nature" as anything other than a series of *probabilities?* And if there are only probabilities or likelihoods, what of alternate probabilities and other likelihoods?

———

And so perhaps we ought to speak more often of an open universe—as distinct from the usually closed universe according to which modern thinking often conforms. Even devout people are tempted to think of the world as clearly divisible into "natural" or "supernatural" elements— and we think we have understood quite clearly which is which. But this dichotomy may be no longer tenable, much less helpful. On the one hand, we live in a world shot through with wonders. Microsurgery, computers, electronic wizardry: the universe is constantly clarified, disclosing fresh possibilities. But on the other hand, this same world becomes, with every fresh disclosure, more mysterious, more opaque.

Science itself has begun to dismantle the mechanistic determinism— the totality of the "laws of nature"—that was once thought inseparable from acquired knowledge and practiced method. The classical "laws" of physics, which we once thought expressed what could not be said in any other way, are now seen to connote *possibilities* rather than certitudes. And statistical "laws" are more and more seen as signs of real randomness—or, perhaps we ought to say, of *apparent* randomness whose deeper pattern we have not yet ascertained. Hence we have the constant possibility of genuine novelty in the universe as it is. Everything is unique.

Therefore it may be not only imprudent but inexact to define a miracle as a suspension of the laws of nature, as an exception to nature. This kind of thinking leads us to consider reality as established and one-dimensional—in other words, closed. In fact, many of the so-called natural laws are, as I suggested, merely statistical: they describe what *usually* happens. A miracle, therefore, does not violate or contravene nature: it elevates nature, it offers a promise and gives a concrete pledge of fulfillment. It reminds us, every now and again, not only *who* we are but *Whose* we are.

Relevant to this is the recent discovery by astronomers and physicists that the atoms of living bodies were forged in preexistent suns or stars. For modern cosmology, then, human beings are woven into the entire cosmic network. Hence we may speak of a kind of functional integrity or unity in the universe, by which everything that is is linked to everything else that is. Exactly how this notion is to be pursued is freighted with exciting, not to say foolish, possibilities of perception, but at the least we can say that this postulate requires an underlying principle of order and stability, of which one indication is gravity. If gravity were one bit stronger or weaker, planets could not form in stable orbits around stars, and life (at least human life as we know it) could not exist.

———

This is fascinating, for it places a very high premium indeed on personal life—indeed, on *personality*—and helps to understand that the universe may not be, after all, the reflection of coldly impersonal forces. We have imposed our own limited understanding on the cosmos, and according to that understanding, existence is something of a ho-hum—everything is ordinary and predictable, a completely logical interweaving of urges and substances, never personal. All is determined, and the notion of a personal Authority behind nature is restricted to poetry. When it becomes thoughtful prose, it is called antiquated thinking or rank superstition, unworthy of "modern, scientific man." At such times we may be trapped by our own cleverness. We do not expect very much, and so we see very little.

Another rationale for abandoning the concept of fixed laws for reality is that they address only the *material* world. The world of thought and art, of wit and creativity, and perhaps most of all the order of moral, aesthetic and spiritual life is not understood by applying systems or inflexible, deterministic principles. Here, freedom operates in all its sublime mystery. Within an open universe, therefore, we come to behold what is beyond the ordinary, everyday, habitual meaning of things. Only in an open universe—not in a closed one—Archimedes speculates and Aristotle contemplates, Plato meditates and Planck ruminates, Mozart scribbles notes and Mendel experiments with plants and seeds. Once you start talking about fixed laws and give up speaking of probabilities and possibilities, they all grind to a halt, stop working and nothing happens.

A closed universe reflects our tendency, at the end of this millennium, to think minimally about almost everything. Even after we express admiration or awe at the latest medical advance, we soon take it for granted and shrug it off as "natural." Love (by which, alas, society generally means only romantic-erotic love) has a biochemical basis, or arises from mere need. Birdsong? Tiny nerves in their little throats click at mating time or feeding time. Puffy white clouds and blue skies? Condensed water and refracted light. Heroism or holiness? Illusions: everyone has an agenda. How little we think of ourselves and our world. But even in our smugness, we yearn for something more marvelous to heal what is still disordered within and around us, to heal what is still afflicted. And even in our tendency to minimize, our desire for transcendence is revealed.

———————

But let us admit this much. Miracles such as those attributed to Jesus do not, ordinarily, fall within the scope of our experience. Did God, then, play favorites with eyewitnesses two thousand years ago? ("Why did he speak to Abraham?")

One might reply that the time of Jesus was the setting for the foundational signs witnessing Him who is among us always. In one sense, we do not need them today in such abundance, for faith and promise are clearer (if not entirely clear) in light of the Resurrection of Jesus, the ultimate miracle that has forever transformed human life and destiny— indeed, the entire universe. And in another sense, we are perhaps given precisely *other kinds* of miracles, those that are best for us today. It may not be wrongheaded to say that God gives each age the kind of "extraordinary" it needs.

In the time of Jesus, people certainly could reject the meaning of his miracles: their worldview enabled them to do so. It is the same today— God acts without pressure against us. We can see the marvelous and minimize it. If God was indeed at work in Jesus, and if one accepts that Jesus is now hidden but alive, then what problem can there be in positing miracles? It is almost "logical" to expect the wonderful.

We ought not to presume that the world was always as it is now or that it will be forever as it is now. Eternal Mystery that we call God, free to act according to His unfathomable guidance of creation, acted "then" according to the needs of other people in other times. He acts now with us, according to our needs. Then as now, the resisting grip of sin is reversed—sometimes gradually, sometimes dramatically, always substantially—by the touch of grace.

————

Throughout his life, Jesus touched others both physically and emotionally because he had first been touched by their needy situations. The blind, emotionally ill, epileptic, bereaved—each came to him or was recognized by him as bearing the sign of an existence uprooted and thrown into the unfathomable mystery of suffering or death. To those within the dark encasement of pain, life seemed very paltry and meaningless indeed: it seemed to add up to very little. In each case, Jesus was deeply shaken—and, suddenly aware of how God could reach out through him, he acted. Decisively.

This is what God is like.

The loneliness, the isolation, the grief of the human heart: the kindness of God reaches out to this as to nothing else.

This is what God thinks of human loss: He fills it.

This is what God finally does in the Resurrection of Jesus, the pledge that all human life is finally saved. God cancels death, condemns it. God kills death forever, nullifies it and its effect.

In Jesus, we see how utterly seriously God takes us and our suffering.

He is no mere God of plans and systems, but the lover of the human heart. Here philosophical language fails, for you and I are not moved to love the Changeless One, the omniscient Creator, the Absolute, the Unmoved Mover. No, we are warmed by the nearness of Him Who is close, Who always draws near.

————

Still, we do not ordinarily see the blind receiving their sight, nor the deaf suddenly hearing. Dead men do not sit up in their coffins and go out to dinner. How are these many episodes of the Gospels to touch us? How is it that—just as before, when Jesus stretched out his hands to heal and to bless—children still die, parents weep, sisters are left abandoned by the death of a brother, the blind go sightless to their graves and then do not return in the flesh to resume a happier life right here on earth? There are, as T. S. Eliot wrote, only hints and guesses allowed us so far—hints followed by guesses. In the miracles of Jesus, the curtain is pulled aside for a moment, and the final destiny of all is revealed. The God Who *can* act is the God Who *does* act.

And the Jesus who acted once, acts now.

In every concrete, physical, psychological and spiritual transformation in a human life, the power of the hidden Jesus may be recognized. The miracles stories of the Gospels, therefore, are a matter of today as much as of yesterday.

There is, after all, a straight and logical line from creation to call to incarnation to salvation: God makes, He summons, discloses Himself, joins Himself to humanity and finally saves what He has made. Considered in this context, miracles are an economy of signs that witness to the process of God's unimaginable kindness at work in our midst. His gratuitous initiatives are unpredictable and inexhaustible.

We could really go so far as to say that one would have to be a fool not to see that miracles have a certain logic. The philosopher Maurice Blondel put it well: "God manifests His more-than-normal goodness by more-than-normal signs."

They are everywhere.

CHAPTER EIGHT

THE NEW ETHIC:
THE PARABLES OF JESUS

One day, an expert on Jewish religious matters, much impressed with Jesus' extraordinary deeds and teachings, asked him, "What must I do to inherit eternal life?"

"What is written in the law?" Jesus countered, drawing the man out by asking him what he had learned from the Mosaic tradition. "What do you read there?"

The man knew his texts and replied with the great *Shema* from the Book of Deuteronomy: "You shall love the Lord your God with all your heart, and with all your soul, and with all your strength, and with all your mind—and your neighbor as yourself."

"You have given the right answer," Jesus said.

But the man was not satisfied. "And who *is* my neighbor?" What, in other words, are the limits of my responsibility? Who has such a claim on my love that my attention to him is the emblem of my love for God Himself?

And so Jesus told a story that carried his entire proclamation. But in doing so, he did not really answer the question "Who ought to be the *object* of the love?" Jesus instead focused attention on the *subject* of the love. Everyone must be a neighbor to one in need. Thus, as usual, Jesus offered a deeper answer in his reply, told in the form of a parable:

A man was journeying from Jerusalem to Jericho. The route involved a dangerous, seventeen-mile descent; the road twisted and turned between limestone crags and bare hills, and the entire area was admirably suited to the business of highway robbers—a class of thugs still busy in the same place two thousand years later.

The traveler fell into the hands of robbers who stripped him clean of possessions and clothes, beat him savagely and left him for dead. Not long after, a priest—the highest religious leader among the Jews—was going down the same road. When he saw the poor man by the roadside, battered and needy, the priest turned away quickly and crossed to the other side; after all, you never know what kind of trouble is ahead if you involve yourself in this sort of thing. Why, *you* might end up hurt! Better to ignore the whole situation.

Some time later, a Levite (one of the most respected lay personnel, assisting priests in temple worship) passed by, and he, too, ignored the hapless victim.

And then along came, of all people, a Samaritan, a man from a people considered contemptible heretics by devout Jews. There was, and remains even in the twentieth century, irreconcilable hostility between Jews and Samaritans.

Samaritans, considered foreigners and treated like pagans, were residents of the district of Samaria. Strict conservatives, they shared a common heritage with Jews but claimed that they were, in fact, the true bearers of the ancient faith of Moses. Nevertheless, they routinely intermarried with Gentiles, and this alone made them despicable to Jews. Considered unacceptable and always unwelcome, a Samaritan caused ritual impurity simply by coming into the presence of a Jew.

Samaritans regarded Jews as heretics; their Scriptures consisted only of the first five books of the Bible; and they worshiped at Mount Gerizim (near the modern city of Nablus) rather than at the Jerusalem temple. The bitterness over this practice reached critical mass when the Jewish king John Hyrcanus destroyed the Samaritan temple late in the second century before Jesus. From that time, the battle lines were drawn and no quarter given, and some twenty years before Jesus' ministry, a group of Samaritans, still smarting over the ravages by Hyrcanus, defiled the Jerusalem temple by strewing it with dead men's bones.

Jesus' listeners were surprised at the turn the story then took, for the Samaritan traveler—this sworn enemy of everything Jewish (like the Samaritan woman at the well with whom Jesus had so boldly initiated a conversion)—then became the hero of the parable.

Moved to pity, the Samaritan stopped, dismounted from his mule and rushed to the aid of the wounded man. He tore off some of his headcloth or a part of his linen garment and used it for a bandage, and he poured oil and wine on the wounds to clean and disinfect them. Then he lifted the man on the animal and took him to an inn. That entire evening, the Samaritan kept vigil and tended the injured Jew.

Next day, the Samaritan went to the innkeeper and handed him two denarii—quite a generous sum, for the cost of a day's lodging and food at a typical inn would have been about one-twelfth of a denarius. But the Samaritan wanted the wounded stranger to be well looked after. He instructed the innkeeper to provide the man with every necessity and promised that on his return journey he would stop in and reimburse any extra expenses.

And then Jesus had a question: Which one of these three men—the priest, the Levite or the Samaritan—acted like a neighbor to the victim?

The religious expert who asked the question in the first place could not bring himself to reply with the hated word "Samaritan." Instead, he answered coolly, "The one who showed him mercy."

"Go and do likewise," Jesus said, ending the discussion.

————

The parable was shocking—surely among the most appalling of Jesus' proclamations. Only against the cyclorama of the long history of enmity between Jew and Samaritan can this account be fully appreciated and the force of Jesus' words be grasped. The idea of a Samaritan as a model of pious behavior and of profound and loving compassion prevailing over ancient strife was as astonishing as if, in a modern story, a Nazi brute or a child molester became the hero of the parable.

And notice: the discussion preceding the parable spoke of love, but once the Old Testament allusion is repeated, the word does not reappear; indeed, Jesus rarely uttered the word "love" apart from the nature of God. Instead of overusing it and turning it into an empty cliché, he described the reality of love in its human reach: he spoke of forgiveness, of compassion, of reconciliation, of a refusal to exact revenge. Love is not a romantic idyll, but a country, an atmosphere one inhabits, in which the wounds of alienation are healed, broken friendships restored. "The 'limits' of love can never be defined by any theoretical projection," as one New Testament scholar has observed. "The command of love is never circumscribed by the nationality, status, or inherent lovableness of the potential 'neighbor.'" My neighbor, in other words, is anyone nearby to whom I can reach out and respond.

The account of the Good Samaritan is nothing less than central to what Jesus of Nazareth is about. The devout man who comes to him is thinking of himself: Just how far do I have to go in this matter of treating people like a neighbor? Who *is* my neighbor, anyway? Jesus shifts the focus: Think of the man's suffering, he implies. Put yourself in his place and you will see that the real question is "Who needs help from me?" Anyone nearby and needy has a claim on my active compassion, on my concrete assistance. Yes, even a despised half-breed, a heretic, a killer, a sworn enemy of my people.

———

Over all this is the forgiveness one asks of God—a forgiveness we beg God to mete out to us in the exact measure we mete it out to others: "Forgive us our sins as we forgive those who have done us wrong." On this matter, Jesus was very clear: "If you forgive others their trespasses against you, your heavenly Father will also forgive you—but if you do not forgive others, neither will your Father forgive your trespasses." And how many times must we forgive? "Not seven times," according to Jesus, who then pointed to the Hebrew way of saying an infinite number, "but rather seventy times seven times."

Forgiveness does not, of course, imply that the offense is negligible, or that everything is suddenly made all right or resolved—much less does it mean that the offender (whether self or another) ought not to offer restitution. As usual, Jesus addressed the situation of the primary motive, the inner reaction to hurt. Forgiveness means that one must seek no vengeance, that one wishes no pain on the offender—indeed, that one wish his conversion and work for it, just as we know ourselves to be in constant need of conversion. As for the offender's restitution and correction of life, that is another matter; in any case, vindictive punishment is, for Jesus and those who heed him, out of the question.

The only model for the follower of Jesus is the model of God Himself, Whom Jesus compares to the owner of a vineyard. The world, he says, is laced with the good and the wicked—what to do? The parable continues:

An enemy came and sowed weeds among the wheat, and then went away. So when the plants came up and bore grain, then the weeds appeared as well. And the servants of the householder came and said to him, "Master, did you not sow good seed in your field? Where, then, did these weeds come from?" He answered, "An enemy has done this." The servants said, "Then do you want us to go and gather them [i.e., cut down and burn the weeds]?" But he replied, "No, for in gathering the weeds you would uproot the wheat along with them. Let both of them grow together until the harvest . . ."

Men, Jesus says, are incapable of separating effectively. God alone will bring about the time for final judgment and separation, and He alone will see to it. We dare not make any ultimate assessment.

No one, Jesus insisted, is beyond the range of love, just as no human being, however dissolute and wicked he may be regarded by others, is beyond the limit of God's embrace. There is always a chance for repentance, always an opportunity for the soul bound in darkness to accept, however silently and invisibly, some mysterious shaft of grace.

These parables continued the pattern of reaction Jesus evoked from bystanders. Jesus continued to lose points in the sight of the religious and political establishment. After all, it was one thing to proclaim boundless charity, but it was quite another to include enemies within the borders of that loving acceptance. Even worse, how could this man Jesus make a sworn enemy of Judaism—a Samaritan, of all people—the hero of the parable? This upsetting of traditional, polite presumptions is getting out of control.

Never mind that Jesus was really giving concrete examples of God's attitude—the "outlook," if we will, of the God Who is proclaimed by the Jewish Scriptures as "a God merciful and gracious, slow to anger, abounding in steadfast love and faithful forever—and forgiving iniquity, transgression and sin."

———

Jesus never lacked for illustrations of this—in fact, everything of moment in his understanding of God and in his teaching was contained in these forceful, imaginative depictions of the realm of God's unimaginable love. Another parable has haunted the world ever since—the story Jesus told about an irresponsible son and the astonishing resolution to a family crisis.

A man had two sons. The younger asked his father for the share of the inheritance that would one day be left to him—which would be one-half the amount eventually due to the older brother, who was favored by the long tradition of Jewish inheritance laws.

At that time, an estate could be transferred either by a will or by an outright gift during the father's lifetime. In the latter case, the heir took legal possession of the land or property but could not dispose of it until after the father's death (and if the son sold it, the purchaser had to await the father's death to take possession). In this case, the younger son demanded not only a settlement but also the freedom to dispose of the proceeds as he chose, so that he could lead a completely independent life.

Having turned the property into cash, the young man left the country and became a dissolute rake. Before long, all the money had been squandered, famine raged across the land where he had settled, and the only job the boy could land was with a farmer, who hired him to feed the pigs. This, of course, was the ultimate degradation for a Jew: contact with the forbidden, unclean animals. ("Cursed be the man who breeds swine," warned the Talmud.) Too disgusted to eat the pigs' food and denied any share of the rations hoarded by the other farmworkers, the boy had to forage or steal what morsels he could.

Finally, the pathetic lad was filled with remorse. In his mind, he imagined his father's hired hands and household servants, comfortable and with plenty to eat, and he saw that his wretched circumstances were the result of his own stupidity and ingratitude. "I will go home," he thought to himself, "and I will say, 'Father, I have sinned against God and against you. I am completely unworthy to be considered your son any longer. Treat me like one of your hired servants.'" He understood perfectly well that in light of his earlier settlement, he had no further claim to anything—not even food and clothing. He asked, therefore, for the chance to earn everything by sheer manual labor.

And so he set off, and after the long trek to his homeland he glimpsed at last the family estate. But even before the boy had a chance to approach the house, to humble himself and to beg forgiveness, his father saw him in the distance, forlorn and limping. Filled with compassion, he ran out to meet his son ("a most unusual and undignified procedure for an aged oriental," as one scholar has noted), threw his arms around him and gave him a kiss, the clear sign, to a Jewish son, of his father's forgiveness.

"Father," said the boy nervously, almost choking with remorse on the words he had so long rehearsed, "I have sinned against God and against you. I am completely unworthy to be considered your son any longer."

But before he could continue and ask to be treated like a servant, his father interrupted him and completely altered the atmosphere. Instead of treating his son like a humbled reprobate and a potential wage-earner, he presented him to the family and the staff as an honored guest. "Quickly!" the father said to one of his servants. "Bring out the finest robe and put it on him"—a mark of high distinction that a king presented to a deserving official at the beginning of a new era. But there was more: "Put a ring on my son's finger and sandals on his feet"—the first gift bestowed authority, and only free men were shod, while slaves went barefoot.

And more still! "And haul out the fatted calf," continued the father happily, "and kill it, and let us eat and celebrate!" Meat was eaten but rarely, and for special occasions a fatted calf was prepared. The three commands to the servants indicated beyond any doubt that the son was completely forgiven and reinstated in his father's good graces—not because the boy had worked his way back or earned anything or even had the chance to express his contrition, but only because he had made the effort to come home. From there, his father's loving compassion took over. Why? "Because," the father concluded as he addressed his servants, "this son of mine was dead and is alive again—he was lost and is found!" So began the feast, with singing, dancing and unrestrained merriment.

But the story was not over. It began as the tale of a father and his *two* boys, and now the focus shifted to the other.

The older son, a faithful man who had never asked for an advance on his inheritance, had been at work in the father's fields. He approached the house, was surprised to hear a celebration and asked what was going on. "Your brother has come home," replied the servant, who shared the general happiness, adding that the master had ordered a lavish celebration "because he has got him back safe and sound."

Instead of sharing the good news and rushing in to embrace his brother and father, the older brother began to sulk and refused to join the party. His father came out and pleaded with him, but the young man retorted: "Listen!"—and he did not address his father with affectionate respect, as did his brother—"All these years I have been working like a slave for you, and I have never disobeyed your orders. You have never given *me* such a celebration—not so much as a young goat to celebrate with my friends. But when this—this—*son* of yours"—he would not even say "my brother"—"when this *son* of yours comes back, who has wasted all his money on prostitutes, you kill the fatted calf for him!" The words almost seared on his lips.

But the father's compassion extended to the hard-boiled older son, too. "My dear boy," he said gently—using the affectionate diminutive form of the word "child"—"you are always with me, and all that is mine is yours. But we *had* to celebrate and rejoice, because"—and now he turned the phrase right back on the older son, gently correcting him and repeating what he said to the chief servant earlier—"this *brother* of yours was dead and has come to life; he was lost and has been found."

The parable was really shocking. God, it says, is a parent who meets us frail, selfish wanderers as a God of healing, welcoming love. He is not the macho, powerful Lord of laws, not the mighty warrior king who frightens and takes hostage, not the harsh schoolmaster or strict account-ant. "He is the good God, and it is difficult to find less trite formulas," as Hans Küng has written with gentle directness. "He identifies Himself with [us], with [our] needs and hopes. He does not demand but gives, does not oppress but raises up, does not wound but heals . . . He forgives instead of condemning, liberates instead of punishing, permits the un-restricted rule of grace instead of law."

Nothing about Jesus conformed to what we might call the academism of the day: he made no special appeal to intellectuals, nor did he shun them. He was instead an inspired storyteller of life experiences.

The lovely story Jesus told of the father and his sons, for example, was not wasted on his audience, and its message was clear. This, he said about the loving father of the parable, is what God is like: this is how much He loves those who not only are lost, but have deliberately gone astray. His love is constant, His mercy lavish, however unmerited. Con-trast that, Jesus seemed to say, to those who believe they have staked a special claim to God's approval. Do not be joyless, unkind and self-righteous, he urged the censorious. Those whose inner lives have faded almost to extinction are rising to new life; be glad with them. Hence this tale was more than a proclamation of forgiveness to the spiritually poor: it was also a response to those who are angry that sinners should be treated so lovingly.

If one had to isolate a single trait that provoked Jesus, it was what might be called spiritual smugness, as he clearly indicated in another example: "to some who trusted in themselves that they were righteous and regarded others with contempt," he told the story of two men who went to the temple to pray. One, a devout Pharisee, stood and prayed, "God, I thank you that I am not like other people: thieves, rogues, adulterers, or even like this tax collector. I fast twice a week; I give a tenth of all my income."

The second man, a tax collector—one of the thieves and rogues, as the Pharisee recognized—stood in the back, not daring even to look up in a prayerful gesture. Beating his breast (a sign of contrition, of the desire for a purified heart), he said, "God, be merciful to me, a sinner!" This humble man, according to Jesus, found God's favor—"for all who exalt themselves will be humbled, but all who humble themselves will be exalted."

———————

The story of the generous father (who is really the central figure in the story, not the "prodigal son") was Jesus' reply to those who scolded him for the table fellowship and camaraderie he shared with sinners. "This fellow welcomes sinners and eats with them," grumbled the enemies of Jesus, the self-righteous who disapproved of his habit of consorting with those they considered inferior. Adulterers, swindlers, customs officers and tax collectors, shepherds—all these were welcome to approach Jesus, to speak with him. He accepted invitations to share a meal with them.

Why did Jesus seem so lax about these thieves and sensualists? Surely he did not countenance these kinds of activities, with their exploitation of others and of self. No, everywhere in the Gospels Jesus enjoined honor and honesty on all, and everywhere he deplored the sadness that came from the tawdry sale of self. On the other hand, he certainly seemed lenient regarding *these* sins compared with those of hypocrisy and the unbridled lust for power.

To understand the moral dynamic of Jesus, it is crucial to see that making a living was very difficult indeed in Galilee, for the political system left people with no margin for error. Some women and men were coerced into work they otherwise would not have chosen—guarding sheep, for example, or even prostitution—and these unhappy people

Jesus could not condemn. Instead, he questioned the civil and religious system that taxed so heavily and forced people into crime.

It is likely that two thousand years later, Jesus of Nazareth would be called a "bleeding-heart liberal," a man without realism, a man without any pity for the victims, a man who dared to defend the victimizer. Such complaints would completely miss the point, for Jesus saw everyone as a victim. But he offered no reward merely for occupying that status, nor did the victims have a claim on privilege (as they often demand today). There was, instead, a way out of the dreadful cycle of being both deceiver and deceived.

The social conditions of Galilee impelled Jesus to emphasize the merciful compassion of a gracious God over the demands of inflexible law. Religious experts and authorities who easily condemn, Jesus told a crowd one day, "tie up heavy burdens, hard to bear, and lay them on the shoulders of others—but they themselves are unwilling to lift a finger to move them."

The image was at once clear to the bystanders. Farmers often placed heavy yokes, wooden poles and beams on the necks of animals pulling the plow. The poor beasts were worn down, often to collapse, in the service of an inefficient way to turn the soil. Instead, Jesus turned to those beaten down by the system: "Come to me, all you who are weary and are carrying heavy burdens, and I will give you rest. Take my yoke upon you and learn from me—for I am gentle and humble of heart, and you will find rest for your souls. For my yoke is easy, and my burden is light."

He brought not a new system of laws, but a promise of a completely new life in which the only law is a condition of inner self-donation to God. And it was because Jesus himself was so open to God that he could speak and act as he did. That was the force and meaning of his openness to sinners, to women and to children—a spirit of liberation unknown at his time.

———

Jesus insisted that God does more than lift a finger, as it were, to help those who are burdened. And Jesus saw the shock on the face of his hearers when he made this analogy: God is like a shepherd Himself.

"Is there no end to the man's blasphemy?" his enemies protested. If this man were of God, he would never compare the Almighty to a *shepherd,* of all people.

But Jesus continued—and this time he would not be interrupted. His parables were not merely ethical teachings: they were invitations to receive mercy.

"Which one of you, if he has a hundred sheep in his flock and loses one, does not leave the ninety-nine and go after the lost one until he finds it? When he does, he lays it on his shoulders and rejoices—and when he comes home, he calls his friends and neighbors and says, 'Rejoice with me, for I have found my sheep that was lost!' " It was not the animal's high value that warranted the shepherd's trek to bring it back, but simply the fact that the sheep belonged to him and could not find its way home without the shepherd's guidance.

It was the same thing with a housewife, continued Jesus, turning to a woman for his example. In his time (and today in the same part of the world), a married lady's headdress was bedecked with the coins of her dowry. Her most precious possession, it had both sentimental and practical value and could not be laid aside, even in sleep. Imagine, said Jesus, a woman with the very modest nest egg of only ten silver coins. "If she loses one of them," he said, looking straight at his accusers, "doesn't she light a lamp"—because the low door lets so little light into the windowless hut—"and sweep the house"—so that the broom may cause the coin to clink on the stone floor—"and search carefully until she finds it?" Just as with the shepherd and his once-lost sheep, the woman shared her good news with friends and neighbors.

———

The parables were carriers of critical proclamations about God's pursuing mercy. Not merely edifying little stories, they compelled Jesus' hearers to make a decision about him and his mission. Parables implied a self-attestation about Jesus: when one of them depicted the goodness of God, for example, that goodness was seen and experienced in Jesus. When a parable spoke about the kingdom of heaven (a Semitic way of reverently avoiding the divine name in "kingdom of God"), Jesus announced the arrival of that kingdom.

The parables were also Jesus' response to those who accused him of irreligious conduct because he consorted with unsuitable people. What Jesus said, what he proclaimed, what he did represented the very nature and will of the Eternal God. In a way that was fundamentally different from every prophet who had preceded him, Jesus claimed that he was God's very legate—that in and through him, God was acting. The parables told what God is like—and Jesus himself represented Who God is. More than fifty times in the Gospels, Jesus is identified or addressed as "Teacher," and this, perhaps more than any other designation, captures the attitude of his contemporaries.

———————

Many of the most famous sayings of Jesus have been gathered synthetically—arranged according to topic and grouped together in what has come to us as the Sermon on the Mount in the Gospel of Matthew. This is a kind of keynote address, and the content is absolutely revolutionary. Every way of thinking is overturned, every expectation shattered, all the established and acceptable norms of conduct reversed. "My thoughts are not your thoughts, nor are your ways my ways" was the Lord's revelation to Isaiah. Precisely how different are the "thoughts and ways" of God, now set forth by Jesus with complete confidence that what he proclaims is the will of God.

Like a new Moses, he goes up a mountain and sits down—the traditional posture of Jewish teachers. He begins by indicating the real sources of human joy; hence the use of macarisms, or statements beginning with the Greek word (*makarioi*) for "blessed," denoting people in a state of happiness.

"Blessed are the poor in spirit, for theirs is the kingdom of heaven."

First of all, a share in the very life of God (living in the realm of the "kingdom of heaven") is a present reality for those who are "poor in spirit"—those who know that God is their only hope and refuge, those with a deep sense of need for God, those who rejoice in their dependence on Him. Even more than in Jesus' time, this may at first hearing be one of the most disturbing aspects of authentic spiritual life.

It may not sound like good news, this reminder that I am completely dependent, that indeed I cannot achieve anything on my own—whether I rely on talent, intuition, stamina, intelligence, strength of will, or genetic encodement. I am, in the core of my being, contingent. There is nothing passive or abject about this humility: to know that one is dependent, that one is not in complete control, is to live each day clinging in trust, dependent on God, Who acts only in love.

One can hear the objections accumulate. "It's all very nice to speak of divine benevolence, but how can this make sense to one who is suffering the ravages of, for example, physical or emotional illness?" There is no easy answer, but for a beginning one can say that sufferers are perhaps more readily aware than any others of their contingency.

That was Jesus' own experience of God—that he was not only marked and sealed for a definitive vocation in history, but that he was sustained by God, the source of all happiness. "Happiness," in this regard, is not to be identified with a smile button, a state of loopy contentment. To be sustained by God does not erase the challenge and pain of life: Jesus on the cross was, after all, rejected, he died a criminal's death, he was utterly abandoned and (from the standpoint of worldly success) was a complete failure.

————

Jesus continues: blessed, too, are mourners, the meek and the merciful— they will rejoice, they will triumph, they will be treated mercifully as well.

How astonishing this must have sounded then, as now—the assertion that those who grieve and those who are humble before God and kind to others will be comforted and will secure an everlasting reign precisely because they do not covet power. God finally consoles and brings to His eternity those who, like Jesus, avoid worldly superiority. The only kingdom sought by those who follow him is the one he established: "a kingdom of truth and of life," as one of the Roman liturgical prefaces puts it with calm insistence—"a kingdom of holiness and grace, a kingdom of justice, love and peace." Not, in other words, a kingdom at all, as we usually understand the word—rather a realm in which only God is adored.

Christian faith in the rightness of Jesus' teaching is very clear in the history of prayer—in, for example, the gentle, concerned nighttime petition that has found its way into the Book of Common Prayer: "Keep watch, dear Lord, with those who work or watch or weep this night . . . Tend the sick, give rest to the weary, bless the dying, soothe the suffering, pity the afflicted, shield the joyous—and all of this for your love's sake." With such confidence, rooted in poverty of spirit, we rely on the mercy of God and recommend one another to Him. Like so many others, the prayer takes its cue from the Beatitudes.

Those Beatitudes take ultimate human needs with absolute gravity. "Blessed are those who hunger and thirst for righteousness, for they will be filled" and "Blessed are those who are persecuted for righteousness' sake . . ." Righteousness has nothing to do with moral arrogance: a hunger and thirst for righteousness means, rather, the desire for a right relationship, for friendship with God.

Such a commitment leads, alarmingly often, to suffering and to persecution in the world. But according to the ethos of Jesus, it is by meeting violence with nonviolence—hence becoming a "blessed peacemaker"—that one belongs to God. "God is the God of peace because He is a God of strength and goodness," as Romano Guardini has written. In the new order that Jesus inaugurates—not only by word but by deed and by what God does in him—everything the world calls great is being leveled, so that authentic greatness might prevail.

Then there are the "pure in heart." They will see God, and not only in the future: those who are dedicated to God see Him active in the world and in neighbors like the poor beaten traveler en route to Jericho. The beatitude refers not primarily, as is so often thought, to sexual desire (although that is certainly included among desires that can become inordinate and exploitive); rather, the pure in heart are the single-minded and sincere, those who are dedicated to the things of God and strive to reflect God's mercy. Like all the sayings of blessedness, Jesus does not principally address one's destiny in the next world. Belonging to God is something that is of the present moment; the nature of the fulfillment of that belonging is up to Him.

Jesus speaks not a judgment of doom but a pronouncement of something unprecedented in human existence, and in this regard he is, indeed, a revolutionary. Every old claim, every value taken for granted— that this world is sufficient unto itself and is the only reality—is to be reversed. As Luke insists, the rich, the satisfied, those praised and honored by the world are in the greatest danger. The poor, the mournful, the hungry and persecuted are blessed—not because their condition is itself desirable or blessed, but because need teaches how inadequate existence is. And Matthew rightly reminds us, in his spiritualized version of the Beatitudes, that if we are not literally poor or hungry, we must at least know the meaning of spiritual hunger, of our own deep poverty before God, our utter dependence on Him.

Of course, hunger can make us obtuse, poverty can make us greedier than plenty, and many wealthy people are singularly detached from excess. But with comfort, with every whim gratified, a certain torpor often arrives. Hence every religious tradition in the history of the world has stressed the need for regular, routine subordination of even our most basic urges and instincts. All good things are made to serve us; we do not exist to serve them.

———

And so continues the Sermon on the Mount, that collection of Jesus' sayings, uttered on various occasions during his ministry and lovingly preserved by the communities. He utters not pious platitudes or interesting aphorisms, much less does he engage in pretty philosophical or poetic musings. It is much harder than that: Jesus quotes Exodus and Deuteronomy: "You have heard, 'An eye for an eye and a tooth for a tooth' "—a Jewish prescription that was set down to *control* excessive retaliation, not to justify it. "But *I* say to you, do not resist an evildoer. If someone strikes you on the right cheek, turn the other also; and if anyone wants to sue you and take your coat, give your cloak as well; and if anyone forces you to go one mile, go also the second mile. Give to everyone who begs from you, and do not refuse anyone who wants to borrow from you . . . Love your enemies and pray for those who persecute you . . . If your right eye causes you to sin, tear it out and throw it away . . . And if your right hand causes you to sin, cut it off and throw it away."

What is this? Are these words not sheer folly?

When Jesus urges us to tear out an eye or cut off a hand, the sense is clearly a form of Semitic irony. The hearer replies something along the lines of, "Well, it shouldn't be necessary to go *that* far to avoid sin!" The rejoinder is then, "How far *ought* one to go?" And that can be answered only by the individual in the particular situation. "Above all, clothe yourselves in love, which binds everything together in perfect harmony," Paul urged the Colossians in a letter that antedated the Gospels and sums up the highest ideal of conduct—a topic sentence for Christian ethics that is the very essence of discipleship.

Jesus certainly does not advocate weak, impassive surrender to force, nor does he—who so frequently healed the lame—endorse self-mutilation. Be decisive, he urges—even radical in your choices. A loving commitment to another requires fidelity; when that breaks down, one sees the wound of sin in the pain, bitterness and even recrimination that follow. Similarly, Jesus is very much aware that those who "lust in the heart"—who intend to translate desire into mere selfish gratification—will lose themselves in the bargain; they will have no higher frame of reference for their actions than the pursuit of pleasure. If alcohol or food, sex or influence become addictive, if they control us, we have to employ radical surgery, just as a gangrenous limb must be amputated, the body invaded with a scalpel so that disease may not destroy, or tons of infected hamburger recalled so that people will not become ill. Extreme measures are thus often called for in the world of the body: is the life of the spirit less important?

There is a modern mania about purity in foods, an obsession with weight, cholesterol, sodium, vitamins, exercise—all of them legitimate issues, to be sure. But while there is high energy spent on what goes into our mouths, where is the concern for what goes into our eyes and ears, for what feeds the spirit? There is so much that is lovely to see, hear, read, behold: why are we so often indifferent to the violence and ugliness that assault and diminish us, often in the name of news or entertainment? In the name of freedom, perhaps something of our humanity is chipped away when we claim so proudly that nothing offends us. A very great deal ought to.

———

The most revolutionary aspect of Jesus' teaching is his implicit insistence that unrestricted, other-centered love—which is a matter of the will, not the emotions—must be the basis of human relations. Defense must never become aggression, nor offense be met with retaliation: "Love your enemies and pray for those who persecute you . . . Be merciful, just as your Father is merciful. Forgive, and you will be forgiven." If we stop to think about it, this is not sweet, sententious, unrealistic counsel from an idealistic philosopher-poet; it is, quite the contrary, the height of pragmatism, the only way for there to be peace between individuals, groups, races, nations. To be sure, it is an ideal—an ideal that, if it guides every consideration, affects human nature at the core of its being.

As long as we consider the transformation of life through unrestricted good will to be unrealistic, or merely a high ideal that is really impossible, then there will never be harmony. As long as we reply that this is impossible, grace cannot infuse human experience, and the world remains mired in improbability. Faith in God's nearness, and in His absolute ability to disclose Himself to us and share His salvific life with us, is about experience—or it is not faith at all, but a pleasant reverie, a kind of feeling-good-about-yourself—and an obsession with "self-esteem"— that have no reference or resonance when reality punctures and the violins are heard no more.

If the commandment of love is fundamentally a new *ethic*, did Jesus in fact enjoin a new *moral code?* Or is it even quite correct to speak of a moral code—one set of rules replacing or refining another?

CHAPTER NINE

BEYOND MORALITY:
JESUS' TEACHING ON SIN
AND FORGIVENESS

The proclamation of universal mercy and the promise of divine benevolence—so clear in the parables of Jesus—have direct parallels in his teaching on sin and forgiveness. He could address these matters, Jesus clearly felt, because he clearly believed that critical times were at hand: that God's ultimate self disclosure in history was imminent, although just what form that would take and how that would be revealed was unclear, even to him.

Jesus was, after all, as orthodox Christian faith insists, fully human. As one of the most respected Catholic biblical scholars of the twentieth century has written: "Uncertainty about the future and about how some of the most urgent issues in life will turn out is one of the greatest agonies of being human. The Jesus who knew exactly what would happen becomes almost a play actor on the stage of time, unaffected by vicissitudes. He is a Jesus who should not have feared death, since he knew exactly how he would triumph, and he should not have found it necessary to pray [to be delivered from so terrible an execution]."

In other words, Jesus indeed shared the ordinary ignorance of every human being. But that he was singularly graced by God with a prophetic mission and voice, and that in his nature, person and wisdom he was God's image in the world—in a qualitatively different way from the essence of every other human being—constitutes one of the core beliefs of Christian faith.

But to imagine the baby Jesus looking up at his mother and knowing Einstein's theory is sheer fantasy. He would not be God's ultimate reaching out to us in *human* life if he knew everything there was to know. He was thoroughly a man of his time, and as for that time, he perceived reality and expressed himself in terms not of dynamic human psychology (unknown to ancient peoples) or of an evolving social order, but in terms of a critical time in Jewish history, a time of decision-making on behalf of God. And these decisions were to be rooted and grounded in compassionate, forgiving love. In this regard, he was indeed revolutionary.

———

"Compassion" and "love" are two words so cheapened by overuse that they set many people's teeth on edge. Many people respond as if compassion means approval, which is ridiculous. Muddled thinking, however, encourages people to think that if we speak of compassion for the criminal, sinner, drug addict and child abuser, we withhold it from the victims of their crimes or we extend automatic pardon to the wrongdoer. But which of us, victim or victimizer, does not need compassion? Jesus evidently thought the worst people he encountered were so deserving. Witness his treatment of the worst of his society—notorious extortionists, prostitutes, thieves, embezzlers, hypocrites. He loved, he forgave, he embraced them as readily as those they hurt. If you don't approve of that, you don't approve of Jesus.

———

But make no mistake about it: he required of the miscreant that he sin no more, that there follow in the wake of forgiveness a fierce effort at leading a new life. It is shocking to realize that Jesus never turned anyone in to the authorities. This does not warrant the assumption that he was in favor of felons freely roaming about: he had the welfare of the poor, the lonely, the old, the defenseless always in mind, and that meant protecting them, too. But his watchword was always that punishment never extract vengeance: "You have heard it said, 'An eye for an eye and a tooth for a tooth,' but *I* say to you, Love your enemies and pray for those who persecute you."

But how *can* we? It seems impossible.

The sayings of Jesus should not be read (like the Mosaic code and the proliferation of laws in Jesus' time) as specific regulations for the life of his disciples, telling them what they are literally to do in every situation. What he proposes, in light of this critical time when God enters our experience and alters human life and destiny by the sheer gift of Himself, is a kind of atmosphere, a scenario, symptoms, signs and examples of what it means when the kingdom of God breaks into the world. He tells us how radically overturned every natural, human expectation becomes. New life is rooted in extraordinary, unprecedented love. The radical nature of the Sermon on the Mount, then—indeed, of every apparently new moral prescription Jesus gives—is not a new law replacing or simplifying or revoking an old law. What he announces instead is the love of God, which challenges humanity to make God the basis for all of life. When this happens, he says, you will see love as a winnowing fire, encircling the globe, cauterizing the wound of sin and beginning the transformation of all creation.

The Sermon on the Mount, then—with its radical ethic of love and its proscription against every kind of hatred, revenge, exploitation, lust and infidelity—reveals the effect of grace incarnate in human relations. These are the signs of God at work in the world. You belong to God's city of light, says Jesus; a new life is growing out of this experience—a radical upsetting of human expectations.

This ethic of love is very different from the legislative mentality that has often besieged Churches since the time of Jesus. Laws have proliferated, codes of conduct have been formulated, strictures have been articulated, sinners have been berated. Jesus was, it has been said, a new lawgiver: that has often been the presumption of certain Church teachers. "Jesus said this" or "Jesus said that," it is too often claimed, as if the Gospels were clear and unambiguous handbooks of what to do and not to do. But Jesus of Nazareth was nothing like a new lawgiver.

When he spoke of a new law, he spoke of only one reality. "This is my commandment, that you love one another as I have loved you." And his love was inclusive, freeing, never condemning, always allowing opportunities for repentance. Churchmen, of all people, do not always like to be reminded of this, nor do they want it always preached: it seems, for one thing, too optimistic about human conduct. And unless you provide *laws* for religion—just as you do for traffic—what will people *do?* The lid will be off, we will lose control, and everyone will go to the bad. In other words, God will be helpless against human perversity unless there is a vast array of sanctions. Religion, to many modern Churches, is tantamount to a system of laws and doctrines: that is the usual thinking, but in the final analysis such an attitude bears no relation to the life of mature faith.

This attitude of moral vigilance—as if faith and morality were synonymous—is closer to a fascist police mentality than it is to the attitude of Jesus, who speaks of a new inner attitude that frees us from a slavish fear of law; he stresses, on the contrary, an attitude of constant conversion, of turning to God. He reminds us that God rejoices over a sinner's repentance. And no one knows better than God that a sinner needs time to repent, which is only one reason why a follower of Jesus can never, under any circumstances, support capital punishment.

This issue is absolutely essential to Christian faith and practice. From the early days of belief in Jesus, those who presented themselves for baptism were prohibited from ever carrying out an execution, however legally permitted. "A soldier who is in a position of authority is not to be allowed to put anyone to death; if he is ordered to, he is not to do it." So stated the *Apostolic Tradition* of Hippolytus (A.D. 215), whose very title witnesses its ancient character and tradition. But there was nothing revolutionary in this work: it simply made explicit for Christian converts in the Roman Empire what was the teaching of Jesus and the faith of the apostles.

To argue that some criminals are beyond the pale of grace and forgiveness—and therefore must be executed rather than allowed a lifetime to repent—is simply to replace God's ultimately free, forgiving and transformative action in the hearts of human beings with one's own presumptive and preemptive judgment. To endorse capital punishment, in other words, is to play God in more ways than one—not only by taking a life but also by deciding who can and who cannot be changed by grace and forgiven by God. "I have no pleasure in the death of the wicked," says the Lord to his prophet Ezekiel. "I desire that the wicked turn from their ways and live." To that end, God has the patience of God.

The offering of forgiveness, which does not mean saying that a sin or a crime is all right or can be forgotten, is not among the doubtful elements of Christian life: it is absolutely at the root of it. The Christian forgives and does not extract vengeance—punishment in kind—precisely because he himself has known forgiveness from God; because he knows that God offers, again and again, a chance for repentance. As Jesus forgave his own executioners, so must his followers forgive theirs (not to say those who extract less). Forgiveness is not something one can take or leave, not something that can sometimes be offered and sometimes not. Forgiveness breaks the cycle of hatred, of revenge, of precisely the attitude that led to the murderous crime in the first place.

One of the most powerful examples of forgiveness emerged from an experience of such horror that it is difficult for us to imagine. During the Holocaust, countless children were exterminated at the Ravensbrück concentration camp. When the place was at last liberated, a piece of paper was found, placed with the body of a dead child; on the paper were words written by an unknown dead prisoner:

"O Lord, remember not only the men and women of good will, but also those of ill will. But do not remember all the suffering they have inflicted on us—remember instead the fruits we have bought, thanks to this suffering: our comradeship, our loyalty, our humility, our courage, our generosity, the greatness of heart which has grown out of all this. And when those who have inflicted suffering on us come to judgment, let all the fruits which we have borne be their forgiveness."

Forgiveness, which is no more than obedience to Jesus' renunciation of the old "eye for an eye" mentality, is in fact an entirely pragmatic way of reordering the world. It puts a stop to retaliation, to anger, to final judgment. "But some people do not *deserve* to live" is a rejoinder one often hears. It sounds suspiciously like Hitler speaking, or a mad serial killer on the loose. As for the risk of executing an innocent person every so often: "What's a life or two? Some people are better off dead!" The words were spoken by a sociopathic killer in a classic movie; he thought his life would be much better without his unloving father, and that another man's life would be freer without a cheap and faithless wife. It all has the logic of "We had to burn this village in order to save it."

The refusal to kill inhibits the process of killing; allowing God alone the final judgment on the worth of a human life—which means one can never say a human being has "forfeited the right to life"—breaks the cycle of the criminal's own arrogance and refuses to imitate his tyrannical act to destroy life. A cold-blooded, premeditating killer says that someone deserves to die, for whatever reason of greed, expediency, lust, revenge or passion. Just so, the cold-blooded, premeditated execution of that killer in the name of state justice repeats the madness—

the act says that someone deserves to die, just as the killer said that someone deserved to die.

God pours His love on the righteous and the wicked; He writes off the debt, searches out the hard of heart, brings to Himself the most errant sheep. Can those who say they live in the name of His son do differently? "Forgive us the wrong we have done as we forgive those who wrong us," we ask in the Lord's Prayer. This is the result of a previous statement of Jesus: "If you do not forgive others, neither will your Father forgive you." Forgiveness, let it be stressed, says not that the offense is negligible, forgotten or unworthy of correction. It *does*, however, refuse to act from vengeance. And it seeks not the death of the sinner, but endless opportunities for his repentance and conversion—a condition that no human can declare forever impossible.

Not incidentally, there is a terrible irony at work in the machinery of capital punishment. If it is indeed a fair and noble way to order society, to prevent crime and to deter criminals (specious arguments in every case, all of them unsupported by evidence), then why are the identities of executioners always kept secret? Why is only one of the firing squad's rifles loaded with bullets, or why does only one of the vials contain the lethal poison? Why is it considered desirable for even the executioner not to know who he is, to be one of a team, and the gesture of only one (unknown to them all) is the fatal gesture? And why do executioners not go about the country proclaiming with pride that they have killed more criminals than other executioners, and so ought to be elected to high government office? The only answer can be because everyone knows that they do something so shameful that their identities must never be revealed.

A Christian by definition cannot support capital punishment, for he believes in and adores one who consistently condemned violence and vengeance—and who was the ultimately innocent man wrongly executed. Jesus took no revenge against his enemies; he did not even scold Peter, who cravenly denied him when Jesus, so needy of friends, was dragged away to a bogus trial and swift execution.

The new attitude of unconditional forgiveness, of granting one's offender the opportunity to repent, is never proclaimed as instantaneous, as the work of a moment or a day. "If God so loved us, we also must love one another." So wrote the author of the First Letter of John to early Christians. Really to love, as Christ loves us and gives himself to us, means necessarily to work toward forgiveness, even if we do not *feel* it. For love is a matter of will, not always or primarily of emotion. No follower of Jesus can encourage his own worst instincts to vengeance.

———

The Sermon on the Mount, with its apparently harsh issuance of a strict moral law—no anger, not so much as a lustful thought, not a whisper of ill will, no divorce and remarriage, no oaths, no retaliation, passive resistance to evil, no accumulation of wealth—seems patently impossible to us at the end of the second millennium. In fact, scholars have been trying to whittle away Jesus' traditional teachings for generations. They contain an impossible ideal, say some well-meaning preachers—an ideal that cannot be fulfilled and so awakens consciousness of our human weakness and shatters our self-reliance. Other commentators have insisted that the apparently uncompromising teachings of Jesus come from a time of imminent crisis issuing in a new world order of which this kind of conduct will be a sign. But the problem with these attempts to make the sayings palatable is evident: they treat his teachings as a kind of new law.

But if we read these sayings (as perhaps we should) as directed to newly converted Christians after baptism, then the difficulties begin to dissolve. The so-called new laws of Jesus are not, then, a handbook regulating the life of the disciples, nor do they contain prescriptions for what they are literally to do in every situation: rather they describe signs of the new order caused by the radical incursion of grace.

———

The injunction to render love real by forgiveness and the refusal to seek vengeance is an important element of the liberating message of Jesus, which is far more than a mere moral code. Very often, a commitment in faith is wrongly identified with morality—rather than a stance toward reality that begins the process of setting everything else in order. And so the sayings of Jesus are often wrenched out of context and made, by preachers, to serve moral matters: sin versus virtue becomes the touchstone of a life well lived, and in the process there is often a failure in translating the spirit of the sayings of Jesus.

One sorry example of this obsession with a new set of laws, which

was precisely what Jesus negated, may indeed be the developed tradition
in some Churches regarding the implications of his evident high regard
for marriage and commitment and his concomitant low regard for divorce and remarriage.

The teaching is apparently unambiguous in the Gospels, and a summary reads thus:

"It was also said," Jesus reminds his listeners, citing the Mosaic law
allowing divorce, " 'Whoever divorces his wife, let him give her a certificate of divorce.' " Such a certificate could be handed to a wife if her
husband grew annoyed or bored with her, or if she committed so trivial
an offense as the preparation of a disappointing meal. "But I say to
you," Jesus continues, "that anyone who divorces his wife and marries
another commits adultery against her." It is, then, well attested that Jesus
pronounced divorce and remarriage as signs of failure in human relationships.

But it is critical to understand the background against which the
prohibition against divorce was issued—both the Jewish customs of the
time and the concept of marriage itself. In both cases, there is a wide
difference between life then and life today.

First of all, as we have already seen, a Jewish woman had to be completely unrecognizable when she left home: her face was hidden by an
elaborate array of double veils, a band on the forehead that attached
bands to the chin and a hair net with complicated knots and ribbons.
A Jewess who ventured from home with her face visible could expect
her husband to hand her a writ of divorce before nightfall, and some
women were so terrified of being seen uncovered that they remained
hidden even at home, lest a visitor or passerby behold her. One rabbinic
tract records that a Jerusalem priest could not even recognize his own
mother when he heard false charges of adultery against her—the penalty
for which was death.

"It is suitable for women to stay indoors and to live in retirement,"
wrote the Jewish statesman and philosopher Philo, a contemporary of
Jesus—who, as we have also seen, ignored every custom and tradition
about not speaking with women. Although Philo wrote from Alexandria
and of its customs, life in Judea was no less strict. Girls stayed shut up
at home before marriage, and never disclosed their identities in public
afterward. In synagogue, of course, women were segregated from men
and were forbidden to teach. They had no right to bear witness, could
not initiate any legal proceeding, and the birth of girls was often greeted

with indifference or even sorrow; the arrival of boys, of course, was cause for celebration.

Only against this cultural cyclorama can the actions and teachings of Jesus be understood. Jesus not only had women disciples and close women friends; he not only addressed them in public, touched, healed, embraced and socialized with them. The most revolutionary and the most freeing aspect of his proclamation about women was in fact in his teaching on divorce. He condemned polygamy, which was quite common among Jews at the time, because it led only to the exploitation and subservience of women. More to the point, he condemned Jewish divorce customs precisely because they were capricious, permitted for the vaguest and most trivial of reasons, and because easy divorce invariably allowed a man's transient lusts to decide the fate of a woman and her children. He outlawed divorce, in other words, because it degraded women.

This brings us to the heart of the matter.

Jesus clearly denounced divorce and remarriage. You may not break marriages, he said: to do so is a sign of sin, of a rupture in human relations. He also proclaimed that we may not steal, may not defraud the poor, may not kill, abuse others.

But Jesus did not go further and say that marriages *cannot* be broken: he said they *may* not be broken, that to do so was forbidden. And the conclusion to his prohibition—"whoever marries another [after divorce] commits adultery"—adds to the force of his prohibition.

The question is whether or not the followers of Jesus may be more rigid than he, unforgiving in a way he never was. The Roman Catholic Church, in particular, has developed an astonishingly harsh praxis regarding remarriage: those who do so are effectively cut off from the life of faith and are regarded as "outside the church" of believers. No other Christian communion has taken so unbending an attitude.

On the other hand, the Roman Church has developed a legal loophole: the conundrum known as a proclamation of annulment, which states that the marriage (because, for example, of coercion, lack of full consent, mental reservation, impotence, unstated refusal to have children) was never valid in the first place; the couple, then, is free to obtain a civil divorce and remarry in the good graces of the institutional

Church. This is an interesting legalism, but very many good people sense an air of hypocrisy about it.

Of course marriages sometimes fail, and of course people sometimes marry for less than the best reasons: for sheer passion, for status, for security, for pride's sake. When Jesus states his prohibition against divorce, he reminds us that human beings deserve more from one another than capricious abandonment. But nowhere else in his teaching is there any situation when he renders a person forever chained to the consequences of sin. His entire treatment of people was to liberate, not to legislate. To repeat: he does not say that a marriage *cannot* be dissolved, nor does he say what should happen when it has been. This concerns the conscience and the healing compassion of the parties involved.

The question remains: Can the followers of Jesus be more rigid than he, and decide that one certain sin above and beyond all others produces irrevocable, excommunicating results? Ought people to be excluded forever from Christian fellowship because of one unique sin? People do make mistakes, they do hurt one another, they do fail in commitments—and no one, in or outside the Church, would say that this is just fine, thank you.

It is likely that very few people go through divorce casually, unscathed by doubt or remorse. But when it happens and people wish to heal the wounds and proceed, is it in the spirit of Jesus to be unforgiving—to determine that a failure dooms one to certain consequences forever? It is self-evident that in fact some marriages simply *do* break down, that commitments are abandoned, that promises are violated and love betrayed. "It is not a writ of divorce that dissolves marriage before God," wrote no less an authority than the great Christian theologian Saint Cyril of Alexandria in the fifth century. "It is bad actions that dissolve the marriage."

Would anyone ever urge a spouse to remain with an unregenerate abusive alcoholic, for example, or with an uncaring hedonist pursuing affairs? Surely the followers of Jesus have no right to be a legislator when he was not, a codifier when he shunned that function. Jesus forbids cruelty, exploitive carnality, revenge and the deliberate rupture of human relations. But he never says they are beyond forgiveness.

There are two critical principles at work here—principles that have to do with understanding both the meaning of the Sermon on the Mount and comprehending the meaning of marriage two thousand years ago and its meaning today. The goal of such reflection is, for the believer, a deeper relationship with the hidden Jesus.

The first people to hear Jesus' absolute prohibition against divorce and his equation of remarriage with adultery were both shocked and cynical: "If such is the case of a man with his wife, it is better not to marry!"

But they could not have been *less* shocked to hear Jesus' other radical requirements, his prohibition of (1) anger as well as murder; (2) a lustful gaze as well as adultery; (3) no oaths at all, not merely false oaths; (4) absolute nonretaliation; and (5) love of enemies. From New Testament times, the disciples of Jesus have had to understand and make practical applications of his teachings to changing circumstances.

It is doubtful, for example, that anyone ever took literally his statement that "if you are angry . . . or if you say, 'You fool,' you will be liable to hell-fire." Mere anger, in other words, may not be compared with murder. Equally so, no one would equate a lustful look or fantasy with actual adultery—just as we have seen that one cannot take literally Jesus' injunction to cut off a limb if one is in danger of sinning with it. And who really thinks that if one is slapped on the cheek, Jesus requires us literally to turn the other? Is self-defense un-Christian? As for oath-taking, Christians, with ecclesiastical approval, have done this for centuries.

Why, then, do some feel that it is absolutely essential to uphold with literal strictness the principle of indissoluble marriage? Rather, is it not the case that Jesus presents us, as always, with the utterly changed life that accompanies the reign of God? These "shocking" and apparently impossible characteristics, he implies, are what life is like when love alone rules in the human sphere.

Contrariwise, Jesus does not say this ideal is always possible. Since the early centuries of Christianity, some women and men made promises to God—called vows by the time of the High Middle Ages. In time, these vows were legalized and solemnized: pronounced "forever" and so binding the soul to God. But one could be dispensed or freed from these vows, for a variety of reasons.

Jesus does not, let it be repeated for emphasis, say that marriages *cannot* be broken: rather he says they *ought not* to be broken. "Man *should* not undo what God has built up," as the Catholic priest and theologian J. P. Jossua, O. P., has written (italics his), "but that does not prevent its being undone in fact." The silent witness of uncountable numbers of people of good will in this matter cannot be ignored.

To put the matter briefly: Jesus had no such mechanistic idea of human relations (much less of human-divine relations) that he saw a kind of magical, eternal bond securing two people together—a bond they formed willingly but that they could never, however equally willingly, dissolve. There is a real danger, in this regard, of substituting juridical or legal abstractions for a spiritual reality. Perhaps it is not tangential to ask, along the way, if a civil or religious *ritual* of marriage necessarily creates a true bond between people. The law has always recognized that marriages contracted under coercion or bribery, or with any circumstance limiting the free will of a partner, is automatically invalid.

Even the Roman Church has admitted this, for a marriage can be proclaimed null and void if the factors listed above (among others) were present from the start—and this despite whether the ritual was duly performed or not. And so perhaps, just as baptism begins the process of becoming a Christian, one might view marriage as the beginning of a process whereby two people intend to establish a spiritual bond that is strengthened or weakened, reinforced or diminished, only through the motions and will of daily commitment.

Another equally mechanistic view seems intolerable in our time: that a marriage is spiritually "consummated"—which means sealed, made perfect, ratified—simply by virtue of sexual congress. There is a long and tangled history of societies having made such a determination for legal and social reasons. But is it not vaguely repellent to believe that God necessarily decides, fulfills and endorses according to human caprice?

———

Which brings us to the second issue: the meaning of marriage centuries ago and its meaning today.

Customs and laws, rites and sanctions, cannot be enforced from the basis of the past. It is, on the contrary, the present social phenomenon in which God continues to disclose Himself. From the time of ancient Israel through to the nineteenth century, marriages were arranged by families for dynastic, economic, territorial or religious reasons; romantic love was scarcely a consideration. If, in time, a man and woman grew mutually fond of each other, that was very nice (and frequently a surprise). That fondness was not, however, required or even expected. Sterner considerations prevailed. Until fairly recently, for example, the postmedieval European tradition of marriage saw the bonding of couples as primarily a means of producing more workers for the farm: children were seen as producers rather than consumers. Later, the rise of romantic literature (and American movies) created an entirely new set of expectations about marriage and the family. Whether these prospects have ever been met by anyone off the page or screen is doubtful.

In the Hebrew tradition, for example, marriage was viewed primarily as an institution for the preservation of the husband's clan—hence a young man who married was not founding a new family but continuing one already in existence. Children, who would in turn preserve his lineage, were counted a blessing and a gift from God; sterility was viewed as a disgrace and a punishment. In Hebrew society, the unmarried were a sign of social decadence, and consecrated virginity was unknown. And the virtually total subjection of women and their lack of rights indicate how impossible it was for them to cross the frontiers of anything like emotional peerage.

But marriage today is, in very many parts of the West, a different matter. Men and women no longer see themselves as carriers of a legacy or of a family or racial tradition, and much less do they see themselves as producers of workers for dynastic territories. Today in the West, people very often live together motivated by a desire for mutual growth and self-giving love. "When that ceases, the marriage ceases," as one Roman Catholic theologian has sensibly (and controversially) observed.

The only people who would disagree with a commonsensical statement like this are those thoroughly rooted in an Anglo-Saxon legal tradition, where the law is seen as the determinative measure of what is permissible. If this worship of law is linked to a juridical notion of religion and Church authority, the only result can be the curious belief that religious laws provide the answers to all questions. It should be remarked that in such cases of prescription and proscription, of warning and of condemnation, there is rarely any mention of the soul's freedom before God, or of how best the ultimate value might be served: the primacy of responding to His infinite love. And that, let it be stressed, has nothing to do with fealty to laws.

We should be very clear about this skewed vision of what constitutes "morality." In an Anglo-Puritan tradition, it is presumed that if freedom is emphasized, people cannot be trusted to do what is right. Everyone will defect to the enemy of selfishness and wickedness, humanity will quickly backslide and religion will lose its hold on people. But is it the function of religious life to have a "hold" on people? Is religion rather not a matter of guidelines, of trying to articulate mysteries beyond complete comprehension? Is religion not a matter of bringing us to the point where we meet God, not human laws? To be sure, it is easy to miss the point, to call the meeting with lazy self-centeredness a "meeting with God." But by the fruits of one's garden shall the healthy plantings be known.

———

How very different is the free response God asks from those who sense the hidden Jesus. Even during his life in the flesh, no one was forced or coerced; it was possible to deny the meaning of his miracles, and his teaching often fell on impenetrable ears. The decisive invitation to accept the offer of infinite love occurred—"occurs" is the better word, for God is not anything at all unless He is present and active—in the glorification of Jesus after death. If our relationship to God is qualitatively different from our relationship with the tax authorities, why do we so often confuse them in our lives?

To put the matter another way: if I truly love my friends, my attitudes and actions are lived out in an atmosphere of devotion and trust. I do not look for ways to cheat, to connive, to cut corners on the extension of my love—nor do I doubt theirs for me. And if I am negligent or curt or impatient, I am at once aware of my failings and try to set matters right. I do not expect my friends to summarily end the friendship. For reasons I can never fathom, they love me.

Is God less? Does any kind of failure incur His wrath? His everlasting punishment? Does not such language turn Him into a wounded suitor, a very limited neighbor—not even a friend? Is there not, as one respected academic Catholic theologian has suggested, a necessity "to accept and forgive those who have found it impossible to live the demands of this [marriage] bond"?

———

So what of the Sermon on the Mount, which, on this and so many other matters, seems so uncompromising? Is a lustful thought the same as adultery? Is an explosion of anger the same as murder? How can we speak of Jesus as the ultimate manifestation of God's will and wish and love if Jesus sounds so unyielding about perfection? Does it not seem as if his teaching is really a matter of all or nothing? Whatever am I, weak to the core, to do in the face of such an ultimatum?

The all-or-nothing preachers seem awfully bloodless—not to say adrift, for they seldom seem to practice their own urgency. The Sermon on the Mount, a message of challenge and mercy, requires not success at everything, but a constant willingness to rise when one has fallen, to keep on. "I am not called to be successful," said Mother Teresa of Calcutta when asked how she could possibly succeed in her mission to alleviate suffering and loneliness. "I am called to be faithful."

The "commands" of Jesus—ought they not to be called rather "invitations"?—are not inflexible prescriptions but a guide to an ever deeper intimacy with ultimacy. At stake is action, not philosophy—and the actions Jesus described as constitutive of the kingdom of God were actions enjoined because a dramatic inrush of that kingdom was at hand.

But how to describe what it is like when God is invited to take hold of us? How to speak of it? "The wolf shall live with the lamb," wrote Isaiah, "the leopard shall lie down with the kid . . . The cow and the bear shall graze together . . . The nursing child shall play over the hole of the asp . . ." Dared the hearers then (or now) think, "Sure, tell me another good one"? No, the message is clear: where God reigns, everything is different. A complete renewal occurs. Everything expected, everything "normal" is transformed.

Every one of the demands of Jesus must be seen in this light. It is not our task to succeed, but to live faithfully: to allow ourselves to be transformed by infinite love. Belief in that unimaginable love—belief that we are forever accepted—does not mean that we are instantly changed, but rather that the beginning of the renewal occurs. The old weakness drags at the will, the old selfishness remains, the impatience, the nagging suspicions. But there is a new beginning.

"To be a follower of Christ," as Romano Guardini has written, "does not mean to imitate him literally, but to express him through the medium of one's own life. A Christian is no unnatural reproduction of Christ . . . The task of the Christian consists of transposing Christ into the stuff of his own daily existence."

Perhaps only the unimaginable splendor of the Resurrection of Jesus supersedes the revolutionary nature of the Sermon on the Mount, which is both challenge and program. The Sermon asks us to forgo our demand for our rights, for our power, for our opportunity to use counterforce to redress offense.

With every statement, Jesus radicalizes the revelation of God to Israel.

Not only are we to place no other gods before Him—not the god of self, of money, of pleasure—but we are to love God with all our heart and energy. The standard for love of God is benevolence toward both neighbor and enemy. We are forbidden not only to kill, but to harbor angry thoughts and words that lead to ill will. Not only are we to avoid adultery and sexual exploitation, but we must not intend to be faithless and grasping, nor may we regard others as simply means for our own comfortable ends.

Morality and ethics, then, are not, at the end of the day, academic matters to be argued and legislated. They have, on the other hand, to be seen as connected to a new life, a life (like that of Jesus then and now) hidden. The disciple is summoned to extend Jesus' own compassion, his healing, his doing good, his generosity to all persons—that is the meaning of morality—and to live in truth with all people. That is the meaning of ethics. The opposite just does not work, which brings us back to the absolutely pragmatic nature of Jesus' teachings and of our faith in him. To live as if only I mattered, to exploit and objectify others, is unethical. To hurt another willingly and knowingly, to deceive, to humiliate, offend or degrade, is a definition of immorality.

Ultimately, morality and ethics are not modes of conduct arising from constraint, from law or fear: the conduct arises from love.

CHAPTER TEN

THE TRUE COUNTRY:
ON FAITH AND PRAYER

Faith is an attitude toward reality—a refusal to admit the final meaninglessness or opacity of the universe. And prayer is not so much what we say to God about that reality as a disposition in which we listen for Him. Faith is not primarily intellectual assent to a complex set of teachings and instructions. It is, first of all, a process in which I try to listen to what God—and God through Jesus—says, and to see what He does, right here and now, ever at the threshold of my life. However interesting, the past—what He once did—is a different country. As the philosophers of the French Enlightenment complained, it is hard to understand why people would place their confidence in a God Who once spoke to someone else and has nothing to say to oneself in the present. The only kind of God Who makes sense, of course, is One Who continues to address me in my experience, in all that makes me. That is the country in which I reside.

But how to speak of this listening and seeing, of being on the alert for the disclosure of the hidden God, or of the mysterious figure of the hidden Jesus in the present? How can I know that it is the living God Who speaks, or the existent Jesus who acted once and continues to disclose himself?

There seem to be about as many Jesuses as there are books written about him. Some of them market the sweet and gentle Jesus who simply told everyone to be nice and good and loving, but this sort of figure would not have aroused much emotion, would not have caused such violent reactions either for or against him. Other books describe a fiery wizard, a frightening figure warning of imminent damnation then and later. Still others present a social revolutionary fighting for the underdog—or a heroic general mustering the troops against moral evil. And others, in a time when celebrity is the ultimate aphrodisiac, have proclaimed him as Jesus Christ, the superstar.

Is he best perceived as a benevolent magician? A cool, confident teacher of right living? A stern lawgiver? A gracious, generous provider of everything necessary to a good life? The angry rabble-rouser? The comforting elder brother? Take your pick, and the library can satisfy every inclination. Because the New Testament provides so few facts about Jesus, preachers and writers have always stepped in to take up the slack, providing an endless variety of portraits limned in the colors of vivid speculation and imagination.

———

No one who speaks or writes about Jesus does so without a viewpoint, a "take" on him. However elaborate or simple the presentation, or however he is discussed in terms of conventional Church doctrine or simply wrapped in warm and pious reverie that can offend no one, we are always left with a dilemma: after working our way through all the thickets and the options, it is "someone else's Jesus" who is presented for our consideration. But it is in one's own experience of him that the true Jesus draws near. And while this sounds hopelessly subjective, it is not completely so, for he is the Jesus of *faith*—not only of my faith, but the Jesus of faith to whom a cloud of witnesses has testified for two thousand years.

———

"Listen! I am standing at the door, knocking."

From the final pages of the New Testament, written about seventy years after his death and Resurrection, those words—placed on the lips of the risen and glorified Jesus—resound through the centuries, challenging us with the fresh possibility of his ongoing presence at every moment.

But there is a tension here. Just as I am connected to a genetic past, so I am linked to a spiritual legacy. The affirmations of those who preceded me certainly do not determine or decide the contours of my faith, but their experiences and their expressions of those experiences retain a powerful emblem. We stand in the tradition—which is just another way of saying we are spiritually daughters and sons—of those who believed, proclaimed and wrote in the first decades following Jesus and in all the centuries since, in which light occasionally transpierced the darkness in the witness of those we call the saints.

The writings that constitute the New Testament provide hints and pointers, guidelines and a kind of norm: they are the carriers of an ancient tradition about him that I simply cannot ignore. For two thousand years, those writings and those claims have in every generation influenced emperors and kings, mystics and sinners, the famous and the lowly, geniuses and ordinary poor folk.

———————

But however primary and constitutive the biblical assertions and meditations on Jesus remain for all ages, an important fact needs to be emphasized.

I do not believe in someone—I do not stake my life and death on the meaning and effect of one's love for me—simply because of what has been claimed and written about him by others, whether remote or recent. Nor do I embark on the journey of faith, which is fundamentally a relationship with a person and not with a set of intellectual propositions, because someone else has advised that belief is a good thing to have, as if it were an academic degree, a possession or a skill like a second language. Rather, I trust, I commit myself, I live in ongoing hope in a relationship only because somehow another addresses me and discloses himself to me. The present (not the past, however gratefully recalled) is the forum of my commitment. Now more than ever, at the end of the second millennium, very many people want to hear Jesus standing at the door and knocking; even more, they want to open and find a real person there.

———————

The earliest New Testament writings, those that predate the Gospels, have virtually no interest in a Jesus of the past.

The letters of Paul, for example, which were written to various neophyte Christian communities between about twenty and thirty-five years after Jesus' execution, allude to a few sayings attributed to the Master and, apart from the unadorned mention of his birth and death, refer only to his last meal with his disciples. Otherwise, Paul's concern is not with a man of the past but with one resoundingly of the present.

But after the eventual deaths of virtually all the original eyewitnesses to the life and work of Jesus and of post-Easter apostles like Paul, a quartet of anonymous documents were written in the last third of the first century; only much later were these writings attributed to men named Matthew, Mark, Luke and John. The narratives do not conform to any standards of chronology or causality, nor do they provide a complete record of Jesus' words and deeds. Like Paul but with a very different content, the authors were not obsessed with past history or anything like the creation of structured biographies; rather, they had religious considerations.

Hence the evangelists framed earlier oral and fragmentary written traditions in literary forms and stories enabling people to meet the living Jesus in the very different circumstances of late-first-century life. They did not manufacture untruth: sometimes they found, with their limited language, startling new ways to reflect on the truth. Everything was passed through the prism of faith: the one presented is the one who speaks to new situations.

The Gospels, then, represent what the early Christians believed of Jesus. Their freedom to meditate on the significance of his life, to expand and to create was not falsification, but rather a freedom to discover the impact and meaning of the life of Jesus—a life that was not over with his death and Resurrection, but was freed from the limitations of time and place. The Jesus of history and the Christ of faith were one person. Just as the full meaning of his reality was hidden during his life in the flesh, so after his glorification: Jesus was hidden but nonetheless real for that.

Still, the four Gospels do not constitute anything like a biography. Since this is so, can we say anything for certain about Jesus from the standpoint of history?

Taking into account the letters of Paul and of others preserved in the New Testament, we can clearly read only a few claims: that Jesus was a Jew of the tribe of Judah; that he attracted a band of disciples, preached to his own people and suffered from the misunderstanding of many in a ministry that lasted a bit over two years; that he linked his last meal with his friends to an interpretation of his imminent death; and—with the involvement of some politically motivated Jews (but by no means all of them)—that he was set up on bogus charges of treason, was tried before a Roman official, was executed and was buried. He seems to have died at about the age of thirty-six or thirty-seven.

But the story did not end there. The amazing and unprecedented claim was made that, after his death, he appeared alive to a significant number of witnesses, who were convinced that he had forever passed from death to a totally new mode of life. It is interesting to note that Paul does not refer at all to Jesus as a wonder-worker during his ministry: on the contrary, Paul's focus was on the living, risen Jesus, present and active among believers: there was no greater miracle than that, and he recalled it to believers in a voice both firm and unwavering.

Like every concept and word we try to exploit in expressing or discussing our relationship to God, "faith" is perhaps so worn through usage that it is in danger of becoming a cliché.

"What must we do to perform the works of God?" Jesus is asked by some friends one day.

"*This* is the work of God," Jesus replies: "that you believe in him whom He has sent"—that is, in the promise of unlimited access to God that shines forth through Jesus himself. So confident was he of the limitless love that he had received from God, and equally sure that such a gift was offered to all people, that he asked for the trust of others. The self-awareness or identity of Jesus was rooted in his profound experience of God.

What did the words "faith," "trust," "belief" mean for Jesus, and how did the Gospels understand the relationship between what Jesus did in history and what he continues to do in the life of the believer?

"If you have faith the size of a mustard seed," says Jesus to his disciples, referring to faith as a nugget of trust in God's infinite possibility— the kernel and embryo always in a state of becoming—"then nothing will be impossible for you." His meaning is clear: to accept God, to rely unconditionally on His infinite and relentless love as the sole foundation of surety in life, is to enter into His omnipotence. Seeing more deeply than with our physical eyes—seeing with the inner eye, just as we know we are loved by another through the clarity of our inner sight—we know from experience that we are infinitely accepted. That is the meaning of Jesus' injunction to "believe in the good news"—to accept that we are accepted. Nothing here about an intellectual endeavor, an exercise of reason: "It isn't a matter of reason," said Thomas More, defending his faith. "Finally, it's a matter of love."

And what is the effect of this trust, this faith? "Your faith has saved you," Jesus says again and again to the wounded, the weak in body and spirit. Something has already happened: in principle, one is saved—for meaning in this life, not only for eternity (which is God's business and in His keeping). "Do not let your hearts be troubled. Believe in God, believe also in me"—that is, "Rely on God, trust Him without limit"—and take with utter seriousness the life and meaning of Jesus. In this regard, the English novelist C. S. Lewis was right: "Relying on God has to begin all over again every day, as if nothing had yet been done." It is the work of a lifetime, a stance toward reality that has to begin daily, for faith, as the author of the Letter to the Hebrews wrote, is "of things unseen"—of things imperishable, beyond decay and death.

"Blessed are those who have not seen and yet have come to believe," Jesus says to his disciple Thomas, who requires visible proof of his master's triumph over death. It is a challenge that rings like an anthem down through the ages.

But as soon as we begin to discuss faith, mystery, darkness—the sheer elusiveness of things—it seems as if we are outside the realm of ordinary human experience. This very much requires correction, for faith is a fundamental human act.

When we go to a physician, we make an act of faith in his competence and good will—that he will heal and not hurt. The faith may be a bit shaky at times, and we may be full of fears and doubts, but it is faith nonetheless—and we act according to faith, awaiting what we hope will be a favorable outcome. This faith in another may have originated in someone's recommendation about this physician, but it is sustained, and the relationship fares forward, only because of one's own experience. It is the same thing with an adviser or teacher: we have to make all sorts of leaps, acts of confidence.

More to the point, faith—a self-giving trust—is really at the basis of all real love. I can see the manifestations and indications of another's devotion, and I would be very foolish indeed not to accept them. But I cannot require multiple, daily *proofs* of that devotion: it exists as an encompassing reality that communicates itself through signs, through gestures, through hints—through experience. In both cases, that of the doctor and of the friend, the relationships begin through chance or counsel, a coincidence of time and place—by learning what might be called the tradition about someone.

Since the time of the apostles, those who have come to consider the truth of Jesus Christ express their reliance in rituals and formulas, as do all who form communities based on common convictions. In Enid Bagnold's play *The Chalk Garden,* a very grand old lady points to her dining table, set for a formal luncheon. Musing on the origins of the setting, the arrangement of glasses and her own simplified life now, she observes wistfully, "Even the table is laid with fragments of forgotten ritual."

"Faith is handed down that way," replies her old friend, a wise judge.

"In You I put my trust," sings the Hebrew psalmist again and again. It is the single most resonant theme that results from a reflection on experience—on a realization that there have indeed been patterns of meaning in my life that have enabled me to discern a mysterious, underlying order and direction despite the apparent chaos and muddle of what I have inherited and what I have done. And ordinarily these patterns of meaning have to do with relationships, for it is often by means of relationships that the direction, growth and meaning of my life are clarified.

Jesus never speaks abstractly or philosophically about the nature of faith; that would be the task of later generations. For him, faith is confidence in God's power to heal and save—confidence, in other words, in the presence and power of grace: "Whoever does not receive the kingdom of God as a little child will never enter it." Few of his sayings have been so sentimentalized and attenuated as this one, for spiritual childhood—a state of utter, humble dependence—is certainly not the same thing as spiritual infantilism, which turns potentially strong, adult Christians into sniveling, petulant creatures who think that simplicity means stupidity and humility means bashfulness.

The Gospels present faith as an attitude of openness: belief is evident when people are accessible to the action of God in their lives—not closed to the surprise of grace. In practical terms, this means what has traditionally been called "not quenching the Spirit," or refusing to deny that God can act out of His absolute freedom to manifest Himself in an infinite variety of ways. In this regard, there is a provocative observation in the Gospels: Jesus could work no miracles for people in a certain region, we are told, "because of their lack of faith." This presupposes a receptivity to the presence and action of God—a receptivity that is itself the condition for the full possibility of His activity.

Faith, therefore, is a process in which one grows, in which one adopts more and more the qualities of the child—undiluted, unruffled trust in the benevolence of another's care. The child meets reality as it is, without presumptions or expectations and with simple acceptance. But true spiritual childhood takes very seriously that one is entirely dependent on God and can trust Him absolutely.

Faith is a process, a daily progress: "I believe," says one man to Jesus—and then he cries at once: "Help my unbelief!" What, then, does it mean to believe? Is faith a matter of intellectual understanding and subsequent assent to unfathomable mysteries? Is it a sheer effort of will? Is it, as various unfortunate forms of American piety would indicate, a matter of intense emotion—of feeling good (or worse, "feeling good about yourself")?

Christian faith is none of this.

It is, first of all, a way of beholding, a way of regarding reality—an attitude of open-mindedness. Faith is a journey in wonder, and so a part of its dynamic must be an acceptance of the sudden occurrences of darkness. Faith is characterized by a refusal to admit that the world and everything in it is finally chaotic and meaningless: faith refuses to assert the opacity of the universe. There are questions about reality, and there is certainly doubt, which necessarily accompanies faith but does not negate it; doubt is emblematic of the infinite desire to understand infinity more deeply. The world, in other words, has not yet fully disclosed itself to us.

Faith is, then, like a lens through which I gaze out at reality and inward at the life of God quietly breathing within me and making my own breath possible. It is essentially a perspective that refuses to deny that there is ultimate meaning, order and purpose. The meaning, order and purpose may often be unclear; they may appear to shift and change, and they may be articulated differently. But in the final analysis, faith is an attitude about reality that is deeper and more realistic than denial, for it takes with absolute gravity the provisional nature of all human knowing. One who denies the existence of anything transcendent is locked into the poverty of his own narrow perceptions; those who are open to transcendence are freed from the constraints of that poverty. They are susceptible to surprise. They can be found, and so they can find.

We are, after all, incomplete and insufficient unto ourselves, despite the insistence of those who chirp with endless exhilaration about being independent.

But in fact if we have a shred of honesty, we must admit that we are plagued by questions and doubts and that in the core of our being we are profoundly restless and dissatisfied. Our need to feel loved and secure, to feel safe and comforted, is always beyond our ability to achieve. Saint Augustine was right: "Our hearts were made for You, O Lord, and they shall not rest until they rest in You." To those for whom this is nerveless idiocy, one has to ask: If placing one's ultimate trust in the reality of God is a fantasy and a delusion, then what do we call placing that trust in riches or romance or anything that is less? Or have we no sure locus for that trust at all?

Taking our poverty seriously requires the uncomfortable admission that we have very few answers other than this utter reliance on God. It is tempting, in this regard, to escape into the false security of law, which at the last only convicts us of failure. But faith involves a conscious acceptance of our contingency—hence we trust unconditionally in an infinite wisdom and goodness that exceed any imagining or expectation. Dependent as we are, we learn to surrender ourselves to this inconceivable goodness; aware of our limitations, we are not enslaved by them.

———

The Christian, therefore, does not place his trust in various "truths," dogmas or doctrines: his trust is in someone who has spoken first, who has issued an invitation and sent a message. It may not be off the mark to suggest that faith is not primarily a matter of my understanding something or accepting someone: it is a matter of my admitting that I have been understood and accepted by the other. Hence, as a "believer," I am always no more nor less than one engaged in dialogue: I listen, I respond—I exist in dialogue that is itself being, action and speech that is beyond words.

And with whom is this dialogue?

One who fills the world and yet does not belong to it: rather, all the world belongs to Him Who has manifested Himself in the risen and present Lord. "All time belongs to him," as the ancient Easter liturgy has it, "and all the seasons."

———————

In no other case is language more forced into metaphor.

The object of faith is a place into which one may step, a room one may enter, a power on which one may lean, a love to which one may commit. And faith itself? It is the act of meeting this reality, of building one's life around it.

In this regard, one does not really believe in the Bible, but in the God Whom it attests. One does not believe in tradition, but in the God Whose sustaining love it witnesses. One does not believe in the Church, but in the God Whom the Church proclaims. Hence, biblical texts; the writings of saints, mystics and theologians; the formulas of the Church's creeds and doctrines—all of these express in human language the straining and striving toward ultimacy by which is meant, in the simplest language, the experience of and the concomitant desire for God. Despite all uncertainties, insecurities and questions, the believer clings fast to God. At this point, there is little distinction between faith and hope. After all, you can long for and hope for only what you already know, however partially, and have glimpsed, however imperfectly.

———————

The process of faith involves, of course, a journey in prayer. The life of Jesus itself was a prayer—not just a series of acts and a collection of teachings, occasionally interrupted by dialogue with God, but a single, constant abandonment of himself.

Everything in the teachings and deeds of Jesus of Nazareth was rooted in his profound inner life, his steadfast communication with God. From that inner life came his unimaginable humility, his obedience to the destiny he saw more and more clearly as God's will for him; from that, too, came the love of God, which radiated through him to those he met, and had its concrete effects in his words and actions. In him the fullest meaning of prayer becomes evident: from his awareness of God there came an unshakable bond of love; from love came connection. In Jesus, we see the point of convergence between love of God and love of neighbor. Implicitly, all this has to do with an understanding that his entire life was prayer—for prayer is never mere words but a condition of being, just as faith is a condition of being. Words make explicit what is always existent when there are no words.

His life was full of examples of this.

"In the morning, while it was still very dark, he got up and went out to a deserted place, and there he prayed."

"When Jesus heard this [i.e., of the execution of John the Baptist], he withdrew in a boat to a deserted place by himself."

"The word about Jesus spread abroad, and many crowds would gather to hear him and to be cured of their diseases. But he would withdraw to deserted places and pray."

"After saying farewell to them, he went up on the mountain to pray"; and "During those days, he went out to the mountain to pray, and he spent the night in prayer to God."

Night and solitude run like motifs through the Bible, reminding us that silence is the condition for awareness of God's presence. As we have seen, there is a deep silence in the birth and infancy accounts; just so, there is the silence and withdrawal of Jesus from the business of the world; his silence at his trial—and the silence that follows his great outcry at the moment of death.

————

After Jesus had been praying alone for one of those entire nights, he returned to his disciples, who apparently had been talking about his frequent need for solitude and prayer. "Teach us how to pray," they said, "as John [the Baptist] taught his disciples."

Jesus replied that the core of prayer had to do with receiving and offering forgiveness: "Whenever you stand praying, forgive if you have anything against anyone—so that your Father in heaven may also forgive you *your* trespasses."

This summary of prayer, found in Mark, the earliest of the Gospels, probably represents the earliest form of the Lord's Prayer. Because the oral tradition of Jesus' sayings was faithful to him even as new, local and specific applications of those sayings were made to the ongoing life of believers, there is an expanded version of the Prayer in Luke:

"When you pray, say, 'Father, hallowed be your name. Your kingdom come. Give us each day our daily bread. And forgive us our sins, for we ourselves forgive everyone indebted to us. And do not bring us to the time of trial."

During Jesus' ministry, prayers devised by Jews—certainly unofficial orations used outside formal worship—were not firmly fixed but spoken freely, with additions and changes made by those who repeated them: this was not to falsify but to elaborate the original sense. And so there is the Matthean form of the Lord's Prayer, which has become the most widely used version:

> Our Father who art in heaven,
>   hallowed be thy name.
> Thy kingdom come,
>   Thy will be done on earth as it is in heaven.
> Give us this day our daily bread;
>   and forgive us our debts,
>   as we forgive our debtors;
> And lead us not into temptation,
>   but deliver us from evil.

And in this version, Jesus adds pointedly, elaborating on the penultimate part of the prayer, "For if you forgive men their trespasses, your heavenly Father also will forgive you; but if you do not forgive men their trespasses, neither will your Father forgive your trespasses."

Elsewhere, the injunction has another aspect: "Pray for those who persecute you," Jesus says, and the reason is clear. God is the Father of all, even of our enemies: "He makes His sun rise on the evil and on the good, and sends rain on the righteous and on the unrighteous." Our enemies, in other words, are included in God's loving plan—an awareness Jesus lived out at the bitterest moment of his life, when he prayed for those who were putting him to appalling torture and death. How different this is from the spirit of contemporary society, so litigious, so intent on vengeance and redressing wounded "rights."

————

The Lord's Prayer begins with a reworking of a well-known Aramaic prayer, the Kaddish spoken at the end of the synagogue service: "Magnified and sanctified be His great name in the world which he has created according to His will . . . May He establish His kingdom . . . speedily and soon." Jesus turns the prayer just a bit: the kingdom becomes an event now, when God's will is done on earth as it is in heaven—that is, the kingdom here below (man's acceptance of grace) localizes and makes visible the kingdom of heaven. The kingdom has dawned and is now growing in our midst, but it is not yet fully realized.

From the outset, then, Jesus took a prayer familiar from Jewish worship: the new element occurred in the series of petitions that follow— for sustenance (daily bread) and for forgiveness of debts or trespasses (the Greek words for these two, used alternately in Matthew and Luke, go back to the same Aramaic word, *hoba*). Each time we pray, we place ourselves in the realm of forgiveness, of sealing our friendship with God—and our witness to this and our sign of it is our forgiving relationship with others.

As for the last petition—"Lead us not into temptation but deliver us from evil"—this has posed difficulty for many good people. How can God, Who is all good lead us into temptation? The meaning of the Greek text (and of the original Aramaic that certainly stands behind it) is simply "Spare us temptation as such," and its meaning is repeated: "Deliver us from evil."

————

"Thy kingdom come."

This simple but pregnant prayer of Jesus inspired the earliest prayer of Christians. In the years immediately following Jesus' death, they expected an imminent end of the world, believing that although the kingdom had been inaugurated in the ministry of Jesus, its fulfillment was something of the future. Soon Jesus (as the glorious figure of judgment, the apocalyptic Son of Man) would return to dissolve this world and establish forever the kingdom of God—so much is affirmed by the oldest preserved Christian document, Paul's first letter to the Thessalonians (which dates from about A.D. 50). The same expectation is implied when, a few years later, he concluded his first letter to the Corinthians with a short prayer well known to them, which he cites in the Aramaic original: *Marana, thà!*—Our Lord, come!

The same formula concludes the *Didache,* that venerable, early collection of Christian prayers and traditions; indeed, these two Aramaic words, according to some modern scholars, may have terminated the celebration of the Eucharist in the primitive Church. The followers of

Jesus, having just gathered for a meal in his memory, believed that it prefigured the heavenly banquet for which they longed—the fulfillment of the kingdom in eternal life. Hence their pious impatience: "Our Lord, come!" Christians prayed for the Lord to be present to them in the Eucharistic meal, and also to come to them definitively.

This simple, heartfelt prayer typified the attitude of the first Christians, who for several decades expected the imminent end of the world and the dramatic, visible return of the Lord. When that was patently not in the divine plan, the obvious delay became one of the concerns guiding the Gospel writers as they selected, edited and modified traditional material so that the life of the Jesus of history would be relevant to those meeting him as the Christ of faith. The clear deferment of the Second Coming demanded certain norms for authentic Christian living in the present.

How could the first generations of Christians cling so courageously to Jesus that they could and did die for the honor of his name? How could they pray so longingly for him to come to them?

Of course they prayed because the enemy was so readily apparent, and because the memory of Jesus and his teachings gave them the courage to do so. But, in addition, and even more important a factor, was that somehow he must have been presented to them as an absolutely extraordinary man who impressed as no other did—and who was eminently lovable because he himself had so loved others. The love of Jesus for all, and the love he evoked from others, was regarded as the basis for all Christian life.

There is virtually a chain of logic here. Jesus showed to the world a face of compassionate love at every instant of his life. Then the unprecedented experience of him as risen and glorified—transformed completely, no longer subject to death but alive forever in God—evoked in those who put their faith in him a vibrant hope and a response of love.

We often speak blithely of this faith, hope and love as if they were three distinct "commodities" or at least spiritual realities. But in fact they perhaps ought to be regarded as three aspects of a single reality, of our experience of another, of a crucial relationship. Faith carries within it an ineffable love, and this is buoyed by hope for the continuance (indeed, for the permanence, somehow) of the love itself. And if faith is both based on and results in love, then love longs to communicate. When our life in God and our relationship to Him is at stake, we call this communication prayer.

Like faith, prayer is not an intellectual exercise: it is a condition of being in the presence of One Who is known and loved. Nor is faith a skill that can be mastered, although certainly some quiet discipline and the dampening of outer and inner noise helps to remember that we are ever in the presence of God.

Prayer, which is essentially listening for God and offering ourselves to Him, is only possible if we admit our contingency, our complete dependence. And if we sit still long enough, we can perhaps hear, as Julian of Norwich heard, that "everything is finally going to be all right"—that we are accepted and loved beyond our wildest imagining and that, whatever the circumstances in which we find ourselves, no matter how ragged and tattered our life, God is present to hold and to heal us.

Real prayer perhaps ought to be considered, again like faith, as a process, a stance we take toward life—an attitude of alertness, of being accessible to God. With those we love, we need to plan time together; we long to find ways to give, and we are not ashamed to receive the warmth and healing we need to go on. But our love for others is deepened, and the presence continues, outside those moments. Although the cold impersonality of so much contemporary work often dulls the realization of it, the fact is that a man working to support his wife and children is loving them even from the distance of his workplace.

So it is with the primal relationship we have, with ultimacy itself. Hence when Jesus urges us "to pray always and not to lose heart," he speaks not of "empty phrases and many words" (which he specifically discourages), but of the condition of constant alertness and openness before God. This is the work of a lifetime—just as with our love for another in this world: God is not less than His creation. Paradoxically, our frailty and our poor efforts at alertness are not to discourage us, for only when we realize how distracted and poor we are do we know that we are such obvious ready targets for grace. Paul was aware of this paradox: "Whenever I am weak," he wrote to the Corinthians, "then I am strong."

As for the time devoted to prayer, Teresa of Avila—that courageous and sharp lady who reformed the religious life of Spain in the sixteenth century—summarized a common misconception. Speaking to pious folks who sighed and said that if only their busy schedules permitted, they would pray more often and for longer periods, she replied, "Don't imagine that if you had a great deal of time you would spend more of it in prayer. Get rid of *that* idea! Again and again, God gives more in a moment than in a long period of time, for His actions are not measured by time at all."

It is tempting to accept the spirit of our cynical age: it is not God speaking to you, we are told, it is your own imagination—a desire for psychological comfort, a residual longing for parental protection, a projection. If this is so, it is astonishing that after many years of lukewarmness to the things of God, one has not succeeded in quenching the desire for converse with Him. If this is so, why does the most abject spiritual indolence not stifle the invitation?

Our task is to be with God, responding to the motions of His Spirit in a moment here, a second or two there, a quarter-hour then. The time of explicit prayer, of "being with" rather than "saying to," simply focuses an orientation of one's being that exists outside those moments; hence, all of one's being becomes an act of dependence, of offering, of adoration, and so one comes to understand the invitation of Jesus to pray always. If our freedom is more and more lived responsive to the touch of God, we will be unafraid to reply in the words of the prophet, "Here I am, Lord!"

Prayer is, then, not so much what we say to God as it is a condition of alertness for His presence. And what we listen for is not a message of words (much less a dramatic announcement that will radically alter our fortunes) but the conviction that we are comprehended, accepted, grasped in the core of our being, loved by infinite Love. Prayer is essentially surrender, and it is this that modern man avoids at all cost. Power is so coveted that we have lost sight of the truth that real serenity lies in abandoning every pretense of it. Imagine what the world, or even your parcel of it, would be like if you and those around you lived in a state of abandonment, of surrender to the benevolence of God.

Imagine what our lives would be like if we took God seriously.

Now, perhaps more than at any other time in history, it is notoriously difficult to hear and heed the presence of God. We have lost touch with the blessedness of quiet. We make noise, it seems, doing just about everything. We do not speak or converse, we shout. Everywhere there is sound, every place seems full of a noisy beat, as if the possibility of hearing our own pulse would be too awful to contemplate.

"Come now, turn aside," urged the great medieval philosopher Anselm of Canterbury in the eleventh century—and he was speaking first of all to himself. "Turn aside for a while from your daily employment, escape for a moment from the tumult of your thoughts. Put aside your weighty cares, let your burdensome distractions wait, free yourself awhile for God, and rest awhile in Him. Enter the inner chamber of your soul, shut out everything except God and that which can help you in seeking Him, and when you have shut the door, seek Him. Say to God, 'I seek Your face—Lord, it is Your face I seek.'" Well did Anselm understand the injunction of Jesus: "Go into your room and shut the door and pray to your Father Who is in secret—and your Father, Who sees in secret, will reward you."

God does indeed reward us, if only we knew how to see the shape of His gift. He does indeed speak to us—or perhaps we should say addresses us—whether we listen or not. The world and everything in it shouts simultaneously to us of the presence and absence of God. Every bit of the sheer beauty in the world, from nature to art, announces something of the loveliness of God's presence; on the other hand, the sheer magnitude of evil, of the exploitation and cruelty wrought by person against person and nation against nation, speaks to us of God's absence—of every realm where the mercy of God is disallowed.

But we ought to be very honest. Even our best religious intentions, like our language, are sloppy and full of vanity, pretension and a satchel full of mixed motives. "Everything evil in man functions also (there all the more powerfully) in his religion," observed none other than the great Catholic philosopher and theologian Romano Guardini, who was so highly regarded by the guardians of orthodoxy during the pontificate of Pius XII (1939–1958) that Guardini was invited to be that pope's confessor, his spiritual father. There is, as Guardini and others have insisted, a wide chasm separating the infinite God from our finite expression of Him and the reaching out to Him that is supposed to mark real religion.

But here the paradox returns with a vengeance: this is itself a heartening announcement, too, for in the final analysis what can we do but throw ourselves upon that great ocean of infinite mercy? What can we do but confide ourselves to the arms of God? I have no reason to feel secure in anything that I consider mine—not my faith, not my prayer. "If you think you are standing, watch out that you do not fall," Paul urged the Christians at Corinth. The process of believing, then, is linked to the process of learning to heed in prayer—and all of this is rooted in the process of becoming human at the deepest level. One is always on the way to becoming a Christian. Faith is nothing one can possess; much less is it a pulpit from which to judge and condemn others. Belief in Jesus Christ is process, it is movement and journey; it is a condition of constant clarification, of loving more.

In this regard, there is a great danger in thinking that one has reached a condition of "being Christian." Usually those who make such a claim glance covertly aside at others they consider *not* Christian. In our time, they do more than glance: they all too often shout loudly about the wickedness and darkness of those they despise. What a pity that the designation "Christian" has, perhaps in America more than anywhere, been co-opted by ideologues whose agenda is founded on bogus "principles" that are exclusive, legalistic, unloving and judgmental—and therefore obviously anti-Christian.

These people seem always to know "what God thinks" and "what God wants" and, most of all, "what God hates." Such so-called Christianity is nothing but a pious form of self-affirmation—a way of establishing one's own imagined moral superiority. It is good to remember that God does not take instructions from people: "My thoughts are not your thoughts, nor my ways your ways," said the Lord through the prophet Isaiah.

————

Living by faith and commitment to prayer may sound to some like a kind of spiritual lollipop—an attitude conjured up or self-imposed in order to avoid confronting the harshness of life.

But faith neither conquers nor diminishes suffering. It does, however, provide the means for both endurance and triumphing over suffering. The believer is not crushed or destroyed by suffering, nor does he despair. Danger, emptiness, loneliness are all embraced by God.

Clinging to God as my one and only certainty—not clinging to assertions about Him, or words about Him, but to God Himself, Who is beyond words and categories—this is the basis of the dark journey of faith. "All my hope on God is founded," run the words of the hymn. Despite my frailty, my unbelief, my spiritual tepidity and timidity—and whatever misfortune befalls—I have no reason to despair.

Even when I am confronted with my own spiritual torpor, with my failures, with the poverty of my achievement and of my muddled heart, I am buoyed by the fidelity of God. "The pain of sin purges us and makes us know ourselves, so that we ask for mercy," wrote Julian of Norwich. "Our good Lord comforts us at once, as if to say, 'It is true that sin is the cause of all this pain. But it is going to be all right; it is going to be all right; everything is going to be all right.' These words [are] said most tenderly, with never a hint of blame . . . It would be most improper of me therefore to blame or criticize God for my sin, since he does not blame me for it."

In doubt, in fear and failure, in mental anxiety and physical pain, then, I try to cling to God—especially when I feel completely empty, forlorn and burnt out, when I have not the focus of heart or mind sufficient for one prayer. This, of course, is basic confidence of the most radical sort. Only by saying "Amen" can we endure suffering, for "Amen" is the ancient Hebrew affirmation of something said, done, witnessed—an expression of confirming belief. It is perhaps the briefest and deepest prayer of all, the conviction, despite all the misery in the world and in oneself, that finally God acts out of love for all.

With all its mystery, its evil and suffering, its deprivation and incompleteness, life in this world can be affirmed because of God—and only because of God. Faith, that commitment to open wonder and a refusal to accept that there is finally no meaning, understands that denial is no resolution to the problem of evil. As a stance toward life, an orientation of one's deepest desires and an attitude of constantly deepening reliance on God, faith alone can bestow order where there is chaos. Faith is that for which we are born, that by which we operate daily in the world.

Of course anxiety and panic can always find a home in us, but they can be routed by faith and endured by prayer, which—as they deepen and root us more firmly—gradually displace dread and establish abiding serenity. Indeed, faith itself is the soul's true country, and prayer is its native language.

CHAPTER ELEVEN

THE BEGINNING OF THE END:
THE REJECTION OF JESUS

After two years of preaching and healing, of extending a radical message of God's friendship to humanity, Jesus had not become terrifically popular, for his limpid compassion and strong sense of self offended very many of his countrymen. By the latter part of the year 29 and early 30, he was in fact a marginal man who aroused suspicion and even hostility wherever he went. And his celibacy: Why did he not contribute to the number of Israel? What sort of grotesque refusal was *that?* What sort of selfishness?

Very few people were firmly allied with him. This simple man from Galilee, who had never studied with a renowned scholar or pious teacher, who had once been with that odd figure John the Baptist and then struck out on his own; this man who thought little of public fasting, who uttered challenges to the status quo and was imprudently antiestablishment; this man without credentials, who was no priest and who clashed with the wealthy and aristocratic urban priesthood—was he not almost inevitably destined to be swept aside as he insistently issued challenges and made promises, in each instance claiming that God Himself was at work in his acts and words?

I think it is not at all clear that Jesus would have enjoyed a better reception two thousand years later, for we live in astonishingly mean-spirited times. Someone would find a way to give the public exactly what it most wants—reasons to believe that a man who goes about doing good is really a no-account hypocrite, a money-hungry crackpot with a checkered past, or an egomaniac with a thirst for adoration. And if those characteristics could not be proven, a list of horrors would be invented, to attest to his flawed character—and the critical report would be immediately and gladly welcomed by vast numbers of people unable to endure the possibility of real goodness and the challenge it offers.

————

Still, even a hasty reading of the Gospels presents one thorny problem, for very often, Jesus does something odd that seems to work against him and his mission.

After healing a leper of his grotesque malady, we read, he sent the renewed man away with a curious admonition: "See that you say nothing to anyone." The cure did not occur on the Sabbath, so there was no question of outrage from the literalist authorities. Why, then, did Jesus seem to muzzle precisely the sort of report that could draw people to him and his proclamation of God?

There were moments like this throughout his life. After restoring the dead daughter of Jairus to life, Jesus turned to her overjoyed parents: "He strictly ordered them that no one should know this." After healing a deaf-mute, Jesus charged everyone to keep silence about this wonderful event—a mandate they understandably ignored. And when the master's wonderful deeds and astonishing teaching inspired Peter to announce that Jesus was the longed-for Messiah ("You are the Christ"), he and the other disciples were at once forbidden to tell this to anyone.

The significance of this motif, of what has been called "the Messianic secret," has been argued by scholars for a century. It is so closely interwoven with the activities and proclamation of Jesus as presented in all the Gospels that it is hard to see it as anything but part of the most ancient material about Jesus. And when everything has been studied and assessed, the reason for this tradition is astonishing: Jesus indeed enjoined silence when people wanted to rush him to celebrity simply on the basis of his actions. And he commanded silence when they wanted to go further, proclaiming him the Messiah desired by Israel. The nature of Messiahship *as he understood it* was not consistent with the expectations of Judaism regarding such a figure.

Far from presenting himself as a political figure or social deliverer, Jesus instead linked his suppression of a Messiah-title with his understanding that in the history of Israel, from Isaiah to the Baptist, God's true prophets invariably suffered misunderstanding and, in some cases, ostracism and even death. And here we are at the very heart of Jesus' own self-understanding, of just who he considered himself to be in the dispensation of God's plan for humanity.

———

First of all, it is important to recall that the era in which Jesus lived was not one in which people spoke or even, it seems, thought very much about their identity; instead, they lived and acted. Psychological self-articulation, metaphysical speculation, philosophical discourse on the nature of the human person, emotional stock-taking—all these were yet to come. Like their languages, Semites thought in terms of concrete action, and so for Jesus the Jew, his role was not a matter of social status or personality theory but one of action. He found his identity and destiny in what he did and, as he gradually understood, in what was happening to him.

But there is another consideration, and it has to do with the misunderstanding Jesus met when he enjoined silence on those most likely to spread abroad his fame—his friends and those he healed. This misunderstanding was in all cases connected to Jesus' intuition that he was destined for suffering, which his disciples did not understand during his lifetime, and which often we do not fully appreciate today.

Immediately after Peter's statement about Jesus' Messiahship, for example, Jesus ordered the disciples not to tell anyone of this. He then began to speak of his own imminent suffering and death—predictions that essentially went back to Jesus himself but that became more explicit in the writing, in light of the (then past) events of his death and Resurrection. Jesus said he would be rejected by religious authorities and be delivered over to Gentiles, who would mock him, spit on him, scourge him and kill him—but after three days he would rise from death.

This revelation, too, was met by misunderstanding: Peter said he would never allow his beloved master to undergo suffering and death—and to this Jesus responded violently: "Get behind me, Satan! You are setting your mind not on divine things, but on human things!" Since Peter rejected the idea of suffering, in other words, he was not yet wholly on the side of Jesus, who moments later said: "If any want to become my followers, let them deny themselves and take up their cross and follow me." And so the most perceptive biblical scholars attending to these predictions of sufferings have seen that the passion and Resurrection predictions, like the unifying idea of the Messianic secret, fit into the total framework of the Gospel.

———

The four Gospels are extraordinarily detailed in their descriptions of his trial, execution and burial—precisely because the oral tradition that preceded the composition had been meticulously preserved. And if we read the four accounts carefully, we see a straight line, a kind of compelling logic. Jesus rejected every known category applied to him, especially that of King-Messiah, for he believed that God was working something ultimate through him—the regeneration and reconciliation, the absolute sealing of friendship between man and God, taken at God's initiative. Of this his marvelous deeds were signs, just as his teaching overturned every pious expectation, sent forth a revolution in human thinking and set out the standards of universal compassion and forgiveness.

But from very early on, his deeds and words evoked resentment and rejection from the establishment, as we have seen. Jesus broke religious laws by healing on the Sabbath; he conversed openly in public with women, Gentiles and Samaritans; he embraced children and regarded them as persons with rights; he dined and socialized with sinners, with the outcast and the ritually unclean. He hated smugness and moral superiority and the kind of self-satisfaction that an exaggerated concern with mere laws, and not their spirit, can engender.

For Jesus, humanity's relationship with God was not established by obeying laws, but by responding to God and by being alert to the needs of others—*that* was the ultimate spirit of the law. Hence Sabbath regulations, pious traditions and ritual acts were empty and purposeless if they obscured human need and prevented one from responding to suffering. And so, as Jesus continually proclaimed this spirit over law—and acted according to it—some pious people and religious leaders, jealous of their positions and prerogatives, "began to plot how they might destroy him." It seemed, day by day, an easier goal to achieve: warned in the presence of eyewitnesses, a Jew could be put to death for a second offense of Sabbath-breaking.

And Jesus was aware of this: "Why are you looking for an opportunity to kill me?" he asked a group of grumblers one day. Of course they dissembled, smiled and said he was crazy, they had no such intentions.

But he knew better. And he did not defend himself by becoming a melodramatic public sufferer—a victim of public misunderstanding, talking about his simple background, his self-esteem or his confusion. He was responsible to God; everything about him radiated courageous directness. His identity was apparent to him and others by what he did, which was to live with and for others. He did not deliver merely comforting aphorisms that made life easy. He did not speak much about love: he lived it.

But direct statements about Jesus should not give the impression that he was or is easy to comprehend: the fact is, he cannot be fitted into any category. Neither sovereign nor anarchist, priest nor revolutionary, he provokes both the lax and the strict; neither political reformer nor scholar, neither royal son nor liberal social worker, he is more radical than both. Both his friends and his enemies mostly misperceive and misunderstand him, and much less do they comprehend the complexity of his personality.

There is a constant element of surprise about Jesus of Nazareth. It is unexpected that his own life should originate and proceed in so humble a setting, astonishing that his friends should be so unexceptional, paradoxical that he should prefer the company of the poor and outcast to the powerful and influential, amazing that he should choose to associate with the impolite and shunned. Jesus was not a fashionable man in any way, nor did he court anyone's approval. He was drawn to those considered unattractive and undesirable, socially unacceptable and of no account. He never rejected the company of sinners.

As far as religion was concerned, Jesus was certainly not the founder of a new one. Nor did he set down a list of doctrines and dogmas. He was *different* from all those who did—and so he remains two millennia later. Jesus came not to offer a new code of conduct, but to announce the accessibility of God for humanity. Utterly free in his response to God, he came to set the world free from a slavery to its own limitations.

Although he was no rebel and remained the most devout of Jews, Jesus had no patience with laws that oppressed—and so he was regarded as a threat to the integrity of the Mosaic law itself, which to scribes, Pharisees and other guardians of orthodoxy was the very heart of Judaism. One scholar has succinctly stated the matter: "Only if their devotion to the law is recognized can the profundity of their hostility to Jesus and their refusal to admit any possible validity of his claims be understood."

All those claims—uttered with terms like "I say to you" and the resonant, authoritative "Amen, Amen"—Jesus put before people as a man of humble background, without money, influence, political power or party support, and without the blessing of any polite group. Attended by a motley crew of men and women who were shockingly ordinary, unremarkable for intellectual acumen, social grace, wit or quickness, Jesus had none of the characteristics of the "successful man" in any era. From the viewpoint of this world's values, he seemed to have got it all wrong, to have made a series of real blunders regarding his choice of friends and acquaintances.

———

This much can be said with certainty about the self-awareness of Jesus: he saw more and more clearly, precisely because of the reaction of authorities in the last months and weeks of his life, that his destiny would be like that of Isaiah, Jeremiah, Ezekiel, Amos, Micah and Zechariah— the prophets who were ignored and finally rejected, outcast and considered martyrs. As he and a group of disciples prepared to travel to Jerusalem for the Passover, Jesus knew the possibility of suffering and death, for to take his message to the Holy City was to risk punishment on the grand scale: "Jerusalem, Jerusalem," he said ruefully, "the city that kills the prophets and stones those who are sent to it. How often have I desired to gather your children together as a hen gathers her brood under her wings, but you were not willing!" Violent confrontation and danger he sought with all his might to avoid, but for sheer safety's sake he would not compromise his fidelity. His fate might turn out to be like those who had been killed in Jerusalem—the prophet Zechariah, for example, was murdered right in the temple as penalty for his unpopular preaching.

That Jesus might well have understood his own death as a ransom for many (as he had offered his whole life as a sacrifice to God) is of decisive importance for comprehending his mission, and it cannot be understood without reference to what inspired Jesus—the central moment of Hebrew faith and worship, which is the Passover sacrifice. The offering of sacrificial animals in the Old Testament (the "blood of the covenant") effected the people's deliverance from sin and judgment, it was believed; hence a covenant bond between God and His people was established and ratified annually.

The implication of the Gospels is that Jesus thought of his surrendered life and sacrificial death as a dedicated self-offering to God in the name of mankind and for their sake—to heal forever the wound of sin and to seal forever man's friendship with God. There is nothing here about appeasing an angry God: Jesus everywhere takes the love of God quite for granted ("God so loved the world that He gave His only Son"). The ideas of ransom, covenant and of surrogate offering for the redemption of others are characteristic of Jewish faith. As we shall see, they are further deepened—indeed, this complex of ideas is altered radically—in light of the Resurrection.

The course of his ministry, then, would have shown Jesus that a violent death was certainly a possibility, if not a foreseen likelihood. He announced the forgiveness of sins, which was a divine prerogative: therefore some of the pious objected, "It is blasphemy!" He cast out evil spirits, restoring the sick to sanity and health, which meant he was practicing magic—the devil's own black arts—and so merited the punishment of being stoned to death. Alternatively, he seemed to some leaders to be a false prophet—and so, according to the law, he could be strangled to death.

And then Jesus does the most dangerous thing of all. Hoping that an appeal to the widest possible audience—and especially to his opponents—might at last be effective in proclaiming the coming of God to humanity, Jesus and his disciples traveled to Jerusalem, at the end of March in the year 30, for the Passover feast.

He went, of course, to the temple, along with devout Jews from near and far; the year-round population of the city was about 25,000—but four times that number flocked in for feast days. When he entered the temple precincts, Jesus saw a madly commercial bazaar. The place was simply a crowded market, not a sacred place for solemn worship. There were noisy merchants buying and selling birds, cattle and sheep for ritual sacrifice; and there were money changers haggling over exchange rates. Because the Holy City had its own coinage, the vast throngs of pilgrims had to visit the money changers' booths when they bought gifts for the temple rites. This requirement, of course, always led to a fantastic windfall for speculators and merchants; it also diminished the reverence due the holy precincts. Jesus was outraged.

"My house shall be called a house of prayer for all peoples—has it now become a den of robbers?" Jesus shouted, quoting from the Old Testament the words of God to Isaiah and Jeremiah as he overturned the tables, set animals free, scattered the money, routed the pigeons and brought forth angry cries from the merchants and bankers. Like one of the ancient prophets, Jesus announced in the most dramatic way that the repentance and reform he had proclaimed in rural Galilee applied as well to Jerusalem, its holy temple and its cultic priesthood.

For his enemies, some of whom were among the richest and most powerful men in the religious establishment, this was the match in the powder barrel: "they looked for a way to kill him, for they feared him—the crowd was spellbound by his teaching." The authority and influence of these self-righteous rulers were being threatened before their eyes, and so, within a matter of days, an unlikely affiliation was formed between a few Jewish leaders and the occupying Roman authorities. Order had to be kept in Jerusalem; an upstart like this Jesus, with his new ways and unconventional preaching, might rouse the people to insurrection or rebellion. Why, he could call for a general religious revolution, just as he had been breaking the Sabbath and defying certain pious traditions! *Then* what would become of the establishment?

No. Like John the Baptist, this Jesus of Nazareth had to be dealt with once and for all. But his enemies would have to ambush him in private, when he was apart from a crowd, perhaps with just a group of friends, preferably at night. They could not risk rousing the reaction of a crowd favorable to Jesus, for whatever reason, at whatever moment. They needed to know his private plans—where, for example, could he be found in the dead of night during the days of Passover? With so much going on in Jerusalem, it should be a small matter to deal with Jesus the Galilean.

———

As it happened, the enemies of Jesus did not have to look far for help.

Judas Iscariot, one of the inner circle of twelve followers especially close to Jesus, had been charged with keeping the small amounts of common cash used by Jesus and his disciples as they traveled from village to hamlet. More than once, Judas had been caught with his hand in the purse, and over time he had grown greedier and greedier—as well, it seems, as more resentful of his colleagues and his master.

Very soon after the melee at the temple, Judas, aware of the authorities' rage against Jesus, approached a group of chief priests.

"What will you give me," he asked them flatly, "if I betray him to you?" They handed over to him thirty pieces of silver—a remarkably paltry sum, exactly the amount a man had to pay if one of his animals accidentally killed another man's slave. "And from that moment," says the New Testament with calm horror, "Judas sought an opportunity to betray him."

There is no indication that Judas acted from any personal animosity against Jesus, nor did he expect, in turning him over to religious authorities, that Jesus might indeed be summarily executed. We are told only that he was greedy, a little resentful—just small-minded enough, in a rash moment, to turn against a friend. Well, these things happen every day, and usually there is a way out—*if* you get caught. After all, Judas had only to point Jesus out to a hostile group: what that group did to Jesus had nothing to do with Judas, who never said he wanted him dead, after all. Everything would be all right in the end; the other disciples would look after things just fine. Really, it was no big deal.

Judas is, alas, not merely of the past, and so we have little reason to speak smugly of his sin. He unmasks the pettiness and disloyalty in all of us, and the easy way to treachery; it is, after all, so easy to find excuses for betrayal.

And so by a gesture of fearful shallowness and negligence—a moment of caprice, one might say, on the part of a man hitherto charged with no significant wickedness—by this terribly common act, conceived and accomplished in a moment as quiet as the night, the history of the world and everything in it, and the route of time itself, were forever changed.

CHAPTER TWELVE

THE SUPPER:
JESUS AND THE EUCHARIST

On Thursday evening, April 6, in the year 30, Jesus of Nazareth
gathered a dozen friends for supper. He was then about thirty-
six and had conducted a ministry of preaching and healing
for just over two years. Friday at sundown would begin the great celebration of Passover, which that year happened also to fall on the Sabbath
(Saturday). On Friday afternoon, Paschal or Passover lambs would be
slaughtered for sacrifice and the ritual meal, and everything had to be
ready by dusk.

In the Passover supper of roast lamb and unleavened bread, Israel
memorializes its deliverance from Egyptian bondage. The Jewish people
recall annually the Lord's "passing over" their houses during the plague
visited on the Egyptian firstborn, and their hasty escape from slavery.
The covenant, or agreement, between God and His people was sealed
in a ritual of blood, always the sign of life in the ancient world; after all,
when either man or beast lost all blood, life was gone. Offering animal
blood in ritual sacrifice by placing it on an altar acknowledged that God
alone was the author of life, and the pact between God and His people
was a sharing of divine life. So much was clear in the Book of Exodus:

> Moses sent young men of the people of Israel, who offered burnt
> offerings and sacrificed oxen as offerings to the Lord. Moses took
> half the blood and put it in basins, and half he dashed against the
> altar. Then he took the book of the covenant and read it in the
> hearing of the people ... Moses took the blood and dashed it on
> the people and said, "See the blood of the covenant that the Lord
> has made with you."

Jesus had been teaching constantly in the Jerusalem temple precincts since his arrival in Jerusalem, probably about a week earlier, in late March and at the beginning of April. Aware that his enemies were gathering for a major assault on him, and that he might be prevented from sharing the Passover meal with his friends, Jesus arranged an evening meal with his closest disciples. The event was neither a Passover nor an anticipation of it—but neither was it an ordinary supper. By planning all the formalities—a private place (a room borrowed just for the evening); the sharing of bread and wine; singing hymns and psalms—Jesus clearly intended something solemn, and it had to do with the significance of his imminent death.

The entire evening was extraordinary.

Before supper, Jesus did something that made his friends uncomfortable. At the time, the trek to someone's home left guests weary and (because everyone wore sandals) dusty and footsore; it was the custom, therefore, for a household slave to kneel before guests, washing and drying their feet. This was clearly a servile task. And so that evening (the Gospel according to John records), Jesus took a basin and a towel and knelt before his friends, washing their feet.

"Are *you* going to wash *my* feet?" Simon Peter asked when Jesus came to him.

"You do not know now what I am doing," Jesus replied quietly, continuing his task, "but later you will understand."

Peter pulled away. "You will never wash my feet," he said, aware that their roles should have been reversed. But with the most loving glance, Jesus prevailed, and Peter—who only later understood how deeply the following of Jesus is identified with humble service—permitted the footwashing.

To this day, the symbolic gesture continues. At every celebration of the Lord's Supper on Holy Thursday night, the celebrant—even the Pope in Rome himself—puts aside precious robes and kneels to wash the feet of others. But the rite must not be simply considered a memorial repetition, and it is much more than a moralistic example. It is a powerful carrier of the heart of the message, for clinging to God in Christ means that, whatever one's task in this world, it is a kind of service to others. The refusal to dominate, to wield power, the willingness to give oneself and to use one's gifts and talents for the good of others—this is the spirit of Jesus and his friends, now as then.

The meaning of the foot-washing is also the meaning of what follows.

Paul, writing to the Corinthians, left us the earliest account of Jesus' last supper with his disciples: "The Lord Jesus, on the night when he was betrayed, took a loaf of bread, and when he had given thanks, he broke it and said, 'This is my body that is for you. Do this in remembrance of me.' In the same way, he took the cup also, after supper, saying, 'This cup is the new covenant in my blood. Do this, as often as you drink it, in remembrance of me.' "

Although they differ in minor details, Matthew and Luke are remarkably similar to the first Gospel account of the last supper, set down by Mark (about a dozen years after Paul wrote to the Corinthians):

"While they were eating, he took a loaf of bread, and after blessing it, he broke it, gave it to them, and said, 'Take, this is my body.' Then he took a cup, and after giving thanks he gave it to them, and all of them drank from it. He said to them, 'This is my blood of the covenant, which is poured out for many.' "

As a devout Jew influenced by the imminent feast of Passover and the rituals of atonement, Jesus was clearly referring to its elements—but radically shifting their focus to the present. He was also drawing on a rich Jewish heritage of prayer and praise. The bread and cup in religious meals of the Jews were accompanied by a *berakah,* giving thanks to God for His blessings. Conversely, to "bless God" and to "praise God"— Who neither requires nor benefits from what is often thought of as human flattery or blandishment—means to consecrate something to God, to hallow it by turning it over to Him.

The meal as a sign of unity is virtually an archetypal symbol: within and outside religion, human beings share a meal to mark the great and small moments in their shared history. From wedding banquets to funeral suppers, from birthday dinners to casual buffets, we express our solidarity and our unity by sharing the same food. The meaning is clear to all, even without our thinking about it: if we share the same meal, we are literally united, made one, for then our very beings are composed of the same common elements. So it is with those who come together in a shared faith. The religious meals of Judaism are among the most highly ritualized, and from them have come the basic structure of the Christian Eucharist: prayers, readings, hymns, consecration of the community to God.

To these simple gestures—breaking and sharing a loaf of bread, pouring and passing a cup of wine—Jesus attached enormous significance. Associating the broken bread and poured wine with his imminent violent death, he at once made visible symbols of his gift of self for all the world ("for many" is a Semitism meaning "for all") and, in speaking of a "new covenant," clearly referred to what was common Jewish currency.

Jesus, on this last night of his life, saw his impending death as linked to the covenant God had made with His people on Sinai, but in place of bulls' blood, the blood of Jesus himself would bring to fulfillment the relationship between God and humanity. The long trek from Egypt through the desert was ending at last. His would be a sacrifice, a ransom for the world—much as the mysterious figure of the Suffering Servant in the prophecies of Isaiah represents a kind of representative personality whose pain and death would earn the justification of Israel.

Jesus, therefore, did not invent an entirely new rite wholesale. Rather he invested the gestures, forms and materials of old rites with a new value. His body would be broken, like the bread before them; his blood would flow, just like this red wine. "This is my body . . . this is my blood" do not refer, then, to sinews and flesh, nor to matters hematologic, for the terms in Hebrew and Aramaic refer to the substance of the whole person and the meaning of his life—by "blood" is meant his entire being.

His circle of companions knew this, for soon after his death, they began to ritualize what he did that night, and so it continues to this day—the faithful gather in remembrance of him who loved his friends, they break bread and share the cup. In so doing, they honor his memory, celebrate his continuing presence among them, give thanks that Jesus gave himself—gave everything that was his being, his life and death—as nourishment for his people. At the same time, the faithful acknowledge that in the future, in God's good time, all will be fulfilled in an eternal banquet that is unending life. This entire complex of meaning is contained in the Christian Eucharist, which means "act of thanksgiving" and which traces its origins to the last supper.

Few matters in Christian life and practice have been so debated and misunderstood as the Christian Eucharist. The right and proper emphasis on the real presence of the Risen Lord in the shared meal, with his people and with each as an individual, has been often preached and presented in terms that have led Christians and non-Christians alike to think that eating the "body and blood" of the Lord is really something cannibalistic—in other words, that when one partakes of communion bread, one ingests the tissues, muscles, bodily flesh of Jesus, and from the cup, one drinks human blood. This is a pathetic misunderstanding of a sublime reality.

The Roman Catholic Church for centuries clung tenaciously to terminology unknown to Jesus, the disciples and the entire Church until the late Middle Ages. The Eucharist was accordingly presented in terms of Aristotelian philosophy: the "accidents" of bread and wine—what they look, feel and taste like—remain; but the "substance"—the actual invisible reality beneath the accidents—is miraculously transformed into the person of Jesus Christ. Unfortunately, popular teaching and preaching have distorted a far richer understanding of this application of philosophy to theology.

Authentic Catholic Christian teaching, on the other hand, proclaims that by the "body and blood" of Jesus present in the Eucharist is meant the glorious, risen presence of Jesus among the faithful—*not* the organism of worldly flesh through which the existence of Jesus was manifest during his earthly life. It is the reality of a risen and glorified Lord—totally transformed—that is present to us. There is no question of devouring the elements of flesh and blood as we use those terms to describe a human life in this world. It is the *presence* of the person that is at stake. To speak of the "real presence" of Jesus in the Eucharist, then, it is necessary to understand just what "presence" means.

———

The word "presence" can be used with a variety of connotations. My books can be present to me: close by and helpful. I can be present at a meeting, exerting influence. I can be present at a party, as a token of my solidarity with a group. I can be present with one who is ill, providing support. I can be present to a friend, which means mutual attention and involves a prior relationship and commitment even before we come together in spatial nearness to each other.

These aspects of various kinds of presence can be very definitely and distinctly understood if we consider the converse. My absent look at a meeting betokens the fact that my will, my thoughts and interests are really elsewhere: I am, indeed, not present at the meeting at this point—or, to put it another way, I am present *only* physically. When we say this, we understand that mere fleshly or somatic presence is not necessarily presence at all—or, more specifically, it is not *real* presence: it does not *realize* something. My presence, in other words, is more like a kind of absence.

It is easy, for one thing, to speak of "being present" to someone merely physically—that is, in a simply *local* way, as when I am present to a stranger who is near me on a bus or an airplane, or in a crowd. But this is only spatial nearness or proximity—it is not actually or really presence, precisely because it does not actualize or realize or make real the personal presence that the other's life has for me. This kind of proximity, therefore, is mere physical contiguity, and that is a kind of absence. Contrariwise, if in a crowded roomful of strangers I spot someone I love, clearly there is an awareness and a presence that transcends the meaning of all the others, who suddenly "disappear"—they are truly no longer present to me. Even in ordinary conversation, we often say to or about someone that he is "somewhere else."

In his new life in God, Jesus does not make himself present in ways that would enable us to limit him or objectify him so that we might consider him just another object or individual among objects and individuals. As God Eternal is at the center of our being, as its origin, cause and sustenance, so the risen Jesus is present in the Spirit. We do not have to look around the room to find him.

Just so, ordinary fleshly proximity does not guarantee personal presence. In this regard, it is one of the symptoms of social pathology in our time that people live, travel and work in increasingly crowded, crushed physical conditions in the great cities of the world, yet they sense an increasing loneliness that very often leads to anxiety and panic.

There is another kind of presence—of students with a teacher, for example, or of a patient with a physician. There is information to be given and received, there are instructions to be handed over, there is care to be provided and accepted. This is a deeper kind of presence than mere proximity, for some degree of attention and trust are required in the transaction—a deeper presence, in other words, than the mere bodily closeness of the strangers seated next to one another on the bus who exchange not a word and who have no meaning for one another.

Often people think of the ultimate presence of one person with another in terms of the most obvious kind of physical closeness—that of sexual intercourse. Clearly, this *can* betoken and represent a very profound personal communion between people who love and trust each other. But equally clearly, it is *not* the sexual element that creates the intimacy and the bond—otherwise every variant of intercourse, including rape, coercion, blackmail, indifference and mere mutual convenience would automatically be a profound commingling of two spirits.

It is not, then, mere fleshly contact that determines the degree and establishes the reality of the presence. The awfulness of forced sexual congress (rape, the exploitation of one held in power) lies in precisely the fact that we understand that if the will of one person is withheld, the act is both shameful and criminal. Hence the coerced person is physically present to the controller or attacker but personally absent—that is, the victim is not, *as a person,* present to the other. The victim exists as an object, a thing to be manipulated and abused.

I can only be personally present to another, or with or for another, if I enter into mutual communication with that other. Again, with regard to sex, it is certainly obvious to many that if it is only physical and not personal presence that is effected, and if this physical presence is not clear *as a sign* of something deeper, then we remain as dissociated and lonely after the act as before. It is only through the spirit or the soul that we really enter into each other and yet remain ourselves. " 'In' is the superlative degree of 'with,' " as the Dutch philosophical theologian Piet Schoonenberg has succinctly written.

———

Whether we are seated with a companion, studying with a trusted mentor, embracing a friend or making love to a devoted other, it is obviously not the mere closeness of the flesh that determines the depth and truth of the relationship, it is the deep connection of the *person*—what we might call the *spirit* of the other—that makes real presence possible.

Rightly did the late French philosopher Gabriel Marcel, while a visiting lecturer in Seattle, say that although his wife was thousands of miles *physically absent* at their home in Paris, she was more *personally present* to him than the students before him at that moment in the Seattle lecture hall. This was meant as no offense to the students: rather, he was indicating the prior depth of commitment, of devotion that sustained the bond of a relationship that could not be attenuated by time and distance. The anonymous audience, for all its good will, its attention and courtesy, its respect and docility, was present to him in another way, to be sure, but this was nothing like the way in which his beloved wife's *presence* was within him, always and ever, more profoundly than the most respectful student who was there to be taught, perhaps even enlightened.

That this is a universal truth and not mere hair-splitting or poetic fancy is indicated when loving friends say, in parting, "You are always in my heart," or words to that effect. Time and mere fleshly distance need not destroy. Personal fidelity, despite physical distance, witnesses authentic love. We are present to one another when we give over our love to another and abide in a relationship of mutual trust.

Personal presence is also made tangible and concrete over a distance by various means—a letter, a souvenir or memento, a gift. These things take on deeper meaning—they become *realizing, actualizing* symbols that communicate personal presence.

————————

In discussing the Eucharist, it is crucial to keep in mind that all human language is metaphor—a struggling and striving with crude human words and human concepts to express an experience of the beyond. The words, the formulae of faith, however necessary and refined, are always conditioned and limited by the culture, the time and place in which they are expressed. So much is self-evident.

This is as it should be, for it is not the formulae, however essential, but the act of giving oneself over to God in trusting faith: this is what matters when we speak the words we have invented to express our experience of the transcendent. With specific reference to the Eucharist, what counts is not that we twist and turn philosophical language (words like "substance" and "accidents," which would have made no sense to Jesus or his friends), requiring them to serve once and for all time an experience of God's gift of Himself to us—can *any* words ever do that justice?

No, what matters is that one accepts that along the journey of faith, receiving this bread and sharing this cup with our fellow pilgrims places us in the presence of him who is our salvation. But there is a danger here: since the Risen Jesus is no longer limited by time and place, and cannot be said to be *here* (in the bread and wine, for example) but not *there* (a few feet away, on an altar table or in a pew), we have to be very careful about a magical interpretation of a sacred reality. Still more careful ought we to be: not to think wrongly that the presence of the Risen Jesus in our midst is due to the "power" of a cultic priest, who "makes" him present on command, by virtue of uttering a few words. That, too, is magic, not the divinely free activity by which God manifests Himself as He wills in the person of Jesus.

Clearly, when we speak of the presence of God we cannot speak in any way of a spatial or physical presence. We cannot attribute to God the kind of body that we have—the body that is defined by and limits our place in space and time. Rather, He fills all matter—but not in a spatial or physical way. When we say that God is everywhere, we mean not that He occupies space, but that the world and everything in it could not exist without His inherent, indwelling presence.

To become aware of the presence of God is for some a very difficult thing to achieve. Often people object that "awareness of the presence of God" is merely a mental fancy, mere autosuggestion or self-hypnosis. But it is none of this, nor does it mean having some sort of romantic feeling or wish that something might be true. It is a matter of something very much deeper. In silence and by withdrawing as far as possible from outside noises and cares, each of us can be aware of a reality very deep within, a reality on which our very existence depends.

"Sometimes—there's God—so quickly!" whispers the tortured, guilt-ridden Blanche Dubois, in Tennessee Williams's *A Streetcar Named Desire*. That may be all that most of us, most of the time, can hope for: the quick, transitory awareness of God, Who manifests Himself most of all by bestowing a kind of awareness on us that we are accepted, loved— that we have, if you will, a meaning and a purpose even beyond our ability to articulate that meaning and purpose.

Some people can dispose themselves to an awareness of this absolute by connecting with nature in all its bountiful beauty—the still, silent majesty of the mountains, for example, or the moment when purple and gold streak the sky at dusk and just for a moment you are almost breathless and know that no artist's canvas does it justice. For others, there might be a moment in literature or poetry that enables them to see beyond—in the absolute rightness of a sonnet, or the dazzling multiplicities of meaning in Shakespeare or Milton, Blake or James.

Art and music communicate more than the artist, too. The intoxicating dazzle of van Gogh, for example, has lifted the souls of millions. Many people become mute with awe when they gaze at the glorious washes of color Monet chose to represent his beloved gardens. The unexpected note in a Chopin étude can leave you gasping, and the aching beauty that came from the suffering of Schumann and Mahler gives new meaning to transcendence.

There are as many ways to draw near to the divine as there are people in the world. In every case, there is a sense of *ecstasis,* of standing outside oneself, of *being beheld* by something greater than our own serious limitations.

"Christ will come like that!" says an old priest in a Flannery O'Connor short story, seeing the beauty of a peacock as he raises and spreads his tail "with a shimmering, timbrous noise [as] tiers of small pregnant suns floated in a green-gold haze above his head." It is the sheer, sudden, radiant loveliness that takes the breath away—this is often how God discloses Himself, just as He does when we realize, with rank humility, despite all our paltriness and pettiness, and despite their knowledge of us, that our friends love us and will never abandon us. How can that be true? Perhaps because such largesse is first true of God, Who knows us even better and still holds us close and calls us His own. It would seem impossible did we not know, in some fleeting, mysterious moments, that it is true.

In being raised from death to a completely new and transformed life—a life in God, as Paul calls it—the spatial, fleshly, merely tangibly proximate presence of Jesus has been entirely done away with. The glorification of Jesus in the Resurrection means that he is freed from the constraints of time and place. No longer limited by the economy of the fleshly life, he is present everywhere, in a presence as infinite as his love. But the *effects* of his presence and his love depend entirely on the openness of the human heart to him, by which I mean the will to believe.

Nothing of Jesus is distant or far away in some spatially imagined heaven—which is, in any case, not a place to which we go, but a state into which we enter.

————

What does all this mean for belief that Jesus is present in the Eucharist?

It means first of all that Jesus the Christ is of course always fully present outside the Eucharistic liturgy, or the Mass. He is really present wherever we are—in a presence that is *réelle parce que réalisante,* as the French theologian Henri de Lubac said: real because it realizes, actualizes, is effective. The elements of bread and wine and the enactment of a formal liturgy are not negligible, nor can we forever do without them. In this regard, there is something significant about the tradition—and, alas, tradition is neither a word nor an idea that carries much currency in our time.

From very soon after the death of Jesus right down to our present times, those who believe in him have gathered to break bread and share the cup. Over twenty centuries, the ritual has changed, become more elaborate at some times, simpler at others. But whether it occurs in a great cathedral, with a thousand-voice choir and the richest panoply that can be arranged, or in a mud hut where a few barefoot poor folk gather in hope, the reality proclaimed by Christian faith is the same. Like the infant imaginatively described as laid "in a manger," Jesus comes to be the food of his people—his presence nourishes and sustains. If we dare to cast aside or even to diminish that tradition, so central to admitting both our need of God and His power to give Himself to us—we are of all generations the most to be pitied.

————

A long list of rites and prayers, of devotions and cults, have come and gone over two thousand years. But just as Judaism would effectively abandon the core of its faith-witness were it to abolish the Passover meal, so it is with the Eucharist. In a sense, it lifts the restrictions on Christians in every generation—they are freed from the limitations of their own particularity, their own narrow ways of doing things. This, the sacred meal witnesses, links us to the faith of the apostles. This gives us a frame of reference outside ourselves. The sheer simplicity of the gestures, of the prayer, of listening to the Scriptures, of breaking bread and sharing the cup—all this overarches every culture and epoch.

So much of this is linked to our need to adore. To kneel, to bow, to join the hands, to keep silence in the presence of the Holy One—these seem stranger to contemporary people than perhaps to any previous age of the world. But the simple, quiet gestures, the humbling of the body, listening to the ancient words, withdrawing from everything that constitutes our busy world and our many cares—is not all this the condition of our knowing the presence of God and allowing Him to enter our lives and claim us for His own?

Through the liturgy, the risen Jesus is not summoned from another world in any spatial way, nor is there a physical or chemical change in the bread and wine. What happens is a change of signs, of what things *mean.* Bread and wine become the signs actualizing the deepest self-giving of Christ to us. The Lord gives himself to us as food, and that is the reality of which these powerful signs speak. It is entirely inappropriate, therefore, to call the bread and wine "merely" or "only" symbols, for in the mystery of God's presence in and among us, the symbols given to us are the closest we can come to the reality. In the realm of faith, symbols are never "just symbols." They are the carrier of the reality.

———

Linked to the event of the last supper is, of course, the idea that this was the time when Jesus instituted a ritual or cultic priesthood. Obviously, such a class has developed in the Christian Churches. But it is not at all clear from the New Testament that Jesus intended to set up an "ordained" priesthood—much less did he intend to found a new religion. Jesus was neither priest nor Levite himself; there were no Jewish priests among his disciples; and one looks in vain through the entire New Testament for the structured, hierarchical organization that later developed.

This does not mean that the subsequent organization is contradictory to the spirit of Jesus, although certain aspects of it are certainly inconsistent with him and his teaching: the wielding of power, for example, and the concomitant failure to serve. Human beings who share beliefs and practices organize themselves, to be sure, and the growth in numbers of those who came to believe in Jesus certainly necessitated the assignment and sharing of responsibilities. But these responsibilities, it must also be said, were primarily of *service,* in imitation of him who "came not to be served but to serve."

The early church developed as an *episcopal* church—which simply means that the faithful always selected "overseers" (the meaning of the Greek *episkopoi* or bishops) to manage and maintain the standards of loving service to the needs of the community. In every community, at first, there were these *episkopoi,* joined by elders *(presbyteroi),* deacons and deaconesses *(diakonoi* and *diakonai).* But for a very long time, these were not clearly differentiated roles.

The important point is that in the New Testament, none of the apostles acted in a way that Jesus did not. Most of all, they were not people who exerted *power,* nor were they cultic priests—indeed, it is not clear that any of the disciples of Jesus is described as presiding at the celebration of the Lord's Supper, or the Eucharist. As for exerting authority, at the very moment he is commissioned to preside and to guide in love, Peter (often wrongly identified as the first pope, a later office to which Peter had absolutely no cultic connection) is told by Jesus to "feed *my* lambs . . . tend *my* sheep." Only Jesus can call believers "mine."

It is crucial to bear in mind that sovereign priesthood belongs to the risen Jesus Christ, and to him alone. "There is one God; there is also one mediator between God and humankind—Christ Jesus, himself human, who gave himself as a ransom for all." On this the New Testament is adamant.

In this regard, the Letter to the Hebrews is the single most important biblical document attesting the relation of Jesus to God and to his followers. The priests of the Old Law, says the author, were many, and they repeated their sacrifices annually. But Jesus is the single high priest of the New Covenant. By his offering of himself in life and death, and by virtue of his being forever in an eternal moment before God *as God and man,* he is the eternal high priest who has made a once-for-all sacrifice:

> When Christ came as a high priest of the good things that have come, then he entered once for all into the Holy Place [i.e., into God's eternity], not with the blood of goats and calves [as in the Old Covenant], but with his own blood [that is, his life, himself],

thus obtaining eternal redemption . . . For this reason, he is the mediator of a new covenant, so that those who are called may receive the promised eternal inheritance . . . Christ did not enter a sanctuary made by human hands, but he entered into heaven itself, now to appear in the presence of God on our behalf . . . He has appeared once for all to remove sin by the sacrifice of himself.

It is easy for Roman Catholics, especially, to translate the phrase "sacrifice of the mass" into the idea that there are as many sacrifices as there are masses, which is very bad theology indeed. There is but one sacrifice, the death and Resurrection of Jesus, which effects a new relationship between God and the world, between God and humanity. The completely transformed, glorified humanity of Jesus, taken up into the life of God in an eternal now, is the only, the single sacrifice that establishes our friendship with God, that makes possible our salvation—being saved for meaning in this world and being saved forever from death. And of this sacrifice, Jesus is the sole and single priest. We have no other mediator.

There is, however, another level or degree of priesthood—and that is the priesthood of all who are Christ's, of all who are baptized. "You are a chosen race, a royal priesthood, a holy nation, God's own people," we read in the First Letter of Peter to Christians in Asia Minor, "in order that you may proclaim the mighty acts of Him who called you out of darkness into his marvelous light." This priesthood involves offering a sacrifice of life and work, of *oneself*—hence Paul, writing to the Romans, urges his brothers and sisters in faith "by the mercy of God, to present your bodies [that is, your lives] as a living sacrifice, holy and acceptable to God—this is your spiritual worship."

The priesthood of all believers demands their service to others, their "living sacrifice" of self to God, the daily attempt to close the gap between the words of prayer and a life that is one seamless prayer. In this regard, it is good to remember that in baptism the Christian is given to Christ, who is priest, prophet and king.

Nor does the representative, cultic priesthood that has developed over the centuries—what we call ordained priests—mean an office of power; it is, on the contrary, about sending people to serve the needs of others.

For a long time, it was thought that designated ministers in the faith (i.e., ordained priests) had "powers" to effect this or that spiritual reality. A priest was "empowered" to consecrate bread and wine; a priest had "power" to forgive sins, or to do this or that. It was presumed that God jumped when the priest lifted a finger; in effect, the "powers" of a priest all but made God the servant.

This is dangerously close to magic; in any case, it is a terrible misrepresentation of Christian life and faith.

First of all, let it be clearly understood that only God has power. Only God can effect the transformation of humanity before Him. God does not depend on human ingenuity or will to embrace us. Somehow, mysteriously and quite beyond our ability to comprehend it, God is present to and among those who seek Him, however lukewarmly. God does not require assistants.

It is, of course, entirely appropriate that a community delegate responsibilities of service—and here we come to the rather more restricted designation of priesthood, the ministerial function for which certain Christians are delegated by the community. They are not given "powers" but rather a mandate of service, and so these priests represent the priesthood of all the faithful. The implications of this are critical, for in the absence of institutionally designated priests, there ought to be nothing that "ordinary" Christian laypersons cannot do, for after all they are priests: hence it is not unthinkable that in extraordinary circumstances, any Christian of good will may baptize, preach, gather the faithful together at the Lord's table, proclaim the word of God, preside at the Eucharist. Such was life in New Testament times.

Although there was a highly developed and stratified cultic priesthood in Israel, it is impossible to find a corresponding Christian development in the New Testament, where no Christian is called a priest in relation to the Eucharist. In fact, the New Testament is silent as to who celebrated the Eucharist; it is, as has been noted by no less than Raymond E. Brown (the Roman Catholic New Testament scholar most honored by the Vatican in the last two decades), an "unlikely thesis that only those manually ordained by the Twelve or even by the larger group of apostles celebrated the Eucharist." In fact, in the New Testament, Brown continues, "there are relatively few references to ordination or laying-on of hands for special ministries, and among them I know of no instance of ordination for the purpose of enabling people to administer sacraments."

Indeed, ordinary presiding at the Eucharist was not the task of designated cultic members of the community until the end of the second century: at that time the term "priest" began to be applied to the bishop—and only later to the elder or presbyter. Before then, appropriate community leaders celebrated the Eucharist. The gradual restriction of the privilege to ministers grew quite naturally from the need to guarantee proper celebration of the Eucharist, to see to it that abuses not creep in, and to ensure that the spiritual needs of believers were met in an organized fashion in growing, complex, far-flung Christian communities. But even then, the special task of presiding ministerially at the Eucharist never replaced the priesthood of all believers.

In the past, it was often said that there was a shortage of priests (meaning ordained, ministerial priests); the opposite may have been and may be true: we may not have too few but too many. It may be that God will, in fact, raise up from His people more and more priests—who will be not only collar-wearing celibates but men and women whose entire lives are dedicated to the service of others, and not only as parochial standard-bearers but as social workers, teachers, preachers, hospice workers— wherever there are human need and human struggle. An ordained ministry of bishops, priests and deacons may well be necessary for the efficient organization and functioning of complex communities, but the officially ordained are no "higher" or "closer to God" than they were by virtue of baptism. And they have, let it be repeated, no power except the mandate to serve and to proclaim the tidings of love, compassion and forgiveness.

In this regard, it is difficult to maintain that women are not called to the ministerial, cultic priesthood. True, there were no women among the chosen twelve in Jesus' apostolic circle: neither, I note, were there any Italians or Poles. The twelve, as we have seen, were chosen (in a society that proscribed any sort of official role for women) for their symbolic function as new patriarchs in the new Israel. But there were evidently women in prime positions of ministry in the early Church, as Paul apparently attests in his letters.

In any case, it is unfortunate cultural baggage to maintain that women are existentially inferior to men and hence excluded from full priesthood—indeed, they already *are* priests, by virtue of baptism. To allow women access to the ministerial priesthood is simply to acknowledge and to formalize what is already a reality by virtue of Christian initiation. That they ought to be able to serve as officially sent (ordained) ministers should not to be a shocking idea. If we take baptism and priesthood seriously in all their implications, women are—no less than men—already sharers in the priesthood of Jesus.

"As I have done to you," said Jesus as he finished washing the feet of his friends, "so you ought to do for one another." The mandate "Do this in memory of me" stands for that humble service as much as for the privilege of holding a cultic position or presiding at a community ritual. Indeed, it is precisely service and dedication that illuminate the purpose, meaning and effect of the Eucharist. Christ's complete donation of himself to the cause of humanity's welfare—even to the point of offering his entire life—is the standard for all who gaze on him with hope.

CHAPTER THIRTEEN

ABANDONMENT:
THE DEATH OF JESUS

The four Gospels are often described as stories about the arrest, trial and execution of Jesus preceded by long introductions, which means everything told about his life. Despite the oversimplification, there is something true about the statement, for if we read the documents, even hastily, we are astonished by the unusual attention to details of time, place, identity, even gesture in the accounts of the last hours of Jesus' life. The passion narrative has the ring of authenticity.

In fact, ancient stories of a person's life and significance often developed backward, from memories and traditions about the circumstances of a notable subject's death. As early as the fifth century before Christ, Ion of Chios wrote short sketches of noted contemporaries like Pericles and Sophocles. For the most part, these fragmentary biographies were highly complimentary, idealizing personalities with grand rhetorical flourishes—variations on the elegy, in fact.

Chroniclers eventually began to give due consideration to the entire last period of a man's life—whence the stories moved backward, to his periods of development; finally, from whatever materials might be available, there was reflection on the person's origins and significance. The result was often markedly heroic and laudatory: Plato's life of Socrates (in the *Apology* and the *Phaedo*) is a good example, yet at the same time it is a superb evocation of a man and his times, while the Stoic biographies of Cato and Brutus typify the second. The *Agricola* of Tacitus (written in A.D. 98, about the time the last Gospel was composed) is another example—a biographical account of the historian's father-in-law, with an assessment of the man's political career. In every case, the final days of the subject's life is almost mythicized, it is so heroic. Plutarch and Suetonius also stressed the final days of their subjects, whatever their biased viewpoint.

And herein lies a crucial difference when we compare the Gospel accounts of Jesus. The first Good Friday (which has inspired more art than any other event in the history of the world) is set forth in Matthew, Mark, Luke and John with a calmness, a sobriety and a lack of hysteria that are remarkable. There is no attempt to exaggerate the struggle, to exploit sentiment, to catalog the physical details of suffering and death. What comes through is a disarming simplicity.

At the same time, the clarity and the almost minute-by-minute chronology of the Gospels when they come to Jesus' final hours often lead modern readers astray: it is tempting to regard the accounts as on-the-spot reporting. But they are as rich and complex as the earlier stories (in Matthew and Luke, as we saw) of the conception, birth and infancy of Jesus. By the time the four evangelists set down their accounts—about forty to seventy years after Jesus' death—there had been many years of early Christian experience. It is axiomatic of Bible studies in the past century that this early experience and the consequent needs of communities dictated the content, arrangement, style and concern of each Gospel. Faith was presupposed.

There had been, too, a final break between Judaism and the sect within it that eventually became Christianity. And there had begun—in the year 64, under the Emperor Nero—the violent persecution of Christians, as no less an authority than the Roman historian Tacitus recounted. To suppress the rumor that the burning of Rome was the direct result of imperial edict, Nero (according to Tacitus, who was no admirer of Jesus or his followers) "substituted as culprits, and punished with the utmost refinements of cruelty, a class of men whom the crowd styled Christians. Christ, the founder, had undergone the death penalty in the reign of Tiberius, by sentence of the procurator Pontius Pilate." Thus the persecution of Jesus three decades before had now spread and was being carried out on a much larger scale against the new fellowship.

Then, in Rome, "the confessed members of the sect were arrested; vast numbers were convicted, and derision accompanied their end. They were covered with wild beasts' skins and torn to death by dogs; or they were fastened on crosses, and, when daylight failed, were burned to serve as lamps by night. Nero offered his own gardens for this spectacle, and gave an exhibition of it in his own Circus. Hence there arose a sentiment of pity, for people felt that Christians were being sacrificed not for the welfare of the state, but because of one man's ferocity." (Among those massacred in this first persecution in Rome were Peter and Paul—the former by crucifixion, the latter by the sword.)

In light of the definitive break with Judaism, the fierce persecution of believers in Jesus and the simultaneous spread of the good news of salvation, the Gospels took shape. Presuming faith in Jesus and in the event of Easter, the evangelists, as we have seen, not only reshaped the material in light of new community needs, but did so in light of the belief that Jesus was alive and present, not a figure of dusty history. It is essential to begin any reflection on the agony and death of Jesus (traditionally called the passion, from *passio,* the Latin word for suffering) with these thoughts in mind.

An intricate process over several decades contributed to the final written form of the tradition. Most important in the process was the unique genius each writer brought to reflecting on the life of Jesus according to the needs and faith of his community. His understanding of the oral and perhaps fragmentary written traditions that had circulated nourished his "take" on the subject, as did his own religious concerns and literary style, his own technique. And the details are everywhere informed by faith in the significance of what had transpired. The passion narratives, like everything else in the Gospels, are not merely documentaries of exactly what happened: that kind of literature would never had occurred to writers at that time. Instead, the Gospels are profound meditations on the *meaning* of what happened.

Readers interested in scholarly examinations of the individual Gospels and careful comparisons of the four passion narratives should consult exegetical, linguistic and scholarly commentaries. For our less academic purposes, I shall select from each of the four Gospels passages that seem to me to illuminate key aspects of early Christian faith in the hidden Jesus that may have special application for our approaching him today.

―――――

By the time their last supper together is over, night has fallen in Jerusalem. Jesus leads his disciples from the borrowed room to a nearby grove, not far from the temple precincts. "Sit here while I pray," he tells them, and then he beckons to Peter, James and John, the trio closest to him during his ministry. As they follow him to a quiet spot, Jesus suddenly seems deeply anxious and agitated. "Remain here," he says, "and keep awake." He then goes a little farther, alone, and throws himself on the ground, praying to be spared the terrible outcome that now seems inevitable: "Father, for You all things are possible. Remove this cup of suffering from me—but let it be not as I want, but what You want." His relationship with God remains inflexible: it is rooted in absolute trust and submission. This does not, however, take away his terror, which is very real.

It is tempting to forget, at this point, that Jesus of Nazareth was entirely, fully human, and that everything human must be posited of him—except the deliberate rejection of grace, the selfishness we call sin. Keeping this firmly in mind, we can better understand the nature of this agony in the garden, for Jesus is the completely other-centered one—committed to the benefit of humanity and to the will of God. That all his efforts and all his commitment should lead to this moment, when everything is on the verge of loss, must have been unspeakable.

"Jesus offered up prayers and supplications, with loud cries and tears, to the One who was able to save him from death," according to the author of the Letter to the Hebrews. The Gospels confirm this struggle in the scene commonly called the agony in the garden of Gethsemane. "Let it be not as I want, but what You want"—his plea reflects perfectly the petition of the Lord's Prayer: "Thy will be done . . ."

But that prayer is indeed made "with loud cries and tears," and precisely because of his fear of torture and death—so often the lot of prophets before him—Jesus returns to his friends for consolation. He could not be more disappointed. "Are you asleep?" he asks Peter. "Could you not keep awake for one hour?" He then returns to prayer as the night grows darker and the hour later; his anxiety is so deep that he is literally sick with fear: his perspiration, we read, is like that of a man bleeding profusely from an open wound. Twice more, Jesus returns to his companions, and twice he finds them unable to stay awake. Embarrassed, they do not know what to say to him. "The hour has come," Jesus finally says, seeing torches in the distance.

And then a band of temple police and representatives from the chief priests, scribes and elders approaches with swords and clubs. They are all led by Judas, who comes up to Jesus, genially calls him "Master!" and embraces him. That is the signal, and so at once the band arrests Jesus.

Significantly, Jesus gives no reply to Judas. Instead he turns to his captors: "Have you come out with swords and clubs to arrest me, as though I were a bandit? Day after day, I was with you in the temple, teaching—and you did not arrest me then." For this they have no reply, perhaps because most of them are acting on orders and really have not the remotest idea what they are doing. Jesus is bound and dragged off.

And then something terrible happens—an event so dreadful as to compare, for an attack on the human spirit, with any of the appalling physical sufferings to come.

Every one of Jesus' companions desert him and flee for safety to— anywhere—anywhere he is not.

From this moment forward, he endures rejection, torture and execution without the presence or proximity of even one friend or relative. For a man whose friends are so precious, men to whom he has poured out every hope, fear and confidence—those who have lived with him for over two years, have shared all that can be shared among friends— his loneliness is beyond our imagining. Jesus watches the flight of those who promised they would never betray him or leave him alone to face his enemies. Those who have said they wanted to leave everything and follow him forever, now leave everything to get away from him. The Gospels do not flinch from reporting this, nor do they try to excuse the conduct of Jesus' closest friends—those who would presently be the foundation stones of the Church.

This is a moment of exquisite fright for one who has spent his entire life doing good. Persuaded that his teachings and deeds have God's approval—indeed, that God is his loving Father—Jesus has seen the effects of both his words and his healing. But now . . . how has it all come to this, to failure?

The terror that grips him is the terror that perhaps all this is happening because he has gotten it wrong—that he has failed God—that he has let down, has disappointed his loving God. After all, there is no one—not a single person—on his side now. How else can he interpret so lonely a fate?

———

Jesus is led at once to the high priest—certainly to the man's home and not to the temple, for now it is the dead of night—and soon there is a gathering of the aristocratic priestly families, the elders and scribes. This assembly is called the Jewish Sanhedrin, a group to whom the Romans cede certain judicial and governing powers for the Jews. Eager to find reasons to do away with Jesus, they try to assemble "witnesses" to swear falsely that he has been guilty of religious offenses worthy of death. A few of the perjurers swear that Jesus has threatened to destroy the temple, but however they try to present this, there is a problem: the liars have not been carefully rehearsed, and because their stories do not conform, this scheme collapses.

Jesus remains silent.

"Have you no answer to make to these charges?" shouts the high priest, jumping from his chair. "What is it that they testify against you?" Well might he ask, for nothing makes much sense. Clearly, the high priest (and doubtless the others present) is thoroughly confused—and how can Jesus respond?—for the false witnesses are ridiculous.

The only charges that can stick are those of defying the Sabbath, consorting with sinners and with women in public, and ignoring ritual prescriptions. This makes Jesus seem like a self-appointed prophet, in the view of these religious authorities—who may well be sincere men who believe that by getting rid of people like Jesus, "they are offering worship to God," as even the otherwise firmly antiestablishment Gospel of John says of them.

"Why do we need witnesses?" the high priest asks rhetorically, triumphantly. And with that, everyone agrees that this is reason enough to put Jesus to death, for according to the Mosaic law, false prophets must be executed. Asked if he can otherwise identify himself—as Messiah, for example—Jesus refuses to answer.

————

But the Gospels are very clear: the handful of (surely not deliberately) blind and shallow religious authorities is no more reprehensible than one of Jesus' closest friends. And here is an ironic subplot to the tragic drama, for while Jesus does not claim to be what in fact he was, another claims *not* to be what he is. Just as Jesus is interrogated by a hastily assembled court, Peter is questioned nearby.

As it happens, Peter has found where Jesus has been taken and had followed him, but from a safe distance. The night has turned cold, and Peter keeps close to a fire in a courtyard.

"You were with Jesus, the man from Nazareth!" says a servant, perhaps roused by the commotion at the high priest's headquarters.

"I have no idea what you are talking about," replies Peter, turning back toward the fire.

There is some commotion, and soon another bystander points Peter out as a friend of Jesus; again, Peter firmly denies the truth of it.

Finally, a third person approaches Peter: "Even your accent gives you away—you're a Galilean—you're with Jesus!" Frightened for himself, Peter swears an oath: he has never heard of this fellow Jesus.

At that very moment, the first streaks of morning light appear in the east, and Jesus is led from the council gathering. Across a short distance, his gaze meets Peter's. Overwhelmed with guilt and regret, the disciple races from the area. "He went out and wept bitterly," according to the Gospel.

Alas, a far more desperate act of remorse occurs at the same time and is similarly recounted. Of Judas, we read: "He went away and hanged himself." Thus two acts of betrayal enclose the trials of Jesus, but one of the offenders allows himself to be touched by grace in his contrition; indeed, Peter becomes what his name signifies—the "rock" of faith for the earliest Christian communities, and his own death by crucifixion under Nero, three decades later, reveals the depth of his post-Easter courage.

———

That same Friday morning, April 7 (perhaps as early as eight or nine o'clock), Jesus is taken before Pontius Pilate, the Roman prefect or procurator—the governor of Judea, then in the fifth year of a decade-long reign. Ruthless, cowardly and mad for power, he has supreme judicial authority in Judea and is accountable to the Emperor Tiberius, whose primary goal is peacekeeping in the provinces. Any threat of insurrection, sedition or public turmoil has to be suppressed at all costs.

The Sanhedrin has Jesus taken over to Pilate's fortress—called Gabbatha in Aramaic, which translates the Greek word for a flagstone pavement. This covered, paved court is adjacent to the northwest corner of the temple area; nearby is a room for Roman guards, who can easily be summoned. Those accused of crimes are then escorted from their interrogation by Pilate up a corner flight of stairs to an outer terrace—whence the public can witness the state of the accused and the stages of judicial proceedings.

The religious leaders want to avoid ritual impurity before the first Passover meal that night, and so they do not enter Gabbatha but remain outside. Pilate, therefore, comes out to them on the upper terrace and asks what charge they are bringing against Jesus. He is a criminal, they reply; but this, of course, is mere tautology—it is not a reply at all. Judge him yourself, then, counters Pilate—but they remind him that they have no authority to exact the death penalty. "Ah, then," Pilate may think, "they are bringing me a capital case!" Only he, after all, can hand down a death sentence. Earlier and later in Jewish history, blasphemers and false prophets could be stoned, but capital punishment is not within Jewish competence under Roman dominion.

Pilate then goes inside to meet Jesus for the first time, inside the fortress; by this time, he evidently knows the charge—blasphemy. But also evidently, somehow a *political* spin has been attached to this otherwise religious issue. It has been suggested to Pilate that Jesus is a threat to stability and public order, for he has made himself a Jewish Messiah, which can be seen by Rome as dangerously close to kingship.

"*Are* you the king of the Jews?" Pilate asks Jesus.

"Do you ask this on your own," Jesus replies, "or did others tell you about me?"

And now it seems as if Pilate himself is being put on trial, for Jesus' questions are relentless. As the morning progresses, it is not so much Jesus who fears Pilate as Pilate who becomes more and more terrified of Jesus and so has to do away with him.

"*I* am not a Jew, am I?" Pilate continues. "Your own nation and the chief priests have handed you over to me. What have you done?"

And now Jesus answers, with the implication that if he is indeed a king, he is no threat to Roman supremacy. "My kingdom is not from this world. If my kingdom were from this world, my followers would be fighting to keep me from being handed over to the Jews. But as it is, my kingdom is not from here."

"So you *are* a king!"

"*You* say that I am a king. For this I was born, and for this I came into the world, to testify to the truth. Everyone who belongs to the truth listens to my voice."

And then Pilate utters one of the most notorious ripostes in literature.

Dismissing this sort of spiritual conversation, he asks, perhaps with a shrug and a sarcastic smile, "What is truth?"

With that, Pilate returns outside to the crowd. "I find no case against him." But when he gives the people a choice, the crowd prefers the release of a convicted revolutionary instead of Jesus. It is interesting to note that all four Gospel accounts make Pilate, at first, virtually a spokesman for the innocence of Jesus: indeed, he is presented as fairer and more judicious than the religious authorities, and he alone seems to understand that Jesus is blameless of political perfidy. Still, at the last he is as covetous of his status and prerogatives as the others.

There is a supreme irony in proclaiming, as Christians have done for two thousand years, that Jesus is indeed Ruler, King and Judge, for these must be read as among the most obviously metaphorical titles in the list of those applied to him. Despite that, a vast army of Christian churchmen have aspired to and imitated what might be called the lifestyles of the rich and famous. Too many leaders have wallowed in the glory and luxury of churchly titles and ecclesiastical deference, and—to preserve their status—some have ruled like petty tyrants, claiming divine authorization for selfish folly. Fortunately, at least at the end of the twentieth century, many ordinary faithful simply refuse to support financially such hollow men. The days of the medieval prince-bishop are certainly past. That is reason enough to believe that the Spirit of God is still guiding His Church—by which of course is meant the whole body of those who hope in Christ Jesus, not merely the clergy called to serve them.

———

Pilate becomes more and more fearful of a political disturbance. And so, to appease the crowd and perhaps to persuade them to be satisfied with corporal punishment for Jesus rather than the extreme of his death, Pilate hands Jesus over to his soldiers, who have him scourged. This can itself be a lethal torture, for it is much more than a sound whipping: a scourge, made of leather thongs studded with bone and metal, tears off chunks of flesh and causes sufficient trauma and hemorrhage that many victims die of shock. Romans are never scourged: it is a punishment reserved for slaves and foreigners, and it is either a prelude to execution or a method of extracting information.

But Jesus survives this stage of the ordeal. When it is over, and before returning him to Pilate, the soldiers drag him back to their section of the fortress, where someone has another cruel idea. If this man Jesus is accused of appropriating royal status—well, then, we ought to treat him like a king. And so they engage in a grim amusement that seems to have combined two ancient customs.

First, way back in collective memory was the hazy figure of the Shadow King. The reigning monarch of an ancient land was regarded as the carrier of fertility and therefore the future of the people. But to guarantee the survival of the earth and of the race, the king had to be ritually sacrificed before he grew too old, and his blood—the life-force itself—had literally to be poured onto the earth in the belief that it would regenerate nature and humanity.

Of course it would not do literally to kill the king, so a prisoner was made to substitute for him. For one day, this poor man ruled as the Shadow King. People took out on him their resentments against the real king: they pushed him about, dressed him in a grotesque parody of royal robes, slapped him, fashioned a crown of rough reeds or branches—and at the end of the day slaughtered him like a sacrificial animal and poured his blood on the ground. His death replaced that of the monarch's; nature would be appeased and the future secured by the prisoner's proxy.

At the same time, the soldiers have only to look at the paving stones in the fortress for inspiration. There are marks, used for a kind of vast board game (similar perhaps to Parcheesi), in which live players move from one stone to the next by throwing dice. The winner makes it to the side where a crown is scratched onto the floor; the loser is forced to the end where a sword is incised.

This game very likely recalls another old practice, that of the Substitute King. During the new year festival in ancient Mesopotamia, and even in the Roman Saturnalian feast, a slave or condemned criminal was treated as if he were king. But when the festival was over, he was executed.

And so Jesus becomes the pawn of their game. The soldiers find a piece of royal purple and throw it over his bleeding shoulders. Someone returns from the temple gardens with a net of thorns, weaves it into a makeshift coronet and puts it on Jesus' head—"Hail, king of the Jews!" the soldiers cry and, treating him like the Shadow King, strike him on the face.

When the soldiers weary of this sport, Jesus is hauled back to Pilate and the tragedy continues, with the action shifting dramatically from inside the fortress to outside and then back again. In the ensuing scenes, Pilate bolts back and forth from the bleeding, weakened victim to the crowd; Jesus is dragged from the fortress to the upper terrace. Inside, there is an ominous, almost deathly calm—and an incisive dialogue in which the battered prisoner is almost the prosecutor of the increasingly frightened and confused Pilate—while outside, as the religious authorities incite the masses, there is a growing demand for blood.

And as this supreme folly moves toward its inevitable finale, what does Jesus do? He certainly does not behave like the typical accused. He neither denies, confirms, blames nor attacks. At the proper moments, he says what he must to defend the honor of God, but never does he protest that he is neither blasphemer, false prophet nor political rebel. But his silence betokens neither frailty nor despair; at this moment he most effectively contradicts ordinary expectations. And in so doing, his silence becomes God's supreme statement. Ultimate reality can only be expressed in the language of paradox: perhaps we can say, then, that this divine declaration was uttered in silence, was heard in silence, was effective in silence.

The motif of silence has been important in this book. At first, there was the quiet of God, which is the deep silence of creation. That stillness is our hint of an explanation, for an inner hush, a tranquillity, as far as we can manage it, is required for prayer. At this moment, too, we find in the poor, condemned Jesus the clue to what ennobles and never destroys humanity. He remains silent, abandoned by his friends, crushed by his enemies. His silence means not nothingness, but fundamental dependence on God, Who alone can save him.

We are, after all, most defined by our neediness and inadequacy, our doubt and confusion, our inability to answer for ourselves. Much less can we provide the ultimate meaning of our lives: that must come from outside us. Just when, with a shock, we realize our fundamental contingency—then it is that we are hurled, broken and bleeding, into the arms of God. Infinite, unimaginable mercy covers and finally heals the wound of our deficiency—which is another way of saying that we are finally accepted, embraced, forgiven, saved for meaning. Then we belong forever to the kingdom of grace. And this is not achieved without an awful struggle.

———

And so Pilate decides to show Jesus to the people. Perhaps (the Gospel implies) the sight of this bruised, defenseless man will soften their hearts, will send them away satisfied and dissuade them from demanding the final penalty.

"Look," says Pilate, gazing out at the crowd, "I am bringing him out to let you know that I find no case against him." The soldiers arrive, dragging Jesus up the stairs. Pilate points to him, still wearing the purple robe and the crown of thorns. "Here is the man!"

The chief priests and their police are not at all mollified. "Crucify him! Crucify him!"

"Take him yourselves and crucify him: I find no case against him!"

"We have a law, and according to that law, he ought to die because he has claimed to be God's son."

At this point, Pilate is more anxious than ever. He orders the soldiers to take Jesus back inside, and there he joins him.

"Where are you from?" Pilate asks. But Jesus does not reply, and Pilate is astonished at this. "Do you refuse to speak to me? Do you not know that I have power to release you and power to crucify you?"

Finally there is an answer, perhaps barely whispered because of his weakness after the scourging. "You would have no power over me unless it had been given you from above."

These solemn, sure words stir something deep in Pilate's spirit—the old hunch about the gods, perhaps, or even a supreme God. In any case, he is more hesitant than ever to execute Jesus, and so he goes back again to the crowd.

But he cannot shout over the commotion. "If you release this man," the people cried, "you are no friend of the emperor. Everyone who claims to be a king sets himself against the emperor."

Now Pilate is terrified of both alternatives—the implication of killing an innocent man and the risk of appearing soft on crime, which will displease Rome.

It is now late morning. Pilate goes back inside for a few words, but moments later he is back outside, this time with Jesus again. The roar from below seems deafening: "Away with him! Away with him! Crucify him! Crucify him!"

Pilate capitulates. Jesus is handed over to the Roman soldiers and dragged away. According to the Gospels, Jesus was put to death on the recommendation of Jewish leaders because of his Messianic and prophetic claims to be a king and the Son of God. Pilate agrees to their will because he sees a political firestorm beginning to spread around Jesus: if he claims to be a king, Rome's supremacy is threatened.

———

At this point, we must confront one of the most difficult and painful matters in the history of the world.

There is simply no way to avoid the uncomfortable fact that some of the New Testament contains a very clear anti-Semitic bias. The earliest Christian document (the First Letter to the Thessalonians, written about A.D. 50) speaks of "the Jews who killed both the Lord Jesus and the prophets," and similar assertions are found elsewhere.

The Gospel according to John is egregious in this regard: it refers to "a Jew" or "the Jews" in sarcastic or critical terms no less than seventy-one times (as compared with a total of eleven such references in Matthew, Mark and Luke). As for the death of Jesus, John was clear: the Jews were responsible for rejecting him, plotting his death and putting him up for capital punishment (on extremely vague and spurious religious charges); the Roman authority felt it was politically advantageous to concur and so carried out the penalty.

It does no good to attempt a softening of this motif by interpreting these passages as referring to only a handful of corrupt Jewish leaders. That is not what the texts say: regarding the death of Jesus especially, they speak of "the Jews," with all the generalized contempt you hear when a bigot today complains about an entire race or group—what "they" are like and so forth.

For their part, Jewish writings contemporary with Jesus make no reference to him at all. This is not surprising, for the Jewish people were fighting for their identity (indeed, for their survival) in the Empire, and there were far more important matters than the life and death of an obscure itinerant preacher from Galilee.

Flavius Josephus, writing at the end of the first century, said nothing about *why* Jesus was put to death. He may not have known, or he may have wanted to ignore the claims of and for Jesus, and the success of the Jesus movement, in the late first century. But Josephus did say that Pilate condemned him to death by crucifixion "on indictment of the first-ranking men among us"—i.e., among the Jews. And later Jewish tradition, too, candidly admitted responsibility for Jesus' death: the third-century work titled *Sanhedrin,* in the Babylonian Talmud, refers to the Jewish people "hanging Jesus on the eve of Passover because he seduced Israel, leading her astray."

There can be no doubt, then, that some of the Jewish leaders and chief priests were indeed responsible for the strategy of Jesus' death (and that there was a strong element of clergy-against-laity in this struggle to the death). Motivated by a fierce desire to protect their own status, they saw Jesus' challenge of hypocrisy as a major threat to that. Others, rigorously interpreting the law to preserve Jewish purity, must have been sincere and devout men who thought they were doing good by ridding Israel of this meddlesome, troublesome Jesus. In this regard, as scholars have pointed out, the trial of Jesus as conducted by the Jewish council of high priests (and so recounted in the Gospels) did not at all violate the letter of Jewish religious law.

Jesus, as we have seen throughout this book, challenged many of the religious assumptions of his day; he flouted accepted customs; he presented his teachings as having a unique approval by God; he associated with sinners; and he repeatedly denounced many pious practices as empty and hypocritical. Some people, deeply affected by his marvelous deeds and liberating preaching, began to believe that Jesus was indeed the Messiah long awaited by the Jewish people, although he himself rejected the term outright because of its political implications.

The support for Jesus therefore caused considerable tension among Jewish religious leaders—a strain that reached critical mass when he criticized temple practices right in the Jerusalem temple at Passover time, days before his death. A council of leaders came to the conclusion that Jesus was a threat to Judaism itself. They arranged for him to be seized and turned over to Roman authorities, who would support their need to get rid of a man apparently responsible for stirring up trouble. If Jesus indeed claimed to be a Messiah or king (or if the council *said* he so claimed), Rome, too, could not tolerate him.

Literalists and doctrinaire fundamentalists in every era are dangerous, as history sadly shows even to this day—in the attitudes and actions of zealots in every country, of every faith. Christians, like the sincere but misguided chief priests, often judge people who seem (to them) to violate what they think is the traditional understanding of God's law and will. Were Jesus to appear in the flesh today, he would certainly be offensive to many religious Christians who think they control the truth. Jesus, correcting ongoing injustice and raising questions about "certitude," would certainly be tossed out of very many parish council meetings.

————————

But it is one thing to specify a handful of Jewish leaders, whatever the mixed motives among them, and another to indict "all the Jewish people" or "the Jews," as the Gospels frequently do—and here lie the unfortunate sources of Christian anti-Semitism, one of the most reprehensible strains in history. To put the matter bluntly: why does the New Testament itself, which supposedly reflects the attitudes and teachings of Jesus, seem to be the basis of this anti-Semitism?

It is critical to recall, first of all, that the followers of Jesus were Jews for decades after his death: Jesus himself, after all, never founded a new religion—much less did he advocate defection. To be a Christian meant to be a Jew who believed in Jesus, and a Christian still observed the Mosaic Law, went to synagogue, was bound by religious practices such as fasting, prayer, the requirement of visiting the Jerusalem temple and so forth.

The rift between mainstream Judaism and the Christian sect within it had several causes and took a period of time to be final (from the early 50s until perhaps as late as 150), but by the middle of the second century, Christianity was seen to represent an entirely new and different religion.

First of all, a few years after his death, the disciples and other Jews who came to believe in Jesus through their preaching began to accept Gentiles without requiring them to convert first to Judaism. Jews who did not believe in Jesus would have been understandably offended when Gentile Christians, freely mingling with Jewish Christians, claimed to be part of the New Israel because they proclaimed faith in Jesus. In addition, there were some Jewish Christians who formed their own local synagogues, and in some places entire synagogues of Jews came to believe in Jesus. All these were seen as encouraging disunity in Judaism and further weakening a faith already threatened by political dissent, Roman imperialism and widespread variations in belief.

But the definitive break between Christianity and Judaism occurred as the result of two specific developments—one in Christian faith about Jesus and one in the crisis of Judaism itself.

By the end of the first century, as the implications of the life and death and (most of all) the Resurrection of Jesus became clearer, Christians came to express their firm belief in his divinity. The community from which came the Gospel according to John, for example, proclaim the fully developed faith that Jesus was both Lord (which means reigning Messiah of the universe, and this by virtue of his Resurrection) and God (by virtue of what would later, in a philosophical term, be called his "nature"). For Jews this was apostasy, and their leaders had to react unambiguously and severely: such a Christian belief was misunderstood by Jews as affirming "two Gods," and this threatened the heart of Jewish monotheism ("The Lord our God is one").

Related to this development of Christian faith was the second factor, the crisis in Judaism. After the failure of the Jewish revolt against Rome in the 60s and the destruction of the Jerusalem temple on order of the Emperor in 70, it was necessary for Jewish people throughout the Empire and beyond it to describe and define themselves. With the simultaneous rise of the rabbinic movement and the gradual dominance of the Pharisees, pluralism was held suspect—and the first people to be challenged and expelled from synagogues for their unorthodox views were Jewish Christians.

And so there was introduced into Jewish synagogue ritual an expansion of one of the most formal prayers, one of the Eighteen Benedictions, to include a curse against all those who deviated from Judaism—especially "heretics and Nazarenes," a clear reference to those who believed in the Messiahship of Jesus. Good Jews were disciples of Moses, while Christians were disciples of Jesus: this alone was enough to warrant malediction and condemnation. This ban of excommunication from Judaism has survived to this day: one ceases to be a Jew, according to that faith, when one confesses Jesus as Messiah.

And so Jews who came to accept him were banned from the synagogue. Without the protection of their identity as Jews—who had civil rights in the Roman Empire and so were excused from the duty of worshiping the gods—these expelled Christians were now exposed to

Roman scrutiny and persecution. It is easy, then, to understand Christian resentment against Jews, and this attitude colored the composition of the Gospels in the last third of the first century: they are the works of disenfranchised outcasts liable to subjugation and death. This is the source of the anti-Judaic strain in the New Testament. On the other hand, growing Christian anti-Semitism was countered by an equally virulent Jewish anti-Christianity, as stories circulated in which Jesus of Nazareth was portrayed as a wicked, adulterous magician, the illegitimate son of an adulteress who had cohabited with a Roman Jew.

When Constantine became emperor in the fourth century, however, Christians won political clout, and the hatred solidified on one side. From that time, Christians oppressed Jews, outlawed them, persecuted them and—in an unrelenting and thoroughly un-Christian betrayal of their own Lord—often sanctioned anti-Semitism. The culmination of this, as everyone knows, was the Holocaust, which could only have happened in a world in which the desire to extinguish the Jewish people forever was almost inevitable. Many Christians failed to witness against this tragic betrayal of their own spiritual roots, as Pope John XXIII (writing in 1962) implied so forcefully in his prayer for forgiveness on behalf of all Christians:

> O God, we are conscious that many centuries of blindness have blinded our eyes so that we no longer see the beauty of Thy Chosen People, nor recognize in their faces the features of our privileged brethren. We realize that the mark of Cain stands upon our foreheads. Across the centuries, our brother Abel has lain in the blood which we drew or which we caused to be shed by forgetting Thy love. Forgive us for the curse we falsely attached to their name as Jews. Forgive us for crucifying Thee a second time in their flesh. We know not what we did.

A second question, of course, is this: How are Christians to reconcile this anti-Semitism with the commonly held belief that all Scripture is inspired?

The only answer is that anti-Semitism is, in fact, as totally irreconcilable with Christian faith and practice as is support of capital punishment.

Some of the attitudes of Bible writers, limited by the situations in which they wrote, are simply not to be repeated or supported today.

And some actions are chronicled as examples of what is antithetical to a godly spirit. Much of the conduct of Hebrew kings in the Old Testament was recorded not for imitation but precisely to detail the ungodliness that unbridled power can release in the world. And in the New Testament, for example, the injunction of the letter to the Ephesians—"Slaves, obey your earthly masters with fear and trembling"—is no justification for the subsequent centuries of subjugating minorities. The first century took for granted that servitude was part of the economic and social fabric of life; additionally, it was presumed that Christian masters would treat servants like members of their own families—with love and kindness and in no way like harsh, punitive pagan commanders.

Specific to the problem of Christian anti-Semitism, the Gospel passages in question are indeed troublesome and embarrassing, but they ought not to be excised on that account in the name of some faddish political correctness. To be consistent, the Jewish people would have to remove all sorts of embarrassing passages from the Old Testament: those referring to early polytheism, for example, or to the inferiority of women; injunctions to slaughter the enemies of Israel; the prohibitions against charging interest for loaning money; the types of punishment exacted for what are today considered faults or cultural habits rather than crimes, and so forth.

Censoring the Bible leads many people to believe that what is finally read ought to be accepted literally; that everything is set down to be imitated; and that ancient writings can be read in precisely the same way as modern ones. This attitude, of course, is disastrous. It fails to understand that all human language is metaphor, and that the Word of God is set down in the words of men; these are by definition always limited words, conditioned by the exigencies of grammar, culture, history, politics, social factors.

"The books of Scripture," as the Second Vatican Council wisely proclaimed in 1965, "must be acknowledged as teaching firmly, faithfully and without error *that truth which God wanted put into the sacred writings for the sake of our salvation*"—and it is hopeless to defend the position that hatred, denunciation or condemnation of anyone (in this case, one's own spiritual forebears, the Jewish people) is consistent with "the truth which God wanted . . . for the sake of our salvation."

That truth lies elsewhere, not in socially conditioned verses that are simply there for us not to repeat. God in His wisdom can teach us by presenting negative options, too. Not every position taken by an author of the Bible is inspired; it is the experience of the people of God that is inspired or guided—and the faith that is the result.

Important, powerful Jews in Jerusalem were indeed hostile to Jesus and conspired with the Roman authorities to ensure his execution. To remove this point from the text because it presents difficulties today is to deny two things fundamental to both Judaism and Christianity: the necessity of forgiveness and the realization that a good, just and innocent man of God was rejected primarily because he dared to challenge the narrowest aspects of cultural accretion in religious (i.e., Jewish) life— not because he was executed by Romans on a political charge.

In this regard, we must be honest. Today, it remains very fashionable to condemn un-Christian Christians for their crimes. But it is not at all fashionable to state an analogous truth: that a few decadent, power-mad Jews—who could not have known what they were doing—were responsible for a terrible deed.

But this ought not to have led to a wholesale condemnation of Jews by Christians decades later, however they felt their sorry state was due to Jewish intolerance of them. After all, the Jewish people did not subsequently condemn themselves because their great prophet Jeremiah was killed centuries before Jesus through the machinations of Jewish priests. More to the point, the persecution of Christians effected by Jewish intolerance of them ought not to have produced anything like anti-Semitism. The Jewish people remain God's chosen, for God does not renege on His promise; Christians are their spiritual descendants. With Pope John Paul II, all Christians ought to kneel and pledge, as he did when visiting Auschwitz in 1995, "Never again anti-Semitism!"

The crucifixion of Jesus has become, after two thousand years, perhaps too familiar through reading, hearing and preaching, and too distorted by paintings and sculptures, crosses and crucifixes. The horror is almost impossible to absorb, perhaps especially given the ubiquity of appalling images and the documentation of violence in our time.

In addition, it is impossible for many good people to take seriously the reality behind an event often distorted through mawkish piety, melo-dramatized by arts and crafts, sentimentalized by music and even falsified by bad preaching. In fact, it may be no exaggeration to suggest that the single most famous event in history has become something of a cliché. The cross itself is now a terribly chic fashion item, studded with emeralds and encrusted with diamonds; any suggestion of nails or blood would be considered distasteful, offensive.

Yet here we are, left with perhaps the most powerful religious emblem in history, and it is disarming in its stark simplicity. Here is a young man, stripped of clothes and dignity, nailed through hands and feet to portions of a felled tree. Alone, battered, dying—this is hardly an image of triumphant victory, not an icon promising a glorious destiny.

The torture and death of Jesus are calmly described in the four Gospels, with utmost and dignified brevity and in remarkably understated tones, without focus on the physical aspects of the suffering itself; it would be foolish to embellish, to dramatize. The evangelists do not portray Jesus as a brave martyr whose death arouses admiration. Nor is he an intrepid warrior, enduring his destiny with solemn detachment. Faithful to the end, he has believed in the unassailable love of God.

This does not mean, however, that there was no psychological, emotional or spiritual suffering; compared with the hideous bodily pain, the inner agony of Jesus must have been unspeakable. Too often a lopsided Christology has been proclaimed or at least implied: the notion, for example, that God's Son never for a moment lost sight of his transcendent identity and so only appeared to suffer. This, of course, is rank heresy. Never must we more fervently cling to the truth of the full humanity of Jesus of Nazareth than at the end of his life. His brokenness, his spiritual desolation, his sense of futility, his failure defined the depth of his agony. And he was utterly alone, without the smallest shred of consolation from anyone, friend or enemy.

———

As the soldiers lead Jesus away from Pilate toward the place of execution, a placard is put over his head and dangles heavily around his neck: "Jesus of Nazareth, King of the Jews," it says in Aramaic (the vernacular), Greek (the most widespread language of the Roman world) and Latin (the official language of the Roman administration). Within hours, some pious folk send word to Pilate that the words should be, "This man said, 'I am the King of the Jews.'" But sarcastic Pilate, who knows a savage irony when he sees one, replies, "What I have written, I have written." And so it remains.

Jesus is too weak from the scourging to bear the crossbeam on his shoulders, as the condemned are forced to do. A passerby is thus dragooned into carrying the beam behind Jesus, and the detail of his name rings across the centuries, for early Christians never forgot the man: Simon of Cyrene, from the countryside, the father of young men named Rufus and Alexander.

Simon, the soldiers and the men to be executed (there were two others whose names and crimes are unknown) make their way from the fortress, along the dusty alleys of Jerusalem, perhaps keeping as close to the city walls as possible for the most direct route. After they pass through the Gennath Gate, they can see the spot just outside the city walls where executions are sometimes held. This is a protrusion of ground very near a quarry where tombs have been excavated; its appearance and its use have caused it to be known as Golgotha, the Aramaic word for skull.

And there Jesus is crucified. This form of execution, which originated with the Persians, is rarely used by the Greeks, but is much employed by the Romans. It is considered not only particularly dreadful but also shameful, for it is meted out only to slaves and non-Romans convicted of murder, piracy, treason and rebellion.

The procedure does not take long. First the victim is stripped naked for humiliation. Then large spikes are driven through the lowest point of the arm, just before the wrist, in the space between the radius and ulna. A crew of soldiers rope the arms onto the beam and the crucified man is lifted to the vertical beam, already in place in the ground. Then the hammers are taken up again, the feet are nailed to the beam, and the legs are bound with ropes to the wood, to prevent slippage.

The identifying placard is removed from Jesus' neck and nailed into the vertical beam above his head. Because the whole weight of the body is forced downward, breathing is enormously difficult: to inhale, the sufferer has constantly to try to push himself with his legs, slightly forward and up.

It is just after noon on Friday, April 7, 30—about twelve hours after Jesus was seized.

In the temple precincts, there begins the work of slaughtering lambs for the feast—lambs whose blood had been, at the first Passover, sprinkled over the wooden thresholds of houses, so that all might be spared the plague of death; and lambs annually sacrificed, their blood sprinkled on the altar and on worshipers, in token of the covenant of life binding God and man, and in token of the forgiveness of sin.

Death by crucifixion can come slowly, through exposure, hunger and thirst; it can also come more quickly, if the victim dies of shock, or if wild animals attack. In the case of Jesus, he has been severely enfeebled by scourging, and very likely his respiration is severely compromised; there also may be clots forming, profuse bleeding, dangerously low blood pressure.

Toward midafternoon, Jesus cries out, "My God, my God, why have you forsaken me?" His entreaty is taken from Psalm 22, well known to all Jews. Because the first words (*Eli, Eli*) sound very similar to a cry to Elijah, some taunting bystanders shout laughingly, "This man is calling for Elijah! Let us see whether Elijah will come to save him!"

"My God, my God, why have you forsaken me?"—the cry must be accepted with all its implication of the abandonment Jesus feels. The words express neither a hymn of trust that God will certainly vindicate him (as is implied by later verses in the psalm), nor is it a shout of abject despair. It is what it is: an appeal, a supplication: "Why have you forsaken me?"

Jesus does not accept death patiently. He endures it in all its agony, screaming out to God Who remains his sustenance at the end. But Jesus feels none of that support. He feels nothing but a complete emptying of himself. His friends and family have abandoned him, and as the sight of guards and bystanders blurs before him, Jesus is, by any standard in this world, a complete failure: cut down in his prime, his work suppressed, his honor destroyed, his loved ones alienated, and, at the end, subjected to an appalling death.

He who has abandoned everything to God seems abandoned by God. Everything seems drenched in futility.

Can it be that the mockers were right all along?

Ought this man—of good intentions, perhaps, but finally a hopeless, even quixotic character—to be compassionately dismissed into the pages of history?

Have not too many people already been deluded for far too long?

So much in the background and life of Jesus seems, after all, to predict the collapse of any grand hope and noble intent. The race from which he comes is of bygone grandeur, its magnificence diminished by the victories of others—and Jesus never tries to revive that race, or to restore its tarnished glory.

There are no real achievements to speak of, either—no work to leave as a monument, no secure body of teachings, no school of teachers to take up where he leaves off. His friends, in fact, are unremarkable people without any greatness to recommend them, and they have no very clear idea of just what he has been about. Jesus has been upsetting expectations and overturning polite religious standards since the very beginning of his ministry. In fact, he is a frighteningly simple man with not much of the world's talent: he simply went about doing good, being accessible to others, reaching out to their needs.

But now his enemies seem vindicated, for his teaching has really taken root nowhere, and now they seem to have stamped it out forever. He ends not with a great accomplishment but on trial and then punished on a windswept patch of desert. His life seems to add up to very little.

And as for his death, there is nothing here of a heroic, trailblazing martyrdom. He is not a great philosopher dying for his ideas. Nor is he a military hero struck down in the glory of battle. He is not a great statesman who, while climbing the ladder of success, falls under the knife of assassins. He is not a wise old man, surrounded by loving companions comforting him. He has no wife, no woman or mate or friend who stays close by during the ordeal. The only people reacting to his death seem to have spoken for everyone, and they mock and challenge him. Every consolation is denied. Everything in creation is against him.

What sort of God treats people this way?

A God Who takes human suffering with great seriousness indeed—a God Who enters fully into it and, as we shall see, does not allow it the final victory. And the sort of God Who completely transforms the meaning of suffering and death . . .

And then, at three o'clock, even the world seems to rebel against the horror of it all. The sky darkens, a cold wind blows across the sands.

In a voice thick with torment, Jesus cries out. There is the sound of one long breath as he exhales—the deep groan of death.

And then there is chilling silence.

———

At the insistence of Jerusalem officials, the body of Jesus must be hastily removed and buried, before sundown marks the beginning of Passover. The two criminals crucified with him are still alive, however. Their legs are broken by the soldiers wielding huge clubs; with this trauma, the poor men can no longer prop themselves up to breathe, and so very quickly they suffocate. But Jesus is already dead.

There is no time for the body of Jesus to be properly anointed with spices, which is the traditional Jewish way of trying to preserve the remains. The burial in a new grave is arranged by a man named Joseph of Arimathea, a devout member of the Jewish council who was fascinated by Jesus and had not participated in the folly of the trial and condemnation. From Pilate, Joseph receives permission to remove the body, wraps it in a linen shroud and supervises its placement in a new tomb, carved out of the rocky hillside very nearby. As is the custom—to prevent robbery, for the dead were often buried with mementoes—a vast stone is rolled across the entrance to the grave; the task requires several strong men. The women who knew and loved Jesus will have to wait until Sunday to do their anointing.

Once the burial is accomplished, there is only an enormous silence about and around Jesus of Nazareth: no visitors to the tomb, no mourners, no public displays of grief for a fallen leader. The Roman soldiers have completed their grim duty, and the city is hushed on Passover eve. It is as if the young man who has been executed has already begun to fade into history.

———

But for those who believe that the eternal God disclosed Himself finally and fully in the historical person of Jesus of Nazareth, the silence shows how much God loves—to the point of giving everything. The God Who dies in Jesus is He Who loves without limit or qualification. He is dead among the dead. This is the extreme point.

But from here, human history, the course of time, the destiny of the world—the meaning of reality itself—are about to be forever altered.

CHAPTER FOURTEEN

OF TIME AND ETERNITY:
THE RESURRECTION

Nothing about Jesus is so misunderstood, misrepresented, trivialized and falsified as the Resurrection. As we have already seen many times, everything in the Gospels has to be understood in light of the Resurrection. Christian faith takes its meaning from the Resurrection—every claim about Jesus, every notion of what it means to live in trusting hope, every view of the world, every take on reality. What the Christian knows of God—with "knowledge" that is qualitatively different from knowledge about anything or anyone else—comes through the experience of Jesus risen, however the experience is articulated. Nothing makes sense without an understanding of the Resurrection, yet understanding seems to collapse against this apparently inordinate claim. Raised from the dead . . . risen from the dead: even the language seems to pitch us into the realm of the impossible. It surpasses understanding.

Understanding.

What a strange and difficult term to use when we come to discuss something we cannot see directly with our eyes or touch with our hands. We take that hard, physical reality of sight and touch for ultimate reality, but in this we may delude ourselves, as we know when we experience love. We can see and touch signs of it, but love (like memory and will, inspiration and understanding itself) is a reality far greater than its signs.

Just as when we discuss love or creativity, art or the meaning of life, so it is with discussing the ultimately invisible and ultimately real reality of faith, the Resurrection. But to discuss it requires, as far as is possible, abandoning all preconceptions and negative stereotypes and attempting to see what the New Testament claims about the primal experience of

231

faith and then how the texts address, confirm or even make possible one's own experience of the Resurrection—not how one's own experience arbitrates and mediates the text!

In other words, rather than subjecting the texts to our prior experience, we make ourselves available to the text, to the experience behind it. Reading and understanding the texts, in other words, enable us to read and understand ourselves. The act of interpretation, which does not mean falsifying or giving the texts a self-invented meaning, interprets the interpreter to himself. And the process of being grasped by the text begins by reading it as something *of* the past but *not limited by* the past.

Christian faith is, in fact, fundamentally not a matter of the past but of the present. It is an experience of, and a relationship with, someone alive, someone whose existence in the economy of earthly life, the life in and of the flesh—in other words, bodily life as we know it—ceased almost two thousand years ago. Faith proclaims, in light of a mysterious but certain experience, that Jesus of Nazareth is completely transformed, forever altered.

To begin, perhaps we need to rethink the entire notion of the relationship of our bodies to ourselves. Are we indeed absolutely synonymous with bones, muscle, tissue, blood and the rest? To judge by today's frantic obsession with maintaining the illusion of youth, and the unrealizable goal of bodily perfection (ludicrous as that may be), one might be tempted to reply, "Yes."

But in our more sensible moments, we realize that when we speak of the body, we mean that aspect of self that expresses us in this world and enables us to see, communicate and act. Might there not be another "world"—another sphere of reality—in which we express ourselves differently?

The a priori notion that resurrection is absurd and impossible (a similar objection is offered to miracles) does not take into account the far more open attitude of many contemporary scientists, who hesitate to make such judgments—not only because of discoveries in the realm of microphysics, but also because of a far more acute awareness that the observation of reality precludes making absolute predictions about what is possible or impossible in every single event. Where all possible conditions and limitations can be accounted for, something might be said—but only theoretically, and only as an experiment: absolute general predictions cannot be made about the process of the world as a whole.

What we call the randomness of the world may, as we have seen, be part of a pattern far more complex and intricate than we are now able to perceive and formulate—a point we considered in discussing miracles. Such limited understanding was certainly, in many ways, the lot of those who have preceded us, and we do not call them stupid or imperceptive. We do not, for example, blame the great surgeons of the nineteenth century for not knowing about lasers. Only God knows how the next century will regard our frail attempts at understanding, articulating and dealing with the world.

Do we not in fact have more than a hint of another world beyond ours when we see how another's influence on us transcends the restrictions of time and space, and how our deepest relationships communicate us to a loved one even without words or touch or gaze?

What Jesus of Nazareth once said and did long ago does not constitute the object of Christian faith. What he says and does *now*, how he reveals himself to us as individuals and as a believing community—this is the field in which faith is planted and where it grows. This is the process whereby we go to God.

Christianity is, then, a way of perceiving reality based on an experience of Jesus as alive and present to *our* present. "He is alive now with [i.e., by means of] the power of God," writes Paul to the Corinthians. Christianity is a way of finding ultimate significance and meaning, a conviction that God acts in love on behalf of what He has made—that He has always acted in love.

In this regard, there is a kind of straight line, a kind of supreme logic.

First of all, there is the God Who stands behind, above and within all that is: out of Himself and His eternal existence, He creates, and creation almost amounts to a description of God's essential "nature." In an evolving process, He then gathers and summons back to Himself.

The straight line moves from creation to the call to the patriarchs of Israel, the fathers of a people who witness to and proclaim God's invitation to all nations. Life is guided over the arc of time: people wander, stumble and fail, rise and praise and listen, then wander and stumble again. The glory of the Old Testament is that it documents the sine curve of human fallibility in listening, heeding, ignoring, responding.

But the straight line of God's offer and pursuit continues. All the time, God speaks through those we call prophets, the guides according to whose witness the people can subjugate what is primitive and savage and become more and more malleable to the presence of God. For that is what the straight line of history—this supreme logic—is about: the pouring forth of the presence of God into time and matter.

The straight, logical line reaches its zenith in the ultimate entrance of God into history—in the Incarnation, the coming of God into the world in the particular life of one man, Jesus of Nazareth. God no longer remains a distant, unknowable mystery, aloof from His creation. The process of His involvement in matter is now complete, for He identifies Himself with humanity in all its implications.

In Jesus, we see what God is and what He is like: attentive, healing, compassionate, completely absorbed in the lot of humanity. And there He subverts totally the standards by which the world judges, for Jesus is the innocent one, the one who goes about doing good, who is rejected by the world. It is he who is transparently open to God—so open that there is nothing separating him from the presence of God at all. Of Jesus there can be claimed something qualitatively different from the claims made on behalf of any other human being: when we encounter Jesus, we encounter God.

Relative to this, one proclaims the divinity of Jesus not because that assertion is contained in a creed that one must not only recite but affirm, as if required of members in a club. Nor does one proclaim the divinity of Jesus because one has been taught it. It can only be affirmed because it is experienced as true—with a believing historical tradition—that one is made a friend of God by Jesus. The encounter with him is an encounter with God as savior—it is he who saves from the limitations of self—and not only saved for eternity, but saved in the here and now for meaning and from chaos. The redeeming purpose we find in Jesus is part of the very being and essence of God Himself, Whose nature is to create, sustain, disclose and save forever.

———

This conviction begins with a moment of history—with the claim that at some point after his body was left in the tomb and everyone withdrew, the whole being of Jesus was taken up into what might be called the sphere of the divine, the very life of God. This emphatically does *not* mean that Jesus the man was somehow "made into God" or "became God" when he was glorified. At a moment of God's created time—in the conception of Jesus of Nazareth—He identified Himself with a parcel of this world: the being of this man, Jesus, whose identity *as a man* is preserved even while he shares the nature of God (and here, of course, we stumble and rely on inadequate philosophical discourse).

But if the Incarnation—which means "enfleshment"—of God in history does not mean that Jesus became something that he was not, it also emphatically *does* mean that *as man* he is lifted to a Lordship or reigning Messiahship over the universe, a function he did not have prior to his Glorification; as we shall see, that is the meaning of the word "Ascension." In a timeless "now," Jesus forever shares that life of God with all who ask and can receive.

The New Testament does not describe the event of the Resurrection. No one was present to see it, and by its very nature as a transhistorical event (an event rooted in the transcendent or eternal, which has effects in the created order of time), it is not susceptible of historical proof or disproof. What can be shown, however, is what we might call the crater left by the explosion. We can see and assess the narratives about the faith of the apostles, who beheld him in some way that transformed their bafflement, fear and hesitation into a confirmed experience of Jesus as alive—the same Jesus, but wholly different in the form and manner of his existence.

The Greek words of the New Testament, the grammar and syntax and usage of human language, seem to slip and slide; there is an attempt—by Paul in his letters and then by the four evangelists—to bend language in an attempt to express something unprecedented and unparalleled in human experience. The accounts of certain visions of the Risen Jesus after Easter, for example, differ widely in the four Gospels. As with everything else, those differences reflect not only the variations in local oral traditions, but also the specific concerns of the individual writers as well as the needs and faith of their communities.

But let me repeat. This is the single reality that suffers the most misrepresentation. It is exceptional in human history and, as an event that transcends time and space, it is not available for examination or description the way, let us say, Caesar's conquest of Gaul might be studied and detailed. But equally so, the Resurrection cannot be disproven. Just as we said regarding miracles, it will not do to say that something cannot happen because it does not happen in my experience or because one has not seen it happen.

To discuss the Resurrection of Jesus it is necessary, first of all, to understand what it is not.

When we say Jesus has risen from the dead, we do not mean that his corpse was resuscitated and that he came back to the same kind of life as we know it: that, after all, would be only a return to impermanence and an orientation to death. The particles of which the human organism is composed cannot in any case be identically reconstituted after death, for they never remain the same: everything in the human body is constantly being replaced. Every atom, every gene is in a constant state of flux that involves an endless series of little deaths and fresh beginnings.

Until recently, matter—and especially the human body—was considered to be made up of solid pieces of inert material. Seen this way, the notion of a transfigured, spiritualized body is regarded as little more than madness without the moon. "Spiritual body" in fact sounds like a bald contradiction. But now matter is understood as a form of energy, and almost each month we hear of new studies in physics, biology and even neuroanatomy in which the nature of matter-energy and brain waves are found to be far more complex and mysterious than we have ever imagined.

Can we say once and for all and with absolute confidence that there is no other type of body but one of flesh? Is it not in fact reasonable that you and I will eventually inhabit not a body of sinew and muscle, blood and tissue, but one wholly different yet continuous with our identity, so that we can say with even more confidence that we shall, like Jesus, survive the grave? The physicist Harold Schilling (in the spirit of Einstein, among others) may be very much on the mark in suggesting that with every new discovery, something previously unknown is not only exposed but also—especially regarding the complexity of matter-energy—that we know just a bit more of "the limitless internal depth and content of physical reality."

So speaking, we can be at home with religious language that is not, after all, so far from the language of physics: in his radically transformed and transfigured life, Jesus is as we, too, shall be. He was always infinitely more than the mere interplay of the particles of physics and biochemistry. He was defined, on the contrary, by love, commitment and fidelity—and perhaps also, as we have seen, by sheer ordinariness. These occur in time and space, but nothing reaches fulfillment in time and space. God lifts up life into His own life. Jesus is indeed as we shall be.

Lazarus, the daughter of Jairus and the widow of Nain's son were resuscitated by Jesus very soon after their physical deaths. They were brought back from death—great news for them and their families, but their returns do not effect the transformation of the world; in any case, it is certain that eventually those three died again and this time were *not* subsequently brought back to this life. The Resurrection of Jesus, on the other hand, is entrance into a completely new form of existence, not restricted by time, place or death and, we may logically add, completely different from the kind of organism of flesh and blood with which I am writing these pages and you are reading them.

But let us be very clear about something else: to state that the risen life of Jesus is an entirely new life "in God," we are not saying that his corpse remained in the tomb to decay as do others. "He whom God raised up experienced no corruption" represents one of the earliest proclamations about Jesus—earlier, in fact, than any material about his historical life. In other words, we are not postulating some "merely" spiritual resurrection, in which "his truth is marching on, glory, glory, hallelujah!" For many good people in our time, the meaning of the Resurrection is just this—that his intent or message survives in the teachings of his love. If this is all the Resurrection means, then Jesus is no different from any great teacher in history, or any great friend. But speaking of the Resurrection is speaking of something else entirely.

The tomb was indeed empty, and no body was to be found. That, of course, does not prove anything except that both the friends and enemies of Jesus agreed that the grave was vacant and the corpse remained absent. Other attempts at explanations were put forward at the time for that bit of evidence, and the Gospels freely admit them: the rumor that the apostles stole the body and claimed Jesus had risen, or that the enemies stole the body to prevent a cult around the corpse. The absence of a corpse neither encourages a community nor advances faith: it is the presence of Jesus that is experienced as real and true—not the absence of something.

What do the Gospels in fact report?

Only that when some women came to anoint the body of Jesus on Sunday morning, there was no body to be found. After that, friends and disciples of Jesus experienced visions and sightings of him as alive and present to them. Eventually, those visions ceased. All this hardly qualifies as evidence. What, then, can be said with any certainty? Faith, after all, cannot be based on a fanciful wish.

Let us backtrack for a moment first, to the person of Joseph of Arimathea, that shadowy figure mentioned only as the man who stepped forward when others did not and took reverential care of Jesus' body. The tradition is unaware of him in any other way except in this regard, and he is not named anywhere else in the Scriptures. His name, with nothing else to recommend him, is a very good piece of historical data, for it guarantees the burial of the dead corpse of Jesus. If Jesus had been buried by friends or relatives, the tradition would surely have been happy to report that, and would have attributed the fact to Peter or another of the disciples. But no: the deed was done by a stranger named Joseph, from Arimathea. He did what he did (to the shame of Jesus' friends, it might be added), and he has otherwise vanished from history.

———

Once we move into the discovery of the empty tomb in the accounts of Mark, Matthew, Luke and John, however, we find a very different character from the burial account.

In Mark's Gospel, three women—Mary Magdalene, James's mother Mary and a woman named Salome—come to the tomb to anoint Jesus. They find the stone rolled back, and they enter the tomb to see a young man sitting. He tells the women not to fear, that Jesus has been raised, and that his disciples will see him in Galilee; the women, trembling with fear and astonishment, tell no one.

According to Matthew, two women—Mary Magdalene and another Mary—come to the tomb; there is an earthquake, and an angel descends, rolls back the stone and sits on it outside the tomb. The angel tells the women the identical message as the young man in Mark, and at this news the women race away with great joy to tell the disciples. En route, they meet Jesus, who calms their fears: "Do not be afraid. Go and tell my brothers to go to Galilee. There they will see me."

Luke's tradition, too, is unique. An indeterminate number of women—Mary Magdalene, James's mother Mary, a woman named Joanna and some others—come to the tomb with aromatic oils. The stone is already rolled back, and there are two men standing inside, who ask the women why they seek the living among the dead. Jesus is not here, they say: he has been raised. This the women tell the disciples and anyone else who will listen. Peter and the others find this incredible, and so Peter goes to the tomb, finds it empty, and goes home completely baffled.

For John, Mary Magdalene alone is the first witness. She arrives to find the stone already moved away. She reports to Peter and another disciple that the body has been taken away. The two men go to the tomb, find it empty and then go home. Mary returns and is weeping outside the tomb when a man asks the reason for her grief. She thinks he is the gardener and begs to know, if this man has taken the body of Jesus, where she may find it. When the man then reveals himself as the risen Lord, Mary falls to worship him. Later, she tells the disciples what has happened.

The oldest form of the tradition was probably and simply this: the women came to the tomb (Mary Magdalene, it will be noted, is common in all the accounts), were amazed that it was empty, and fled. The later tradition that the other verses in each Gospel represent answer questions such as "Why did the women come to the tomb, and when? And what did they do when they found it empty?" The other details link the story of the empty tomb to the message of the Resurrection as it was preached, based primarily on the experience of the first appearances of Jesus. The function of the angel or angels, as we have seen, is an element of style— the literary device by which a divine message is proclaimed to humanity. In other words, very early in the oral tradition the *meaning* of the discovery of the empty tomb by women was stylized in the form of an angelic proclamation.

Even the incredible silence of the women (thus Mark) serves a literary purpose: it intensifies their astonishment and emphasizes that Resurrection faith is not a conclusion based on the discovery of the empty tomb alone. Nor did it rest merely on the word of women, who were not admissible as legal witnesses in Jewish law. Faith in the risen Jesus is grounded exclusively in experience of him as alive and present.

———

Although, let me reiterate, we cannot prove the Resurrection of Jesus, we can certainly adduce historical considerations supporting the validity of the Gospel tradition. We can, in other words, show that belief in the Resurrection of Jesus is not folly.

First of all, the disciples would not have been able to preach the Resurrection if they could be contradicted by a tomb with Jesus' body in it. This was especially true because of the Jewish notion of the unity of body and spirit: the Resurrection proclamation could not have lasted one day in Jewish territory if there were a tomb with Jesus' corpse in it. The idea of "soul" as distinct from body, it should be remembered, derives from Greek philosophical anthropology.

As an interesting aside, Matthew records the following. Some of the guard at the tomb go into the city and tell the chief priests about the earthquake and the appearance of an angel. The priests give the soldiers a large sum of money, saying, "You must say, 'His disciples came at nighttime and stole him away while we were asleep.' If this comes to the governor, we will satisfy him and keep you out of trouble." So the guards accept the cash, "and this story is still told among the Jews to this day." Thus concludes the episode. Note: there would have been no need for such action on the part of the high priests if there were a tomb with the body of Jesus in it, so everyone agrees on the empty tomb.

As for the explanation that the apostles stole the body: what advantage would this have been to them? This frightened group of mediocre men was anything but a band of heroes! Is it psychologically defensible that these men of little faith and less courage would have stolen a body to invent the story of a revived, renewed Jesus? Such action could only lead them to the same fate as their master, the same persecution and death (which in fact was their destiny in any case, but they did nothing to seek it).

And would their own fraud have aroused in them the kind of complete transformation that history records—the preaching, the journeys, the fearless confrontation of authorities, the strength to endure martyrdom? It is a basic premise of sound sociology, incidentally, that great movements in world history do not begin with a fraud or a hoax; if such is involved, the movement dies an early death.

And what of the alternative—that the Jews stole the body to prevent the rise of a Jesus cult? If that was so, why then did they not produce the corpse as soon as the disciples began to preach? As for the likes of imaginative writers like Hugh Schonfield (author of *The Passover Plot*, published in 1965), his explanation is almost comical. Jesus did not really die on the cross, he claims: Jesus simply went into a brief coma, was revived by the coolness of the tomb and then somehow made his way out.

Even granting the physical possibility of this, would such a briefly revived Jesus have strengthened the disciples' faith or given the impression that he was the Lord who had conquered death and the grave? His friends would only have been further disappointed in any case when at last they saw him die of his wounds. Other fantasists have Jesus meeting up with Mary Magdalene and hopping off to Spain, where they marry, settle down, raise a family—and presumably work on their memoirs or obtain a Gucci franchise. This is the stuff of Hollywood, not of historical-religious exploration. Need I add that, for tales like this, there is, of course, not a shred of reliable historical evidence?

If the empty tomb is a late fiction invented by Christians to express faith in Jesus' ongoing life among them, why would it be framed almost exclusively in terms of women witnesses, who were illegal and inadmissible according to Jewish principles of evidence? Or were these women in the tradition precisely because that was what happened, and they could not be removed from the accounts? It is also hard to explain why the disciples were not brought to the forefront as discoverers of the empty tomb if the story is fictitious: in other words, if a tale is concocted to seem credible, why are the most forceful elements lacking? No, the best historical judgment to make on the tradition is that things happened as they are written. There is very much in favor of that, and nothing decisive against it.

More to the point, if the Resurrection, the message and proclamation about Jesus and the spread of the Gospel were an invention, one must ask, "For what purpose?" The only results of this faith and this commitment were danger, the loss of both religious and civil liberties, torture and death. For what purpose? To give one's life to a message bound to encounter opposition? "Nobody believed in Socrates deeply enough to die for his teaching," wrote the first Christian philosopher, Justin Martyr, in the second century. "But for Christ, even uneducated men have made light of fear and death."

Still, we do not place our faith in the empty tomb: that would be a very empty faith, as some wag once complained. We place our faith in a living person.

As it happens, there is an earlier witness than the four Gospels to the tradition of the Resurrection of Jesus. It is found as early as the year 56 (about a dozen years before the composition of Mark), in Paul's first letter to the Christians at Corinth.

Of Jesus, Paul says that "he died and was buried, and was raised on the third day in accordance with the Scriptures . . . he appeared to Cephas [Peter], then to the [other disciples]. Then he appeared to more than five hundred at one time, most of whom are still alive, though some have died. Then he appeared to James, then to all the apostles. Last of all, he appeared also to me."

This is the oldest literary witness to the tradition of the Resurrection of Jesus, but it represents a faith that long antedated Paul, who draws on a fragment of very early hymnic material well known to early Christians. It is fascinating to consider the key phrases in this early material.

"He died and was buried." The last three words italicize the finality of Jesus' death, and it is interesting to see that until the Gospels, neither Paul nor any other New Testament pre-Gospel writer thought it significant to mention the empty tomb. It was the encounters with and experience of the Risen Jesus that were at the core of faith, not the fact of a bodiless grave. And the fact that no nonbiblical writers made any such note in history is hardly remarkable: the circumstances of the death and burial of an insignificant non-Roman Jew, and rumors of an empty tomb shortly thereafter, made no impact in a world in which the word "media" meant only "middle" or "amid." To the world, Jesus was no more significant in death than he was in life—until his followers claimed extraordinary experiences of him after death and equally extraordinary claims for him over the next several years.

"He was raised on the third day in accordance with the Scriptures." The word "raised" is of course a metaphor based on the analogy of sleeping and waking. It refers, in this context, to the whole passage of Jesus from an earthly mode of existence to a spiritual mode of existence. As we have already seen, this does not mean the mere resuscitation of a corpse and a return to life in this world. Rather the implication is that Jesus in his Resurrection or Glorification is entirely interpenetrated with spirit. He has become a "life-giving spirit," says Paul in the same letter.

The analogy Paul draws out is that of a seed planted in the earth which comes up a living stalk:

"Someone will ask, 'How are the dead raised? With what kind of body?' Foolish! For what you sow does not come to life unless it dies. And as for what you sow, you do not sow the body that is to be, but a bare seed, perhaps of wheat or of some other grain.

"So it is with the resurrection of the dead. What is sown is perishable, what is raised in imperishable. It is sown in dishonor, it is raised in glory. It is sown in weakness, it is raised in power."

And now comes the crucial statement: "It is sown a physical body, it is raised a spiritual body . . . The first man, Adam, became a living being; the last Adam [i.e., Jesus] became a life-giving spirit."

But Paul wants us to be very clear about this revelation: the world of the divine is not a tangible, material, perishable realm of existence: "Flesh and blood cannot inherit the kingdom of God, nor does the perishable inherit the imperishable. Listen! I will tell you a mystery! . . . We will all be changed, in a moment, in the twinkling of an eye, at the last trumpet . . . The dead will be raised imperishable, and we will be changed. For this perishable body must put on imperishability, and this mortal body must put on immortality. When this perishable body puts on imperishability, and this mortal body puts on immortality, then the saying that is written will be fulfilled: 'Death has been swallowed up in victory. Where, O death, is your victory? Where, O death, is your sting?' "

———

Based on Paul's own experience of the Risen Jesus and the experience of hundreds of others after the Resurrection, the transfigured and transformed Jesus cannot be described; he can only be compared—to the harvest that results from the seed that is planted, and to something that is immortal and undying and no longer "of" this world, of this economy of the flesh. The person of Jesus would have had to go through such a complete transformation from the body of flesh to a body of spirit in order for Paul to be able to speak of the final state of us all, which is like that immortal and undying body. By "body" is meant all that makes for individuation, for specificity, for the uniqueness of each human personality. And that individual becomes not part of some cosmic swirl, nor of some vague, indeterminate universal force. With personhood intact, like that of Jesus, who was the same person but totally transformed in his manner of existence, all who die unto God live for and unto God.

The word invariably used by the New Testament to describe these visions is important: Paul reports that Jesus "appeared to Peter," for example. The Greek verb (*ophthē*) means a coming forth from invisibility to visibility—it emphasizes, in other words, the objectivity of the event, not the subjective imagination of the viewer. But even the word "appeared" must be understood analogously: this seeing of Jesus must have been an extraordinary kind of perception, a reality not visible to everyone who simply happened to be present at a particular place at a particular time.

That is an important consideration for today. The grounding of faith, and the establishment of a faith community that we call the Church is not based on the occasional extraordinary encounters and revelations that occurred two thousand years ago: it is based on the experience of transformation and empowerment through Jesus that countless generations of people have known down the ages—and that continues to the present.

————

In the passages in which it addresses the Resurrection, then, the New Testament witnesses not to the resuscitation of a corpse, and certainly nothing like a return to the life of this world. It addresses rather the entire passage of Jesus from earthly mode of existence to a spiritual and eternal mode of existence.

Regarding the appearances of Jesus, sometimes called the "visions" beheld by others, some would dismiss everything with a wave of the hand. Mass hysteria, some people say: forlorn disciples will see and believe what they need to see and believe. But this is sociologically naïve, for no movement in the history of the world was based on mass hypnosis or epidemic delusion. Within a short time, any movement so dependent fades into oblivion, and it surely does not alter the course and shape of world history.

A hallucination or a hoax, in the final analysis, cannot be reconciled with the dramatic and historically remarkable movement that, within twenty-five years after Jesus' execution, and under the most agonizing conditions, created Christian communities across the Mediterranean world. People do not amalgamate and deepen a sense of personal and group purpose without the forceful presence of a single charismatic individual and sensational, primal, formative events. In other words, if *some* astonishing experience was not at the foundation of the Christian movement, then what accounted for the improbable beginning, the astonishing expansion and the distinctive writings that reflect its origins?

The Jesus whom faith proclaims as the Lord of the universe is no longer defined and limited by time and space, as he was during his life in the flesh; he is, however, accessible to human beings who are still defined by time and space. And if some reply that the only way for "an intelligent person" (whatever that means) to accept the Resurrection is to reduce it to something only historical and verifiable, then we are in the realm of what the American Scripture scholar Luke Timothy Johnson has called "epistemological imperialism," a denial of any realm of reality outside one's control—which is neither good history nor good science. Such objectors have made a prior judgment that material explanations are the only rational, sound justifications for everything in reality. The problem with this narrow perspective is that it has no room for artists, poets, composers, for those who give their lives to another in love and for those who give loving lives of service to many.

The language of faith, like that of the poet, the lover and the mystic, does not simply relate secular facts about what occurred in history at a particular moment in time. Faith experiences and speaks of the divine initiative and intervention in the world, and that claim (as the distinguished Jewish Talmudic scholar Jacob Neusner has said) "does not come before the court of secular history, to be judged true or false by historians' ways of validating or falsifying ordinary facts."

No doubt about it: the Resurrection of Jesus is the central fact of Christian faith and life; it is not a poetic afterthought, a pleasant fancy or a proof of anything—and it is not something of the past, but of now. With a kind of powerful gentleness, Paul puts the matter succinctly: "If we have placed our hope in Christ for this life only, then we are of all people the most to be pitied."

————

What, then, does it mean to say, "Jesus is risen from the dead?" Let me try to offer a summary reply—but not a definitive answer, which can never be given to this inexhaustible mystery.

It means that Jesus has entered into a new and permanent manner of existence—immortal, deathless, no longer limited by our categories of space and time. His life is not a return to this life as we know it: it is a life in God. But it is also a bodily resurrection. The tomb was empty. But the body that went into the grave emerged completely changed.

Jesus, risen and alive—not a soul or a memory, a ghost or a force, but the beginning of the transformed universe—is no longer present *in* a place. He is rather, we might say, present *to* a place; he is no longer contained by any spatial situation. He is present to us wherever we may be. Before his Glorification, he was limited by his corporeality. Now his whole person is with us, and nothing of him is far away in some spatially imagined heaven.

This present moment is the first moment of the Resurrection of Jesus, for there is no passage of time in the realm of God, and Jesus has not changed in any way since that first moment. "All time belongs to him, and all the ages." Every moment of every day in what we call the passing of time is embraced by the eternal present of the Resurrection of Jesus.

At this point we are closer, perhaps, to articulating the meaning of the "sacrifice of Jesus." Totally transformed as man, he now possesses the distinctive title Lord—reigning Messiah over the universe. By virtue of being glorified by God, he is raised to Lordship which *as man* he did not have prior to his death.

————

That Lordship is the meaning of the Ascension, which is not a geographical term or a separate event in time, but a metaphor indicating the transfer of Jesus to the world of the divine—his being raised by God to reigning Messiahship. In saying "he ascended into heaven," we proclaim the invisible transcendent accession of Jesus. The Lukan accounts in his Gospel and in his second volume, Acts of the Apostles, describe the last appearances and are to be read as theological statements of faith.

"He withdrew from them and was carried up into heaven . . . He was lifted up and a cloud took him out of their sight." The language represents not a physical journey up into the skies, for the passage of Jesus is not a progress from one place to another, but from one form of existence to another. The cloud, a repeated symbol in the Scriptures, signifies not the absence but the presence of God with His people, just as it was with the Israelites in the Sinai desert.

To speak of the Ascension, then, is to focus on the enthronement aspect of Jesus' Glorification, which is an immediate corollary of his Resurrection without any interim period. Resurrection and Ascension focus on different aspects, from our point of view, of his Glorification.

To be sure, Luke writes of forty days of appearances of Jesus to his friends after his Resurrection. Forty is a recurring number in the Bible: the rain of Noah's flood lasts forty days and nights; Moses and Elijah fast forty days, and Jesus does the same. Forty represents the length of time necessary for something to be duly accomplished. The event Luke describes (". . . as they were watching, he was lifted up, and a cloud took him out of their sight . . .") is a visible way of describing an invisible reality that had already occurred with the Resurrection. The Jesus who somehow mysteriously manifested himself to his disciples as risen had already entered fully into the glory of eternity at the Resurrection.

One more thing, which I suggest at the risk of irreverence, for we can never know the reality of it: it may be that Jesus was the most surprised person of all when he passed through death and was definitively transformed—not "turned into God" or "made God" but changed utterly in his humanity and taken up into the life of God Eternal. In that humanity, he may have hoped for but dared not presume to expect that God would, after all, completely vindicate him by a total transformation. And in that humanity, he could not, of course, have known precisely what form the transformation would take in any case.

In addition to the Resurrection and Ascension, the third aspect of the Glorification of Jesus—which proposes the effect of it on humanity— is what we call the outpouring or gift of the Spirit, whose first effects were seen fifty days later, in Jerusalem, on the Jewish feast of Pentecost.

The power given to those who had experienced the Risen Jesus first manifested itself and had real results when the disciples broke out of their isolation and went forth to meet Jews who devoutly returned to the Holy City for another feast.

Now the friends of Jesus, empowered with courage where before there was only fear, sensed the first effects of the bestowal of the Spirit, of *God's Spirit,* through the transfigured humanity of Jesus and straight through to the heart of the world. From this time forward, the process of the world's being saved for meaning and being saved for God definitively began. The bestowal of Spirit guarantees the continuing presence of God in history.

But let us be very careful: the gift of the Spirit is not the *control* of the Spirit. The promise that God will always guide His people does not mean that His people will invariably follow that guidance—as history, alas, reveals only too clearly. In forming a community of believers, there has always lurked the clear and real danger that the institution is confused with the community—just as Church administrators, comprising people as weak as the disciples themselves, sometimes wrongly claim that laws, formulas, regulations and even creeds entirely capture the mystery of God.

———

Jesus, in his Glorification, anticipates by a total transformation the ultimate destiny of all the dead. His transformation is the revelation, guarantee and first fruits of the future complete resurrection of all; thus we can say that his Resurrection is the beginning of the transfiguration of the world.

In the Incarnation, God united Himself once and for all to a portion of this world and its concrete reality. In view of the material unity of the universe—the basic oneness of the world according to which all things are related and influence one another even before that influence is understood or articulated—it is absolutely central that the body of Jesus be glorified. Thus all creation is now in process of reaching in and through the Risen Jesus toward that final state in which God triumphs. The successful outcome of the material universe, all sin and evil to the contrary notwithstanding, already exists in the risen body of Jesus.

In this regard, the Christian proclamation of the Resurrection reveals precisely what was *not* anticipated: that this rejected, murdered Jesus was right, and that God—in totally transforming him beyond death—vindicated the one who had given himself totally to God and humanity. God has approved of Jesus—his message, his deeds, his teaching and miracles—and has not sided with the enemies of Jesus. The God of the beginning—of creation, of the call to Israel, of the summons to the prophets, of the revelation in Jesus' life and death and Resurrection—is also the God of the end, Who creates and Who completes. Death no longer has the final word; suffering is no longer the final experience. The Eternal God, Who calls into creation from nothingness, can also summon from death to life.

Is there not, after all, a real logic to all this? The creator God reveals Himself; the revealing God embraces and summons; the summoning God finally acts in love to save what He has made.

CHAPTER FIFTEEN

THE HIDDEN JESUS:
HIS NEW LIFE AND OURS

The announcement of the good news or Gospel—the proclamation of God's coming to humanity in saving power—turns out to be not the political vindication of old Israel, but something unimaginably greater: the Resurrection of Jesus. It is impossible to make too much of this mystery, and of its impact on all reality.

The title of this book indicates for me the single most important aspect of the meaning of faith in Christ. During his earthly life in the flesh, Jesus was hidden: the full implications of his identity as God's ultimate disclosure of Himself were veiled not only from his family, friends and disciples but even perhaps from his own full consciousness.

Certainly Jesus of Nazareth had not the ability to articulate that identity within the limitations of his language and culture. Nevertheless, in that hiddenness, God was at work revealing Himself—and what was revealed was infinite friendliness toward humanity, infinite patience and compassion, infinite mercy.

Of equivalent significance is the complete overturning of human expectations. Everything defied what one might have anticipated for the definitive entrance of God into time and matter. First of all, it was an inauspicious moment in history, and it all happened in an unlikely place, amid a battered, fragmented and subjugated people. The embrace of humanity by God began in lowliness even more extreme than the infancy depicted annually in our Christmas cards and crib scenes.

And then there was the life of the man: hidden, unremarkable, possible to ignore and reject if you were a casual observer. The ministry of Jesus seemed to have an air of improvisation: there were no flourishes, he coveted no political or social power, nor had he any of the equipment of the great men of the world. Everything seems arranged to bear the mark of an astonishing simplicity. God identifies not with the great or famous or beautiful people of the world, but with those whose lives are utterly simple, unfettered by excess and unchained by obsession with self.

Instead of pursuing the routes of success, popularity and notable achievement, Jesus is simply the man for others. Even the dead are not beyond his reach: the long arm of God's compassion reaches through him right into the depths of darkness and turns apparent finality and futility into the surprise of life. God is not to be confined—especially not to action or events in the past.

The relation of past to present is analogous to that of any living human relationship, which is not dependent only on the memories of the original meeting, bonding and series of past events but on what happens now, what deepens and increases commitment. My bond with a friend is not verified or dissolved by defining who we were when we met, but rather by what happens now and what we do to determine where we are going together. It is no less with Christ.

He is of now, and it is his presence now that is the object of Christian faith.

I believe, in other words, not in some more or less reconstructed historical figure of Jesus, nor do I give myself to what he once said and did. It is only to the living and forever risen Lord that I direct my gaze: to him who is hidden but no less present for all that. "I was dead, and look—I am alive forever and ever," says the glorified Jesus in Revelation.

I do not think there are too many other words that inspire as much awe as these. Fewer statements are full of more promise, more comfort, more sheer undiluted confidence that (as Julian of Norwich reminded) all shall be well. Perversity does not finally have the victory; death has not the last word—and failure is not to be so simply conceived.

In Jesus, the very meaning of failure and folly must be reconsidered. He *is*, and he is *hidden* again—yet now as then, he is revealed. In fact, he is revealed in even more ways now than then—in the depths of our yearning to be loved without condition, in our prayer, in our compassion for the needy, in our recognition of our contingency, in the lives of countless people who through the ages have dedicated themselves to the welfare of others, in the deaths of those who lived and died witnessing to human dignity, or who have died innocent of crimes for which they were accused.

————

If anything sensible at all can be said of God, it must be that He exists both involved in and outside of time. And if indeed all time belongs to Him and indeed everyone is alive to Him, then we must consider just what we mean when we speak of time and history.

First of all, what is time but a convenient way of measuring experience? It is commonly thought that we live entirely under its dominion. But this is not so. The present, after all, exists only as a span of practical measuring. For God, with God, there is no time. God does not "see" the past, "observe" the present or "know" the future, as if He were in a cosmic movie theater as the sole spectator, watching all time unspool before Him—but knowing the whole plot and each line of dialogue in advance.

In fact, we have in a real sense invented time, decided its terms and units—and arbitrarily changed it, when opportune, to conform to measurements. In 1582, for example, it was determined that the calendar was "off" by ten days, and so the day following October 4 was decreed to be October 15. No one got very upset by this: it did not seem to matter much what you called the day. Just so, January 1 did not mark the beginning of a "new year" until relatively recently. For a very long time, the year began in March, and for economic purposes it began at other times in different places. Even today, we have vestiges of that in the fiscal year, the academic year and so forth.

————

What really deserves some consideration in this regard is what we call the past, for it is built, rather like the parts of a telescope, into what we call the present. The moments that slip by as you read these words gather meaning only by being connected to a collective past: words in a sentence make sense only by making of each unit of "present" a link in the chain to the "past." The time it takes me to write and you to read these words is, in fact, a succession of little "pasts." But we experience them as a unit we call "the present" in order to measure and identify it as a unit of experience.

It may be more accurate to say, then, that the present is composed of a kind of "bunching" of immediately past moments. We stretch the rubber band of perceived experience backward to include all that is necessary to comprehend reality, to sift through all its components and relate it to our inner life, which is where we live.

This is evident, for example, when we look up into the night sky. As the Danish astronomer Ole Rømer demonstrated almost three centuries ago, light travels at a finite speed, and so, as we gaze at the beauty of the stars and planets, we now know that we are not looking into space but into the past. The light we behold has been on its way to us for a very long time, so that as we continue to gaze we are looking back through centuries of time, even though the heavenly body is visible to our sight only now.

As we scan the heavens, we know that we are in fact beholding a range of time. The moon is to us as it was over a second or so ago; the constellation Sirius we behold as it was more than nine years ago—the farther an object in space, the more remote in the past. Some of what we see does not even exist any longer—but there it is! And all of it, in an instant, is beheld and held existent in the presence of God. Is it any wonder that such nighttime gazing has been known to shatter the hard convictions of more than one atheist?

But just where do we stop stretching the rubber band of time? How far back must we go to comprehend and identify experience, to make sense of it? Five minutes ago? This morning? Last year? When we were born? Conceived? How much of the perceived and meaningful past is built into and alive in our present?

You experience your life as meaningful, for example, since you found a fulfilling career, or since you fell in love—or were released from an empty relationship that for a time bore a credible disguise. Your life began a new volume of time when you became a parent, or produced a meaningful work, or came to terms with maturing or aging or found a mechanism to work your way toward meaning in life.

Most likely, these units of experience or chapters of life are described and measured by relationships of trust, which we may call the love of friendship, and friendship is at the root of all true loves, in whatever category. Being accepted by another, by others, provides an envelope of meaning like no other in life.

And so we come to the central question: How much of the past can really be said to be dead? And the answer has to be that none of it is dead that continues to affect our present. The past is very much alive in everyone inspired by the great lives and deeds of those who went before. And from physics, and the notion of subatomic particles, we know that matter never dies, but simply changes its form of existence.

The past and its people are indeed with us. This we know from genetics, for it is a truism that we did not in fact begin at birth or even at conception. Biological components that flourish in us began with the familial genes—when? How many generations ago? Does this collective past not take us as far back as—yes!—the first moment when there was something? the first moment when God "began" to work? Are we not in fact connected to a past that antedates our own specific pasts? How far back can we stretch the arc of history in order to understand ourselves? Is this not why we are fascinated by history and biography—because we *sense* that in some mysterious ways we are linked to what happened before our consciousness, and to those whose consciousness preceded ours? Are we not, in other words, connected to the first moment of creation?

In a sense, that first moment of creation is *now,* for there is no time with God Who acts. He immerses Himself within it but is not contained by it. Beyond the ebb and change by which life is measured, what we call past and future are all present to God in an eternal now.

In this context, what we call the transhistorical event of Jesus' Resurrection is in fact his entrance into the eternal now of God. *This moment*—as I write and you read—is the first moment of Jesus' Resurrection, for he is alive in the sphere of God. And because the eternity of God encompasses our time, he who is risen, in the fullness of his being as human, is unrestricted and accessible to us, freed as he is from the past and the change and chance and fog of history.

We understand fragments of experience, then, by measuring them: this we call time. Segments of the past are comprehended by memory and reflection; portions of the future are anticipated by expectation, hope, hunch. But to God all is present, "for a thousand years in Your sight are like yesterday when it is past, or like a watch in the night," as the psalmist sang. The past that seems dead to us is still alive and present to God, gathered up in the single, once-for-all simultaneity of His universal present.

And now we are, at last, very close to the ultimate logic of all—our final destiny, which is the eternal present of God's life. What we call life after death is part of the inexorable logic that began with creation and continued in the call to Israel, the summons of the prophets, the Incarnation of God in Jesus, the Resurrection of Jesus to a life unto God. Every life, linked as it is to every stage in the lives of its genetic predecessors, is also linked to every other life—by virtue, as we have seen, of the material unity of the universe. In this context, the dead are not nonexistent: they are taken up to be participants in the life of God Himself, to Whom a way was made by Jesus when God raised him from death. In that Glorification, God began the process of healing the past.

Just as you and I have not been summoned from nothingness, just as our connection to the past flourishes in our individual present, so we do not dissolve into nothingness. In some way we cannot fully understand, as I have suggested several times, God loves what He has made and saves it. Just as creation moved toward the formation of Israel, and Israel brought forth Jesus of Nazareth, in whom God overcomes death—so, too, the great chain of being, always present to God, is being constantly transformed, and we with it.

To repeat the line of the divine plan: creation, call, amalgamation, purposeful guidance, Incarnation, Resurrection, the promise of life eternal in God—all of these moments describe the intersection of time with God's eternal now. Human language, for convenience and measuring, relies on the tripartite metaphor of past, present, future.

During his life in the flesh, Jesus of Nazareth was bound by the limitations of space: when in one place, he could not be in another; what he did at one instant he was not doing at another; event followed event. Then comes the Resurrection. In all his concrete humanity, Jesus is raised to a new and permanent form of existence, no longer separated from us in time and space, no longer distant from us because of the exigencies of the flesh.

And the heaven into which he enters?

It is, of course, not a place to which he and we go, but a state into which he and we enter—the very life of God. None of this can be explained. All we can do is to fumble about with vague metaphors, for all language is metaphor. At the end, we stop thinking and speaking and sit quietly with folded hands. Awe stops our words, slows our breathing and disabuses us of the illusion that we have comprehended anything very deeply.

In Thornton Wilder's great play *Our Town*, the bereaved young George Gibbs comes to the grave of his wife Emily, who has died giving birth and has just been buried. As he weeps, Emily (seated, in the scene, with all the dead she has known) turns to George's mother, who is among those she has joined in eternity. "Mother Gibbs," she says wistfully, "they don't understand, do they?"

And Mrs. Gibbs replies, with great wisdom and calm and gentleness, "No, dear—not very much."

———

Indeed, we do not understand very much.

But the recognition of our own darkness, frailty and contigency pitches us into the arms of God. Our share in eternal life begins even now.

Every act of God since the first measured moment of creation, every word ever uttered by Jesus, every touch and healing, is—by virtue of the life of God into which he has fully entered—a present reality. Christ Jesus: he who *is,* not he who was.

In the Gospels, as we have seen, the meaning of the risen life of Jesus is set down for all who come to him in new circumstances. There was no need for the writers to hanker for the past, or to rummage about filling in gaps in "historical" knowledge about Jesus, for he was not then and is not now Jesus-of-the-past. He lives forever, and this makes possible our new life.

———

Just how God would finally enter, embrace and save history was a matter of considerable debate among devout Jews right up to the time of Jesus' birth. How would the faithful sons of the covenant recognize him? Perhaps he would be born at Bethlehem, David's city, and his birth would be made known to Israel and to all the world?

It is the same today: Where is he? How are we to know, how to find him?

God, who defies and surpasses every human expectation, is ahead of us now as then.

Expecting power and might, fame and perhaps a little majestic glamour, we look in the wrong places. "Truly, You are a hidden God," we read in the book of Isaiah.

But the eternal hiddenness of God, and that of Jesus in his present life, is not distance; much less is it remoteness.

A confident hope in the hidden Jesus is not a comforting intellectual posture, nor is it a poetic-romantic fancy to which we cling, as if it were a life raft in the chaotic sea of our world. No, our confidence—our intuition that, yes, all this is the truest true thing that happens—is a conviction born of experience.

The experience happens in the silence and hiddenness that is deep within us, not far away at all, for God's nature is always and ever to draw near and enter, to re-create us at every moment, to sustain our breath by His, to gather us to Himself. And He never imposes but works with what He has given us—our talents, our capacity to love and be loved and, perhaps most of all, our need of Him.

Born in obscurity, living in humility, dying in shame: how inappropriate the threads of Jesus' life seem, and how we stumble around in the dark to comprehend God's ways for him and for us. But the darkness is the light of God, Who embraces everything that is the ordinary lot of ordinary people, and identifies Himself not with the powerful or the princely, but with the one who loves unconditionally, with him who is rejected and tossed aside by the world. The hiddenness of God in Christ, then as now, is in fact the condition of revelation.

In Jesus, God does indeed speak, but in silence; He shouts over our noise, but in a whisper. Now as then, He remains hidden—and so forever discloses Himself. In stillness, we hear Him. In allowing ourselves to be loved by God, we find the hidden Jesus, who, quietly and gradually, transforms our jaded lives.

Upon our old, insistent blindness, light shines down in living beams; mercy falls like summer rain. Our depth of dimness, our long night of fear and gloom, are banished.

It is so. In His unimaginable and enduring mercy, God claims us as His own forever.

NOTES

This book makes no reference to the apocryphal Gospels or other noncanonical early works, for very simple reasons. Early Christians selected from a wide variety of documents those that represented their faith; writings bearing the names Gospel of Thomas, Protevangelium of James and so forth are late, fantastic writings rejected by Christian communities from the first century until the canon or list of officially accepted writings was finally settled in about the fifth century. This rejection was part of the natural process of defining Christian belief against the kinds of irregularities (heresies) precisely like those found in the apocrypha. The apocryphal works offer no light on Christian faith; they are for the most part fantastic legends whose style and content are immediately recognizable as very different from the quadriform Gospel. At the end of the twentieth century, the hyperbole (and the hype) about apocryphal Gospels is part of a general commercialization about biblical literature that loses a cautious sense of history.

CHAPTER 1

1. On Francis of Assisi and the origins of the Christmas crib, see Leclerc, *Francis of Assisi*, and Thomas of Celano, *St. Francis of Assisi* (Chicago: Franciscan Herald Press, 1982).

1. The manger is mentioned only in Lk 2,7.12.16.

1. *The ox knows its owner*   Is 1,3.

2. *A decree went out*   Lk 2,1–5.

3. On the attestations that Jesus was a descendant of David, see Jeremias, *Jerusalem in the Time of Jesus*, 290–97.

4. *Wise men*   Mt 2,1–16.

4. On the magi, see the entry *magos* in Balz and Schneider, eds., *Exegetical Dictionary of the New Testament*, vol. 2, 371–72.

5. On the midrash of Abraham's birth, see J. D. Eisenstein, *Ozar Midrashim*, cited in Myles M. Bourke, "The Literary Genius of Matthew 1–2," *Catholic Biblical Quarterly* 22 (1960) 160–75.

5. *A star shall come*   Num 24,17.

5. *Arise, shine*   Is 60,1.3.

5. *The wealth of nations*   Is 60,5–6.

259

5. On the midrashic elements in Mt 1–2, see Bourke, *art. cit.*

6. *Amram's wife*   Josephus, *Antiquities of the Jews* (Loeb classical edition, vol. 4), 2.205,210,215.

6. P. Saintyves in P.-L. Couchoud, ed., "Le massacre des Innocents ou la persécution de l'Enfant prédestiné," *Congrès d'histoire du Christianisme,* vol. 1 (Paris: Rieder, 1928), 229–72, has listed a number of ancient literary accounts about a wicked ruler seeking to kill a hero whose birth had been foretold: stories set in India, Persia, Mesopotomia, Greece and Rome that concern such heroes as Gilgamesh, Sargon, Cyrus, Perseus and Romulus/Remus.

7. *While they were there*   Lk 2,6–40.

7. Regarding the placing of Christmas on December 25: this goes back to the fourth century, as a kind of counterstatement to a Roman feast honoring the "unconquered sun." This was considered the time when once again the days began to lengthen—at the winter equinox, then thought to be December 25 (not, as later determined, the twenty-second). It was appropriate, therefore, for Christians to have their celebration of the conquering of darkness by the birth of light. The exact date of Jesus' birth is unknown.

8. On the manger, the swaddling bands, the shepherds, etc., see Brown, *The Birth of the Messiah,* 418 ff.; and Charles H. Giblin, S. J., "Reflections on the Sign of the Manger," *Catholic Biblical Quarterly* 29 (1967) 87–101.

9. On the Jewish tradition about shepherds, see Jeremias, *Jerusalem in the Time of Jesus,* 310–11. Brown, *The Birth of the Messiah,* has a different view: he prefers (420–24) to see the shepherds as connected to royal Bethlehem and the tradition of the shepherd boy David.

9. On the correct rendering of the angelic hymn, see Joseph A. Fitzmyer, S. J., " 'Peace Upon Earth Among Men of His Good Will' (Lk 2:14)," *Theological Studies* 9 (1958) 225–27.

9. The Italian citation from Dante is in the *Paradiso,* canto III, line 85.

10 ff.   On the Old Testament antecedents to the infancy accounts in Matthew and Luke, see Brown, *The Birth of the Messiah,* and also his *Reading the Gospel,* 27–31.

14. *by night*   Lk 2,8.

14. *While gentle silence*   Wisdom of Solomon 18,14–15.

14. *resounding mysteries*   The Greek is clear and sublime: *mysteria kraugēs, 'a tina 'en 'ēsychia 'eprachthē, 'ēmin de 'ephanerothē:* "mysteries for shouting about, wrought in silence but manifest to us." Ignatius, *Epistle to the Ephesians,* 19; see J.-P. Migne, *Patrologiae Cursus Completus/Series Graeca* (1857), vol. 5, 754.

14. *the mystery that has been hidden*   Col 1,26.

15. *The Lord is in his Holy temple*   Hb 2,20.

15. *the incomprehensible mystery*   Rahner, *Foundation of Christian Faith*, 434.

15 ff. On silence, see McBrien, ed., *The HarperCollins Encyclopedia of Catholicism*, 1191; also, Latourelle and Fisichella, eds., *Dictionary of Fundamental Theology*, 1001–6.

16. *Be still*   Ps 46,10.

17. *Now there was*   I Kgs 19,11–12.

CHAPTER 2

This chapter has a particular debt to Brown, *The Birth of the Messiah*, and to Meier, *A Marginal Jew*, vol. 1.

18. On the Herodian dynasty, see Perowne, *The Later Herods: The Political Background of the New Testament*, and Sandmel, *Herod: Profile of a Tyrant*.

19. On dating the death of Herod, see the works cited above and T. D. Barnes in *Journal of Theological Studies* 19 (1968) 204–8.

19. On the birth of Jesus about 7–6 B.C.: According to Mt 2,16, Herod is concerned about all the children two years of age and under, and this is just before his death in 4 B.C. On the paradox that Jesus was born "B.C.," see Brown, *Birth of the Messiah*, 167, and Meier, *A Marginal Jew*, vol. 1, 416, n.24. Meier rightly cautions that "it is not always clear . . . at what time of year an event is occurring, what calendar is being referred to, whether parts of years are being counted as whole years, and whether years are being counted inclusively (i.e., with both ends of the series being counted)" (ibid., 417, n.34). There were, in the ancient world, several calendars used by various civil and religious groups.

19. On Jesus' birth during the latter time of King Herod: Mt 2,1 and 1,5.

19. On Nazareth, see the entry under that place in Freedman, ed., *The Anchor Bible Dictionary*, vol. 4, 1050–51; Fiensy, *The Social History of Palestine in the Herodian Period;* Malina, *The New Testament World;* Matthews, *Manners and Customs in the Bible;* and Meyers and Strange, *Archaeology, the Rabbis, and Early Christianity.* Strange, in *The Anchor Bible Dictionary*, estimates the population of Nazareth as 480 at the time of Jesus; Meier, vol. 1, 277, gives the number as 1,600–2,000.

19. On betrothal and marriage in ancient Judaism, see, e.g., Joachim Jeremias, *Jerusalem in the Time of Jesus*, translated by F. H. and C. H. Cave (London: SCM Press, 1969), 364–69.

20. The sketchy tradition about Mary's parents, supposedly a couple named Joachim and Anna, derive from the second-century apocryphal *Protevangelium of James*, rightly characterized by Meier as "a hilarious mishmash of the infancy stories of Matthew and Luke, with a heavy dose of novelistic folklore [and no] knowledge

about the historical Jesus" (*A Marginal Jew*, vol. 1, 115). The *Protevangelium* has absolutely no historical value.

21. Hannah, long infertile, finally gives birth to Samuel and dedicates him to God's service. The parallels to the birth of John the Baptist, also a forerunner of Jesus, are typically Lukan. He has also taken an early Christian hymn (thus Brown, *The Birth of the Messiah*, 334–38, 355–64) and placed it on Mary's lips (the so-called *Magnificat*, 1,46–55): it is largely based on Hannah's hymn (1 Sm 2,1–10). The New Testament is silent on the genealogy of Mary.

21. On the genealogies, see Meier, *A Marginal Jew*, vol. 1 217, 238; Brown, *The Birth of the Messiah;* Jones, *New Testament Illustrations*, 171.

21. The problem of genealogy raises, of course, the larger question of historicity, and in this regard one must point to the profoundly dissatisfying work of John Dominic Crossan as well as the framers of the so-called Jesus Seminar. Crossan, for example, presents a politically correct revolutionary, and to make his points he prefers any of the apocrypha to the Gospels. Luke Timothy Johnson, who has offered a properly scathing critique of this kind of methodology, summarizes the problem: "The criteria that matter for determining authenticity [for Crossan] are those that make up the predetermined portrait that Crossan wishes to emerge. His use of cross-cultural patterns reduces Jesus to a stereotyped cultural category, that of a member of 'peasant culture.' Into this *historical cipher* [Johnson's italics] Crossan can pour his own vision of what 'Christianity' ought to be: not a church with leaders and cults and creeds, but a loose association of Cynic philosophers who broker their own access to the kingdom of self-esteem and mutual acceptance" (Luke Timothy Johnson, *The Real Jesus*, 50).

21. *the Messiah, the son of David*   Mt 1,1.

21. On the background to Luke, see I Sm 1–2.

21 ff. On the genealogies: the notion that Mary was the source of the material in the Lukan infancy narrative will not hold water: there are too many errors of fact in Luke 1–2—errors regarding specifics of Jewish life and cult that Mary never would have made. As Meier concludes, "Either Mary was not the source of this story . . . or else she had a remarkably poor memory about important events regarding Jesus and herself. Either way, the case for the historical reliability of the Infancy Narratives is not enhanced" (*A Marginal Jew*, vol. 1, 210).

21. *son of God*   Lk 3,23–38.

22. *the child conceived*   Mt 1,20.

22. Regarding the term "Holy Spirit," Brown is succinct: this phrase should not lead us to assume that there is here a developed Trinitarian theology. "Perhaps the broader category of divine agent best covers the evaluation of the Spirit throughout most of NT Christian thought . . . Behind such a conception would be the images of the spirit as the God-given life breath, as the force by which God moved the prophets to speak, and as the animating principle of Jesus' ministry which de-

scended upon him at the baptism and was communicated by him to his followers after the resurrection" (*The Birth of the Messiah,* 125).

22. *but had no marital relations*   Mt 1,25.

23. *You will conceive*   Lk 1,31–35.

23. Regarding Gabriel in Luke, see Brown, *Responses to 101 Questions,* 83: "Since Gabriel is the revealing angel in the [Old Testament] Book of Daniel who explains the great vision of the end times, his presence in Luke's infancy narrative is a signal that what Daniel had prophesied is now coming true—the end time is at hand in the conception and birth of Jesus." Although Brown invariably interprets angels as equivalent to a pictorial representation of divine revelation itself, he (to me, surprisingly) admits to a personal belief in them as distinct spiritual beings. I do not share this viewpoint.

24. *Nothing shall be impossible*   Lk 1,37.

24. Brown, *The Birth of the Messiah,* 270–71, has elaborated the parallels between Gabriel to Zechariah in Luke and Gabriel in Dn 9–10.

24. *Is anything too wonderful*   Gn 18,14.

25. *tested as we are*   Heb 45,15.

26 ff. On the problems and possibilities of comparing ancient nonbiblical birth stories to the infancy narratives, see Meier, *A Marginal Jew,* vol. 1, 243, n. 68; Brown, *The Virginal Conception and Bodily Resurrection of Jesus,* 62, 66–67; and Brown, *The Birth of the Messiah,* 523, n.13.

26 ff. On the problem of requiring faith in the virginal conception, see O. Knoch, "Die Botschaft des Matthäusevangeliums über Empfängnis und Geburt Jesu vor dem Hintergrund der Christusverkündigung des Neues Testaments," *Zum Thema Jungfrauengeburt,* 37–59, esp. 57–58: cf. Joseph A. Fitzmyer, "The Virginal Conception of Jesus in the New Testament," *Theological Studies* 34 (1973), 548.

27. *Child, why have you*   Lk 2,48.

27. *to restrain him*   Mk 3,21 and Jn 7,5.

28. *Where did this man*   Mt 13,54–56.

28. *his parents*   Lk 2,27,41.

28. In support of the theological focus of the teaching on the virginity of Mary (rather than on biology), see the instruction of the Congregation for the Doctrine of the Faith, dated July 27, 1960, cited in McBrien, ed., *Encyclopedia of Catholicism,* 1314–15.

30. *According to the faith of the Church*   Ratzinger, *Introduction to Christianity,* 208.

31. *A virgin shall conceive*   Is 7,14.

31. On *'alma, parthenos* and the Isaian/Matthean texts, see Is 7,14 and Mt 1,23: cf. Meier, *A Marginal Jew,* vol. 1, 222, and Brown, *The Birth of the Messiah,* 148 and 524.

32. *Here am I*   Lk 1,37.

32. *Look, your mother*   Mk 3,32 and Mt 12,47.

32. On, e.g., James as "the brother of Jesus," see Gal 1,19; and Josephus, *Antiquities of the Jews,* 20.9.1, §200. See Meier, *A Marginal Jew,* vol. 1, 327.

32. A number of Roman Catholic scholars consider the brothers and sisters of Jesus to have been true siblings: see, e.g., Pesch, *Das Markusevangelium,* vol. 1, 322–25, and Knoch, *art. cit.*

32. *No linguistic evidence*   Jerome Neyrey, in the entry "Brothers of Jesus," in McBrien, ed., *Encyclopedia,* 198–99.

33. *One may ask*   John McKenzie, "The Mother of Jesus in the New Testament," *Concilium* 168 (1983), 7.

33. On the replacement of martyrdom with chastity, see Brown, *The Birth of the Messiah,* 304, n. 23. He also mentions a Coptic text of the early-fourth-century Church in which the example of Mary was set before chaste Egyptian women.

34. *the Books of Scripture   Instruction Concerning the Historical Truth of the Gospels,* 1964; translated with commentary by Joseph A. Fitzmyer, S. J., in *Theological Studies* 25 (1964) 386–408. See also *Catholic Biblical Quarterly* 26 (July 1964) 305–12; and *The Tablet* (London) 218 (30 May 1964) 617–19.

34 ff. See also Pannenberg, *Jesus—God and Man,* 149.

CHAPTER 3

37. *Early in the year 28*   Luke (3,1) places the critical time of John the Baptist's ministry as "in the fifteenth year of the reign of Emperor Tiberius," who was acknowledged to rule Rome from August 19 in the year 14. Luke, it seems, used the Julian calendar for reckoning, and considered the first "year" ended on December 31, 14. Hence the fifteenth year of his reign would have run from January 1 to December 31, 28. See Meier, *A Marginal Jew,* vol. 1, 385–86 and 419, n.55.

The gospel bearing the name of John (the disciple, not the Baptist) represents a highly developed late-first-century Christology, and an important part of this includes what most scholars consider a kind of anti-Baptistine motif. This attempt, which derives from the need to counter the proponents of John the Baptist who did not accept Jesus, is reflected in the verses of the Gospel according to John that underscore the Baptist's subordination to Jesus: 1,8, 15, 19–22, 24–25, 30; 4,1. Throughout my remarks on the relationship between John the Baptist on Jesus, my debt is very evident indeed to Jerome Murphy-O'Connor, "John the Baptist and Jesus: History and Hypotheses," *New Testament Studies* 36 (1990) 359–74; and Meier, *A Marginal Jew,* vol. 2, esp. 110–29.

37. *Repent*   Mt 3,2.

37. The people of Jerusalem: Mt 3,5–6.

38. That the Baptist's parents were old: Lk 1,7. The Greek is quite specific: Elizabeth was *steira* (i.e., sterile, barren), and both she and her husband were *probebēkotes 'en tais 'ēmerais 'autōn* (advanced in their days).

38. On the Baptist's food and clothing, see Mt 3,4; on his garb, see Mk 1,6; on Elijah's costume, see 2 Kgs 1,8.

38. Barbara Thiering's hypothesis—that the Dead Sea Scrolls refer obliquely to John the Baptist and to Jesus, and so they must have resided with the Essenes at Qumran—must be rejected, for almost everything in the Scrolls is from the centuries before Christ. See Fitzmyer, *Responses to 101 Questions.*

38. *You brood of vipers*   Mt 3,7 and Lk 3,7.

38. *Prove your repentance*   Lk 3,7.

38. *repentance*   The Greek word is *metanoia,* "change of mind" or "change of heart."

39. *Even now the ax*   Mt 3,10; Lk 3,9.

39. *The one who is more powerful*   Mk 1,7–8; Mt 3,11; Lk 3,16.

39. *a good man*   Josephus, *Antiquities of the Jews,* 18.5.2, §116 ff. The complete works of Josephus are published in ten volumes in the Loeb Classical Library edition, translated by Henry St. J. Thackeray (Cambridge: Harvard University Press, 1978).

39. *I will sprinkle*   Ez 36,25–26.

41. *merrymakers . . . I sat alone*   Jer 15,17.

41. *I am with you*   Jer 1,8 and 3,11.

41 ff. For further reading on Judaism in the time of Jesus, see, e.g., Senior, *Jesus: A Gospel Portrait,* 39–45; Rousseau and Arav, *Jesus and His World;* and Witherington, *The Jesus Quest.*

43. *Whoever has two coats*   Lk 3,10. Only Luke records the specifically social nature of the Baptist's proclamation. Since the theme of radical poverty and communal sharing is consistent throughout Luke/Acts, some scholars consider this a redactional element—and therefore not traceable directly to John the Baptist himself. Although Mark and Matthew are quite clear that the Baptist charges people with sin, these two evangelists are less clear on the precise nature of the proclamation. But the Baptist had to hold *something* as sinful, and the tradition that Luke received—especially in light of the Baptist's own history—rightly specifies the lack of social justice. This of course also makes the Baptist's proclamation consistent with (later) that of Jesus.

43. *What should we do*   Lk 3,12–13.

43 ff. On the social radicalism of John the Baptist, see F. Herrenbrück, "Wer waren die 'Zöllner'?," *Zeitschrift für die neutestamentliche Wissenschaft* 72: 178–94; P. Hollenbach, "Social Aspects of John the Baptizer's Preaching Mission in the Context of Palestinian Judaism," in *Aufstieg und Niedergang der römischen Welt,* (edited by H. Temporini and W. Haase), 2/19/2: 850–75; and D. Oakman, *Jesus and the Economic Questions of His Day* (Lewiston: 1986).

44. *All regarded John*   Mk 11,32.

44. *Do not extort money*   Lk 3,13.

44. *Be satisfied*   Lk 3,14.

45. *I did not know*   Jn 1,33. In conflict with the surviving partisans of John the Baptist at the end of the first century (see note above on the anti-Baptistine motif in John), the fourth evangelist omits the baptism of Jesus altogether—although the Baptist strongly asserts Jesus' superiority to himself and on his lips is a report of a marvelous theophany or appearance of God—for the benefit of the (inferior) Baptist; see Jn 1, 29–34. Even John, then, records the spiritual importance of the baptism of Jesus.

46. The final version of the event in Mt 3,14–15 adds an exchange between Jesus and John that, consistent with the faith of the late-first-century church, established the superiority of Jesus and subordination of John. This is certainly an editorial contribution that reveals the significance of the moment for faith, not an actual conversation that occurred, for otherwise Jesus' baptism was simply an empty ceremony he underwent for the edification of people whose estimation of Jesus (as the rest of the gospel indicates) remained completely unenlightened and unchanged! The "fulfilling of righteousness" mentioned by Matthew is, on the other hand, compatible with the ethical theme of justice that runs through the first gospel (see also Mt 5,6, 10).

46. Only later, in light of the Resurrection of Jesus, was it clear to believers that the one for whom John the Baptist was preparing was indeed Jesus of Nazareth.

46. *And just as Jesus*   Mk 1,10–11; see also Mt 3,16–17 and Lk 3,21–22 (although Luke does not specify that John did the baptizing, nor could his account taken alone deny that it was a disciple of John who performed the ritual for Jesus).

46. *O, that you would*   Is 64,1.

46. *You are my Son*   Ps 2,7.

46. *[the] chosen*   Is 42,1.

46. Scholars debate whether the Aramaic fragments of a work called the *Testament of Levi* contain mysterious parallels or foreshadowings of the baptism of Jesus or, more reasonably, whether in fact they demonstrate late Christian editorial influence on the *Testament* in light of the gospel event of the baptism. "The heavens will be

opened. From the temple of God's glory there will come upon him holiness through a father's voice, as from Abraham to Isaac. And his glory will be pronounced upon him. The spirit of wisdom and knowledge will rest upon him in the water"— *Testament of Levi* 18: 5–9 in Stone, *The Testament of Levi,* 125. See also the critical assessment in Collins, *The Scepter and the Star,* 92.

47. On the dove as an affectionate name for Israel, see Ps 74,19 and Song of Solomon 2,14; 5,2 and 6,9.

47. *more than a prophet*   Mt 11,9 and Lk 7,26.

47. On John's disciples Andrew, Peter and Philip joining Jesus, see Jn 1,35–43.

47. *The one who was with you*   Jn 3,26; see also Jn 4,1: some of the Jews hear that "Jesus is making and baptizing more disciples than John." In Jn 4,2, the final editor of John backtracks: "it was not Jesus himself but his disciples who baptized." This is the redactor's attempt to distance the work of Jesus from that of the Baptist; it also, of course, alluded to the life of the readers of John, who were baptized in the late first century not by Jesus himself but by his disciples.

48. Mt 28,19, if read literally, suggests that the Risen Jesus himself verbally commissioned disciples to baptize "all nations . . . in the name of the Father and of the Son and of the Holy Spirit," but it is the *Risen Jesus* who speaks through his hidden, mysterious life in the community. As Brown has pointed out (*Responses to 101 Questions on the Bible,* 108): "If that statement were made immediately after the resurrection in precisely those words, the Book of Acts would become almost unintelligible, for then there would be no reason why Jesus' followers should have had any doubt that he wanted disciples made among the Gentiles. Nevertheless, the debate over the acceptance of the Gentiles went on for the first twenty years of Christianity. Similarly if, as suggested by the Matthean text, such a developed baptismal form . . . was known from the immediate days after the resurrection, the common expression that we find elsewhere in the New Testament of baptizing in the name of Jesus becomes very hard to understand."

52. *There are also many other*   Jn 21,25.

54. *increased in wisdom*   Lk 2,52.

55. The prohibition against marrying a brother's ex-wife is found in Lev 20,21: "If a man takes his brother's wife, it is impurity."

55 ff. The arrest and execution of John the Baptist presents numerous problems if we are to take the New Testament episode (Mk 6,17–29 and Mt 14,3–12) as a literal historical account in every detail. Meier (*A Marginal Jew,* vol. 2, 171–76) has persuasively argued that Mark errs on several important matters of fact, and this throws into question the reliability of this particular chronicle by Mark. Antipas's second wife, Herodias, for example, had not been married to Herod Philip (thus Mk 6, 17), but to another half brother of Antipas. Also militating against Mark's historicity—and of considerably greater interest—are the Old Testament antecedents for the arrest and death of the Baptist (the prophet Elijah's conflict

with King Ahab and the wicked queen Jezebel [in 1 Kings 19 and 21], and the folklore and legends found in Esther and Judith). Among others, Meier has made a convincing case that—apart from the core fact that John was indeed executed on Antipas's orders—the other details in Mark and Matthew (omitted entirely by Luke) provide a religious excursus, not videotape reportage. This religious meditation includes the Markan details popularized by Oscar Wilde's play and Richard Strauss's opera—e.g., Herodias and her daughter conspire to have John's head on a plate, despite the hesitation of the weak Herod who feared going back on his word to gratify any caprice of his stepdaughter, the sultry dancing girl (unnamed in the Gospels, but identified by Josephus—though not as a type of Mata Hari—as Salome).

55. *Because the crowds*   Josephus, *Antiquities of the Jews,* 18,5.1–2, §116–119, documents Antipas's fear and subsequent execution of John.

56. *When Jesus heard*   Mt 4,12–13.

56. *The time is fulfilled*   Mk 1,15. Earlier, Mt 3,2 had put the same proclamation on the lips of John the Baptist, but this is not found elsewhere in the Gospels: Matthew has harmonized the message of the Baptist with that of Jesus to fit his pattern of making them parallel figures. Also, Mt 1–2 have already proclaimed the arrival of the kingdom in the marvelous birth of the Messiah Jesus.

57. On the comparison of Jesus with John the Baptist, see, e.g., Jeremias, *New Testament Theology,* vol. 1, 48–49.

57. *God rules*   Guardini, *The Lord,* 37–38.

58. *How is this possible:*   Guardini, 39.

58. *Why do we and the Pharisees*   Mt 9,14–15.

58. *a marginal Jew*   This is the title of John P. Meier's study of Jesus, already cited.

58. On John the Baptist and the spirit of late Judaism, and on the kingdom of God, see Guardini, *The Lord,* 475 and 37–39; on the different message of Jesus, the literature is (of course) vast. A terse reflection, emblematic of the best sort of scholarship made comprehensible, is offered by Dennis Hamm, "The New Age, 2,000 Years Old," *America,* 18 January 1997.

58. *a friend of*   Mt 11,19.

CHAPTER 4

59. Apart from the New Testament, there are very few substantial allusions to Jesus in ancient literature or history, which is not at all remarkable, for he was (thus Meier, *A Marginal Jew,* vol. 1, 56) "a marginal Jew leading a marginal movement in a marginal province of a vast Roman Empire," and there was, it seemed, nothing astonishing about him until after his death and the subsequent claims made for him by his followers. On the few, almost parenthetical nonbiblical ref-

erences—in Josephus, Suetonius, Pliny and Tacitus—see Johnson, *The Real Jesus,* 113–16; Meier, *A Marginal Jew,* vol. 1, 56–69 and 89–92; and Senior, *Jesus,* 11–13.

59. On the difficulty of reconstructing any kind of life of other great religious figures, see, e.g., Küng, *On Being a Christian,* 146–53.

59. The oldest New Testament fragment contains portions of the words of Jn 18, 31–33 and 37–38. Dating from about 150 (a generation after the author), it was found in Egypt in 1920 and is now in the John Rylands Library at Manchester, England. The fragment has writing on both sides—hence it was not part of a scroll but of a codex, what we now call book form. The so-called Codex Sinaiticus, at the British Museum, was found in a monastery on Mount Sinai and brought to England in 1933. Written in the fourth century on vellum, it contains all of the New Testament, some of the Old Testament and two other early, nonbiblical Christian writings. The Codex Alexandrinus, also at the British Museum, contains almost the entire Bible; it dates from the first half of the fifth century.

61. The Roman Catholic Church, which does not recognize fashionable intellectual fads and is slow to endorse any theory or theology, has long since admitted what is now taken for granted in biblical studies: namely, that there were three stages of development that culminated in the written Gospels. In 1964, the Pontifical Biblical Commission, as was seen in Chapter 2, above, issued an Instruction on the Historical Truth of the Gospels, the full text of which may be read with a readable commentary in, e.g., *Theological Studies* 25 (1964) 386–408.

61. On the Gospels that were not included with the four—the so-called apocryphal Gospels—see Brown, *Responses to 101 Questions,* 18–19. Justin Martyr (who died in 165) was the first to use the word "gospels" in the plural, thus shifting the meaning from a proclamation to a connotation of written accounts of that proclamation. See Lienhard, *The Bible, the Church, and Authority,* 33.

61. By the end of the second century, Christian communities had agreed that the Gospels that traced their origins to communities represented by men named Matthew, Mark, Luke and John represented the apostolic faith; the final, twenty-seven-book New Testament was not fixed until about A.D. 400.

61. *proclaim Jesus as*   Senior, *Jesus,* 118.

62. *The substance*   Pope John XXIII, on the occasion of opening the Second Vatican Council, 1962.

62 ff. On the nonliteral nature of the Gospels: "The truth of the story is not at all affected by the fact that the evangelists relate the words and deeds of the Lord in a different order, and express his sayings not literally but differently." (*Instruction of the Pontifical Biblical Commission on the Historical Truth of the Gospels* [1964], Section IX.)

63. On the development of doctrine, see the instruction *Mysterium Fidei,* issued by the Congregation for the Doctrine of the Faith, 24 June 1973.

64. On ancient storytelling and biography, see Dennis O'Brien, "The Silence of the Gospels and The Silence of Our Lives," *America,* 28 October 1995.

67. *They went back*   Lk 2,39, 52.

67. On Jewish life in the time of Jesus, see Henri Daniel-Rops, *Daily Life in Palestine,* 430–35; William Foxwell Albright, *The Archaeology of Palestine* (Harmondsworth, England: Penguin Books, 1949), 214–15; Daniel J. Harrington, S. J., "The Jewishness of Jesus: Facing Some Problems," *Catholic Biblical Quarterly* 49 (1987) 1–13; and Paul Hanley Furfey, "Christ as *Tekton,*" *Catholic Biblical Quarterly* 17 (1955) 204–15.

68. *Hear, O Israel*   Deut 6,4–5.

68. *on the Sabbath day*   Lk 4,16

68. On going to Jerusalem at Passover, see Jeremias, *Jerusalem in the Time of Jesus,* 76.

68. *When the festival was ended*   Lk 2,43 ff.

69. On the finding in the temple: the case against seeing this as a parable of the resurrection is the fact, often indicated by scholars, that the phrase "after three days" appears nowhere else in Luke. But the *hapax*—the only use of a word or phrase, in this case with a specific connotation—does not necessarily rule out its presence here.

70. On the language Jesus spoke: The bystanders at Peter's denial of Jesus note the difference between Galilean Aramaic and that spoken in Judea: "Certainly you are also one of them [i.e., the followers of Jesus of Galilee], for your accent betrays you" (Mt 26,73).

71. *to put together*   Harrington, *art. cit.,* 8.

71. *The child grew*   Lk 2,40, 52; Heb 2,17 and 4,15.

71. On the caution that must be exercised in discussing the specifics of Jesus' development, see Meier, *A Marginal Jew,* vol. 1 254 ff.

71. *If Jesus' knowledge*   Brown, *An Introduction,* 73.

73. *He who does not*   Cited in Jeremias, *Jerusalem in the Time of Jesus,* 3.

73. On the trade of Jesus and his father, Meier, *A Marginal Jew,* vol. 1, is very good; see esp. 279–83, 317 and 352 n.6.

73. The assertion of Jn 19,27 that Mary went to live with one of Jesus' disciples after Good Friday also strongly implies her widowhood, although it is not entirely impossible that she could have been abandoned by her husband's desertion rather than by his death. But in a civilization that placed so high a value on family honor,

it would have been odd for this family scandal not to have been intimated in the Gospels or, more to the point, brought into the open by the enemies of Jesus.

CHAPTER 5

76. On the likely chronology for the life and death of Jesus, see esp. Meier, *A Marginal Jew,* vol. 1, 372–409.

76. *In the morning*   Mk 1,35 and 6,46.

78. *Then Jesus was led*   Mt 4,1–11; see also Lk 4,1–13.

These come from the so-called "Q" collection, a tradition of sayings of Jesus that circulated orally, and which were known separately by both Matthew and Luke. The existence of the hypothetical "Q" is axiomatic among serious New Testament scholars. The Markan account is far more laconic: "The Spirit immediately drove him out into the wilderness. He was in the wilderness forty days, tempted by Satan; and he was with the wild beasts; and the angels waited on him" (1,12–13). On the temptation narrative, see esp. Jacques Dupont, "L'arrière-fond Biblique du Récit des Tentations de Jésus," *New Testament Studies* 3 (1956–57) 287–304.

79. *the devil departed*   Lk 4,13.

79. *You are those*   Lk 22,28.

80. *All authority*   Mt 28,18.

81. *Get behind me*   Mt 16,23.

82. *to restrain him*   Mk 3,21.

82. *not even his brothers*   Jn 7,5.

82. *Who are my mother*   Mt 3,33–35.

82. *Prophets are not without*   Mk 6,4–6; see also Mt 13,53–58.

82 ff. On the execution of John the Baptist, see Josephus, *Antiquities of the Jews,* 18.5.2, §§116–119. The Markan account of Salome, the dance, Herodias's idea, etc. (on which Matthew also draws), is most likely based on legend and folklore. On this, see Meier, *A Marginal Jew,* vol. 2.

84. *Get away from here*   Lk 13,31.

84. *Why does your teacher*   Mt 9,11 ff.

85. *Look, a glutton*   Mt 11,19 and Lk 5,34.

85. On women in Judaism, see Jeremias, *Jerusalem in the Time of Jesus,* 360–61, 374–76.

86. On women as deacons and elders (presbyters), see Brown, *The Critical Meaning of the Bible,* 141–42.

87. *She had been suffering*   Lk 8,48.

87. On Junias, see Rom 6,7.

88. *Follow me*   Mk 1,16 and Mt 4,19.

88. *the fish of the sea*   Hb 1,14.

88. *I am now sending*   Jer 16,16. On the transformation in the lives of the first disciples of Jesus, see the thoughtful meditation by Dennis Hamm, "The New Age, 2,000 Years Old," *America,* 18 January 1997.

88. The word "apostle" (from the Greek meaning "sent out") is generally mis-understood to identify the twelve, with the rest being disciples. But this is not what the New Testament says. "Apostle" was a title given only after the Resurrection of Jesus, when those who believed in him were definitively sent out on a mission. As such, it refers (seventy-four times in the New Testament outside the Gospels) to a much broader group of people than the twelve, or even than the disciples who knew Jesus personally during his life in the flesh. When the word "apostle" is used, very rarely, to refer to the twelve in the Gospels (never by John, only once in Matthew, twice in Mark and six times in Luke), it is by analogy with the larger group of the post-Resurrection community. On this, see J. Dupont, in *L'Orient Syrien* 1 (1956) 267–90, 425–44. There is no question that the twelve had a place of honor before and after the death of Jesus, and that when Judas was replaced by Matthias immediately after the Resurrection, there was no attempt to replace any other of the twelve when they died.

89. For Peter as rock and stumbling block, see Mt 16,18 and 23.

89. *the hot-head brothers*   Mk 3,17. The Aramaic is *Boanerges,* i.e., "sons of thunder" or "sons of rage."

89. On the difficulty of identifying or describing the twelve, see Raymond E. Brown, "Aspects of New Testament Thought," in Brown et al., *The New Jerome Biblical Commentary,* 1379.

90. *Judas Iscariot*   Lk 6,16; see also Mt 10,4 and Mk 3,19.

90. *Whoever welcomes one such*   Mk 9,37.

90. *with such authority*   e.g., Mk 1,22; Mt 7,28; Lk 4,31.

91. *Whoever does not receive*   Mk 10,14.

91. *to the lost sheep*   Mt 10,5.

91. *I am sending you*   Mt 10,16.

92. *What are you arguing about*   Mk 9,33.

92. The citations are from Mt 9,36; 14,14; 15,32 and 20,34. There are parallels in Mk 6,34 and 8,2; and the concept appears again in Lk 7,13 and 15,20.

CHAPTER 6

93 ff. On the synagogue, see Meier, vol. 1, 308.

93. *Hear, O Israel*   Dt 6,4–9 is called the *Shema,* named after the first Hebrew word of those verses ("Hear").

94. *The Spirit of the Lord*   Cited in Lk 4,18 ff. Scripture scholarship has demonstrated that this Lukan account of Jesus reading from Isaiah is clearly the evangelist's religious rendering of the tradition. The Isaian text, for example, is composed of portions of verse 1 of chapter 61, part of verse 6 of chapter 58, and then part of verse 2 of chapter 61—and Luke presents the Greek text of the prophet, not a literal rendering of the Hebrew original. There are other difficulties if one insists that the Lukan account is historical in every detail rather than important as an expression of faith in what Jesus did in his capacity as a synagogue worshiper. On this matter, see, e.g., Meier, vol. 1, 303, and R. Alan Culpepper in *The New Interpreter's Bible,* vol. 9 (Nashville: Abingdon Press, 1995), 104 ff.

94. *Today, this scripture*   Lk 4,21.

96. That the imposition of hands was unknown in Old Testament times and in rabbinic literature has been established by Fitzmyer, *The Gospel According to Luke* 553.

97. On the healing touch of Jesus, see Guardini, 48.

97. *If you choose*   The account of the curing of the leper is found in Mk 1,40–45; Mt 8,1–4 and Lk 5,12–16.

97. *Your sins are forgiven*   Mk 2,5; see also Mt 9,2 and Lk 5,20.

97. On the limitations of Jesus' human knowledge, see Brown, *An Introduction to New Testament Christology,* 31–59.

98. On the Pharisees, see Bowker, *Jesus and the Pharisees;* Neusner, *From Politics to Piety;* Rivkin, *A Hidden Revolution;* and the standard Biblical dictionaries: Kee, 419; McKenzie, 668–69; Anthony J. Saldarini, "Pharisees," in Achtemeier, 782–83.

98. *Why does this fellow*   Mk 2,7.

98 ff. The Matthean version of the healing of the paralytic sharpens this idea that Christian forgiveness continues and makes real, after the Resurrection of Jesus, the meaning of the healings he performed during his ministry: the bystanders, writes Matthew, praise God "who had given such authority *to men*"—i.e., to those after Jesus who offer forgiveness in his name.

99. *no secular everyday work*   Meier, *A Marginal Jew,* vol. 2 682–83.

99. *Come forward*   Mk 3,3; see also Mt 12,9–14 and Lk 6,6–11.

99. *Look . . . why are they*   Mk 2,23–28; see also Mt 12,1–8 and Lk 6,1–5.

100 ff. The account of the healing of the man born blind, one of the richest and most highly artistic episodes in the Gospels, occupies the entire ninth chapter of John.

100. *from the dust of the earth*   Gn 2,7.

103. *Ephphatha*   Mk 7,34.

103. *Then the eyes of the blind*   Is 35,5–6.

CHAPTER 7

106. The raising of Jairus's daughter and the healing of the hemorrhaging woman are found in Mk 5,21–43; Mt 9,18–26; and Lk 8,40–56.

107. On the New Testament words *dynameis* (manifestations or deeds of power); *semeia* (signs); *erga* (works), see, e.g., the entries under those words in Balz and Schneider.

107 ff. The literature on miracles is, as one might expect, enormous. Among the most helpful and comprehensible of available materials that provide a solid introduction: Brown, *An Introduction to New Testament Christology,* 63–65; Fuller, *Interpreting the Miracles;* Charles C. Hefling, Jr., "miracle," in Joseph A. Komonchak et al., *The New Dictionary of Theology;* John Paul Heil, "miracles," in Achtemeier, ed., *Harper's Bible Dictionary,* 639–41; Howard Clark Kee, "miracles," in Metzger and Coogan, eds., *The Oxford Companion to the Bible,* 519–520; René Latourelle, "miracle," in Latourelle and Fisichella, *Dictionary of Fundamental Theology,* 690–709; John L. McKenzie, "miracle," in his *Dictionary of the Bible,* 578–80; J. B. Metz and Louis Monden (respectively), "miracle" and "miracles of Jesus," in Rahner, ed., *Encyclopedia of Theology,* 962–67; Donald Senior, "The Miracles of Jesus," in Brown et al., *The New Jerome Biblical Commentary,* 1369–1373 and his bibliography on 1369; Gregory E. Sterling and Michael L. Cook, "miracles," in McBrien, *HarperCollins Encyclopedia of Catholicism,* 867–69; Theissen, *Miracle Stories.* In addition, the best commentaries on each Gospel (by, e.g., Brown, Fitzmyer, Jeremias, Schnackenburg, Schweizer, et al.) provide substantial references in periodical literature.

108. The citation from Bernanos is from his play and his libretto for Francis Poulenc's opera *Dialogues des Carmélites* (Milan: Ricordi, 1957), 29.

111. *a man whom God sent*   Acts 2,22.

111. On the differences between Jesus' miracles and those of the pagans, see, e.g., Louis Monden, in Rahner, ed., *Encyclopedia of Theology,* 967.

113. *You divided*   Pss 74,13 and 89,9; also Pss 65,7 and 89,9.

113. *Peace! Be still!*   See Mk 4,35–41; Mt 8,23–27; Lk 8,22–25.

113. *Take heart*   Mk 6,50.

113. On the nature miracles, see, e.g., Meier, *A Marginal Jew,* 905–33.

113. *There was, in their synagogue*   Mk 1,23–26; see also Lk 4,33–37.

114. *Fundamentalists tend to forget*   McBrien, *Catholicism,* 341.

117. The account of the son of the widow of Nain is found in Luke 7,11–17.

117. The raising of Lazarus is recounted in John 11.

118. For a scholarly treatment of the Gospel miracles, see Meier, *A Marginal Jew,* vol. 2, 509–874. His meticulous erudition withstands the most intense scrutiny.

123 ff. On the functional integrity of nature, see a number of recent articles in the popular press—e.g., Margaret Wertheim, "God Is Also a Cosmologist," *The New York Times,* 8 June 1997.

127. *God manifests*   Maurice Blondel, "La notion et le rôle du miracle," *Annales de philosophie chrétienne,* July 1907.

CHAPTER 8

128 ff. The parable of the Good Samaritan is found in Lk 10,25–37. On the background to it, see two books by Joachim Jeremias: *The Parables of Jesus,* 202 ff.; and, more popularly, *Rediscovering the Parables,* 159–61.

131. *Forgive us our sins*   Mt 6,11; Lk 11,4.

131. *If you forgive*   Mt 6,14.

131. *Not seven times*   Mt 18,22.

131. The parable of the weeds is found in Mt 13,24–30.

132. *a God merciful*   Ex 34,6.

133. The parable of the Prodigal Son is found in Lk 15,11–32. See Jeremias, *Rediscovering,* 101–5.

133. *Cursed be the man*   Cited in Jeremias, *Rediscovering,* 102, n.1.

133. *a most unusual and undignified*   Ibid., 102.

135. *He is the good God*   Küng, *On Being a Christian,* 213 and 313.

137. *tie up heavy burdens*   Mt 23,4.

137. *Come to me*   Mt 11,28.

138. The parables of the lost sheep and the lost coin are found in Lk 15,1–10.

138. On Jesus and the stringent laws, see Freyne, *Galilee from Alexander the Great,* 155–207.

139. Matthew, who sees Jesus as both the new Moses and the corporate representative of a new Israel, appropriately gathers many sayings of Jesus into what is called a Sermon on the Mount (Mt 5,1 ff.), which is not so situated in the Lukan parallel (Lk 6.20 ff).

139. *My thoughts are not* 　　Is 55,8.

139. The Beatitudes are found in Mt 5,3–12; the Lukan version is in Lk 6,20–23. Among the best commentaries are Guelich, *The Sermon on the Mount;* Hamm, *The Beatitudes in Context;* and Metz, *Poverty of Spirit.*

142 ff. On these verses of the Sermon on the Mount, see Guardini, *The Lord,* 71–75, and Dennis Hamm in *America,* 20 September 1997.

142. *You have heard* 　　Mt 5,38–42, 44,29–30.

142. *Above all, clothe yourselves* 　　Colossians 3,14.

CHAPTER 9

145. *Uncertainty about* 　　Brown, *Critical Meaning,* 91.

147. *This is my commandment* 　　Jn 15,12.

148. The social, humane and secular arguments (as distinct from the Christian religious arguments) against capital punishment are well articulated. See the vast literature compiled and published extensively by, for example, Amnesty International USA (322 Eighth Avenue, New York, NY 10001) and by the Death Penalty Information Center (1320 18th Street, N.W., Washington, DC 20036). An important recent text is Prejean, *Dead Man Walking.*

148. *A soldier who* 　　Hippolytus of Rome, *The Apostolic Tradition,* in Deiss, *Early Sources of the Liturgy,* 53.

148. *I have no pleasure* 　　Ezek. 33,11.

149. The prayer cited has been memorialized in Appleton, ed., *The Oxford Book of Prayer,* 112.

149. *What's a life or two* 　　Bruno Anthony (played by Robert Walker) to Guy Haines (portrayed by Farley Granger) in *Strangers on a Train;* screenplay credited to Raymond Chandler and Czenzi Ormonde, based on Patricia Highsmith's novel *Strangers on a Train;* directed by Alfred Hitchcock in 1950.

149. *We had to burn* 　　Infamously spoken by an American serviceman during the Vietnam War, defending his wasting a Vietnamese village and its citizens in order to save it and them from being taken over by Communists.

152. The sayings on divorce are found in Mk 10,11–12; Mt 5,31–32 and 19,9, and Lk 16,18. Matthew, written for a Jewish Christian community, adds the exceptive clause that divorce is forbidden except on the ground of *porneia.* The Greek word is often wrongly translated as "unchastity" or "adultery," but that is not its meaning. *Porneia* is a technical term used in the Greek Old Testament for an incestuous marriage, a union within the forbidden bonds of consanguinity. Such marriages, Matthew implies, *must* be broken when Jews become Christians.

152. On Jewish divorce customs, see Jeremias, *Jerusalem*, 359–61 and 374–76. The rabbinic tract he cites is *Pesiqta rabbati* 26, 129b. As for women in royal households, things were freer: Jeremias discusses several powerful women at court.

154. *It is not a writ*   Cited in Peter L'Huillier, "The Indissolubility of Marriage in Orthodox Law and Practice," *St. Vladimir's Theological Quarterly* 21 (1988) 199–221.

155. *If such is the case*   Mt 19,10.

156. On understanding the Sermon on the Mount with specific reference to divorce, see Theodore Stylianopoulos, "The Indissolubility of Marriage in the New Testament: Principle and Practice," *Greek Orthodox Theological Review* 34, no. 4 (1989) 335–45; also, "Divorce and Remarriage," *Theological Studies* 33 (March 1972).

156. *Man* should *not undo*   J. P. Jossua, O. P., "The Fidelity of Love and the Indissolubility of Christian Marriage," *Clergy Review* 56 (1971) 172–81.

157. On the shifts in perspective about marriage, see, e.g., Richard de Ranitz, O. P., "Should the Roman Church Recognize Divorce?" *Listening*, winter 1971, 60–70; and John D. Catoir, "When the Courts Don't Work," *America* 125 (1971), 254–257.

158. *to accept and forgive*   "Divorce and Remarriage," *art. cit.* in *Theological Studies.*

159. On the uncompromising tone of the Sermon on the Mount, see also Guardini, *The Lord*, 94–97 and 452–58.

159. *I am not called to be*   Mother Teresa of Calcutta, quoted in Dennis Hamm, "Who Loves First?" in *America*, 26 April 1997.

160. See Küng, *On Being a Christian*, 264–65.

CHAPTER 10

165. On the etymological study of the Greek words *pistis* (faith) and *pisteuein* (to believe) and their relationship to and difference from the Hebrew words and concepts about faith, see, e.g., Balz and Schneider, *Exegetical Dictionary*, vol. 3; Latourelle and Fisichella, *Dictionary of Fundamental Theology*, 309–15; McBrien, *Encyclopedia of Catholicism*, 510–15; McKenzie, *Dictionary of the Bible*, 267–71.

Two densely provocative studies on the nature of faith are Schillebeeckx, *The Language of Faith,* and Rahner, *Foundations of Christian Faith,* but the reader must be warned that these are not easy bedtime reading.

165. *What must we do*   Jn 6,29.

165. *If you have faith*   Mt 17,20.

165. *believe in the good news*   Mk 1,15.

166. *Your faith has saved you*   Lk 7,50.

166. *Relying on God*   C. S. Lewis, *Letters* (New York: Harcourt Brace Jovanovich, 1966).

166. *of things unseen*   Heb 11,1.

166. *Blessed are those*   Jn 20,29.

167. *Even the table*   Enid Bagnold, *The Chalk Garden,* revised acting edition (New York: Samuel French, 1956), 63.

167. *In You I put my trust*   Ps 143,8.

167. *Whoever does not receive*   Mk 10,15.

168. *I believe*   Mk 9,24.

169. On spiritual poverty, see Metz, *Poverty of Spirit,* esp. 27–30.

170. On the metaphors for faith, see Guardini, *The Lord,* 199–200.

170. On hope, Paul Tillich delivered a compelling sermon, "Waiting," which he included in the collection *The Shaking of the Foundations,* 149–152.

170. On faith, Küng is very good: *On Being a Christian,* 428–36.

171. *In the morning*   Mk 1,35; see also Lk 4,42.

171. *When Jesus heard*   Mt 14,13.

171. *The word about Jesus*   Lk 5,16.

171. *After saying farewell*   Mk 6,46; see also Mt 14,23.

171. *During those days*   Lk 6,12.

171. *Teach us how to pray*   Lk 11,1.

171. *Whenever you stand*   The earliest version of the Lord's Prayer seems to have been Mk 11,15; Lk 11,2–4 is a further development, and Mt 6,9–15 is the longest version and that which has survived as the settled form of the prayer in liturgy.

171. On the various versions and verses of the Lord's Prayer, see, e.g., the exquisite work by Oscar Cullmann, *Prayer in the New Testament,* esp. 37–69.

172. *Pray for those*   Mt 5,44–45.

173. On the proper understanding of the final petitions of the Lord's Prayer and their linguistic background, see Cullmann, *Prayer in the New Testament,* 62.

173. On *Marana, thà!,* see M.-E. Boismard in *Revue Biblique,* 2 (April 1956) 182–208.

173. On the *Didache,* see Deiss, *Early Sources,* 16.

175. *everything is finally*   Julian of Norwich, *Revelations of Divine Love,* 104.

175. *to pray always*   Lk 18.1.

175. *empty phrases and many words*   Mt 6,7.

175. *Whenever I am weak*   II Corinthians 12,10.

176. On surrender, see the eighteenth-century French spiritual classic by Jean-Pierre de Caussade, *Abandonment to Divine Providence.*

177. *Come now, turn aside*   Ward, trans., *The Prayers and Meditations of St. Anselm,* 239 (from the beginning of the "Proslogion").

177. *Go into your room*   Mt 6,6.

177. *Everything evil*   Guardini, *The Lord,* 506.

178. *If you think*   1 Cor 10,12.

179. *The pain of sin*   Julian of Norwich, *op cit.*

CHAPTER 11

182. *See that you say*   Mk 1,44; Matthew and Luke have, as often, followed him: Mt 8,4 and Lk 5,14.

182. *He strictly ordered them*   Mk 5,43; Lk 8,56; Mt 9,26, however, omits the prohibition and reports the result: "The report of this spread throughout all that district."

182. *You are the Christ*   Mk 8,29; see also Lk 9,20. Matthew, in light of Easter faith in the divinity of Jesus, adds "the Son of the living God"—a confession Peter certainly did not make during the ministry of Jesus but that makes logical the extraordinary praise of Peter by Jesus that immediately follows. For reasons that will be later discussed, no serious New Testament scholar would claim that an explicit acknowledgment of Jesus' divinity could be made during his lifetime.

182. On the Messianic secret, see, e.g., Vincent Taylor, *The Gospel According to St. Mark* (London: Macmillan, 1952), 122–25, and Georg Strecker, "The Passion and Resurrection Predictions in Mark's Gospel," *Interpretation* 22 (1968) 421–42. The literature on this is vast, and a bibliography may be found in any standard work of New Testament criticism or of individual Gospel commentary; see. e.g., *The New Jerome Biblical Commentary* and Fitzmyer, *The Gospel According to St. Luke.*

183. The passion predictions are found in three sections of the tradition: Mk 8,27–33, with its parallels in Mt 16,13–23 and Lk 9,18–22; Mk 9,30–32, with its parallels in Mt 17,22–23 and Lk 9,43–45; and Mk 10,32–34, with its parallels in Mt 20,17–19 and Lk 18,31–34.

183. *Get behind me, Satan*   Mk 8,33 and Mt 16,23.

183. *If any want*   Mk 8,34; Mt 16,24; Lk 9,23.

184. On the Markan concept of soteriology—that is, on Jesus' life, death and resurrection as the reality procuring salvation for the world—see, e.g., Taylor, *op cit.,* 124–25.

184. *began to plot*   Mk 3,6; Mt 12,14; Lk 6,11.

184. *Why are you*   Jn 7,19.

186. *Only if*   McKenzie, *Dictionary of the Bible,* 781.

187. *God so loved*   Jn 3,16; see also 1 Jn 3,16 and Rom 5,8.

187. *It is blasphemy*   Mk 2,7.

187. For the dating of the visit to Jerusalem and Jesus' subsequent death, see, e.g., Meier, *A Marginal Jew,* 372–433. And on the disparity between the Synoptics (who place the cleansing of the temple at the end of Jesus' life—hence the act that was the last straw in the anger of his enemies) and the Gospel of John (who places the cleansing at the start of the ministry), see Brown, *The Gospel According to John I–XII,* 117–18. His conclusion, shared by most New Testament scholars today, is that "it seems likely that Jesus' action of cleansing the temple precincts took place in the last days of his life."

187. Jerusalem had its own coinage: see Jeremias, who gives historic sources for this: *Jerusalem,* 33; on "those who bought and sold" indicating dealing in cattle, see ibid., 49.

188. On the cleansing of the temple, see, e.g., Senior, *Jesus,* 123; Joachim Jeremias links this to the larger theme of the passion predictions and the motif of the suffering servant in his *New Testament Theology,* 276–87.

188. *they looked for a way*   Mk 11,18; see also Lk 19,47.

188. On Judas' larcenous habits as the group's bursar, see Brown, who makes a good case for the historicity of the fourth Gospel as compared with the material in the Synoptics (*The Gospel According to John I–XII,* 453).

189. *What will you give me*   Mt 26,14; cp. Mk 14,10–11 and Lk 22,3–6.

189. According to Ex 21,32, a man must pay thirty pieces of silver if his ox kills a slave belonging to another man. See, e.g., Schweizer, *The Good News According to Matthew,* 488. Meier and others also see a reference to Zechariah 11,12, in which thirty silver pieces is the sum paid to a rejected shepherd: Meier, *Matthew,* 31.

CHAPTER 12

190. Regarding the complex and not entirely certain dating, see the persuasive comments of Meier, *A Marginal Jew,* vol. 1, 386–409; on the Last Supper (p. 399), Meier is particularly succinct.

191. The account of the foot-washing is found in Jn 13,3–11.

192. *The Lord Jesus*   1 Cor 11,23–26.

192. *While they were eating*   Mk 14,22–24. The meal is not documented in the Gospel according to John, and for good reason: it has already been treated symbolically and mystically in chapter 6, in the marvelous event of the multiplication of loaves and fishes. Additionally, John elaborates, in the foot-washing of the disciples by Jesus, the nature of service that is at the root of his self-donation at the last supper. On this, see, e.g., Brown, *The Gospel According to John, XIII–XXI.*

193. See Ex 12 and 24, and Is 52,13–53,12.

194. On the reality of the Risen Christ present in the Eucharist, in the proclaimed Word, in the liturgy, in the community, in the life of the believer, see the brilliant article by Piet Schoonenberg (translated by Mary Pierre Ellebracht), "Presence and the Eucharistic Presence," *Cross Currents,* winter 1967, 39–54; the article originally appeared in the author's native Dutch, in *Tijdschrift voor Theologie* (1966).

196. *'In' is the superlative*   Ibid., 47.

198. The quotation is from scene 6 of Tennessee Williams, *A Streetcar Named Desire.*

199. *Christ will come*   Flannery O'Connor, "The Displaced Person," in *The Complete Stories* (New York: Farrar, Straus and Giroux, 1971), 226.

202. *came not to be served*   Mk 10,45.

202 ff. The theological and exegetical literature on the origin and development of the priesthood is, as one might expect, vast. There are several good places to start: "An Example: Rethinking the Priesthood Biblically for All," in Brown, *The Critical Meaning of the Bible,* 96–106; H.-M. Legrand, "The Presidency of the Eucharist According to the Ancient Tradition," *Worship* 53 (1979) 413–38.

202. *feed my lambs*   Jn 21,15–17.

202. *There is one God*   1 Timothy 2,5.

202. *When Christ came*   Heb 9,11–26.

203. *You are a chosen race*   1 Peter 2,9.

203. *by the mercy of God*   Rom 12,1.

204. *unlikely thesis*   Brown, *The Critical Meaning of the Bible,* 77.

206. The injunction "Do this in memory of me" is found only in Lk 22,19 and 1 Cor 11,25—it is notably absent in the Marcan/Matthean accounts—but to peceive those words as addressed *only* to the twelve there seated is to miss the point of the meal, which was certainly to extend beyond itself. It means only (thus Brown, *The Critical Meaning of the Bible*, 77) "that in the tradition represented by Luke (and perhaps by Paul) there was a memory that the Twelve could and did celebrate the eucharist. Otherwise the NT gives us no definite information on the subject."

CHAPTER 13

208. *substituted as culprits*   Goold, ed., *Tacitus: The Annals*, vol. 5 283–84— from Book XV, §XLIV.

209. Regarding scholarly commentaries, see, e.g., Brown, *The Death of the Messiah*—a masterful two-volume, 1,608-page study of the four Gospel accounts of Jesus' final hours.

209. *Sit here*   Mk 14,32 ff.; see also Mt 26,36–46; Lk 22,40–46; Jn 17,1–26.

209 ff. In all that follows, I must acknowledge an enormous debt to the scholarship and the pastoral reflections of the great American exegete (and, thirty years ago, one of my professors) Raymond E. Brown. In addition to his monumental two-volume study cited above, I recommend the terse but rich meditations in his seventy-one-page book. *A Crucified Christ in Holy Week.*

210. *Jesus offered up*   Heb 5,7.

211. That those who had left everything now leave everything to get away from Jesus: this, Brown rightly suggests, is the symbolic meaning of Mk 14,51–52: "A certain young man was following him, wearing nothing but a linen cloth. They caught hold of him, but he left the linen cloth and ran off naked."

212 ff. There is considerable scholarly debate about the historicity of Jesus' interrogation before the Jewish Sanhedrin. Doubts are raised, first of all, by the unlikelihood of a judicial session in the middle of the night so close to a major feast. In addition, the conduct of the high priests and their cronies (as described in the Gospels) violates every prescription of civil and religious law. It is also never made clear, as Brown has pointed out, why, having condemned Jesus to death, the Sanhedrin then handed him over to the Roman procurator. (Only the fourth Gospel states that the Sanhedrin did not have the right to exact the death penalty—which is itself doubtful, as the case of John the Baptist revealed: Herod needed no approval from the occupying administration to behead John.) "If the portrait of the Sanhedrin is unrelievedly hostile, we must remember that [the evangelists wrote for] Christians who themselves have suffered from confrontations with synagogue leaders" (*A Crucified Christ*, 38). Matthew, as usual, is especially unrelenting about the Jewish role in the death of Jesus: only he writes that "*all* the chief priests and the elders of the people took counsel against Jesus" (27,1).

212. *Have you no answer*   The Markan passion narrative continues with Jesus

before the council and with Peter's denial at 14,53–72; the parallels are Mt 26,57–75; Lk 22,54–71 and 22,56–62; Jn 18,13–27.

212. *they are offering*   Jn 16,2.

212. Dt 13,1–5 states the requirement that false prophets be put to death.

213. *He went out and wept*   Lk 26,62.

213. *He went away and hanged himself*   Mt 27,5.

213. There is nothing in Scripture or in the tradition of the Church to support the frequently held popular opinion that Judas Iscariot, or anyone else, is eternally denied the benefit of the redemption won by Jesus in his death and resurrection.

213. On the dates for Pontius Pilate, see Meier, *A Marginal Jew*, vol. 1, 373, and note thereto.

213. On the character of Pontius Pilate and his extrabiblical reputation, see Blinzler, *The Trial of Jesus*, 177–85.

213. On the fascinating archaeologial excavations of Gabbatha, see McKenzie, *Dictionary of the Bible*, 290–91.

214. The most detailed and dramatic scenario of the trial before Pilate is contained in Jn 18,28–19,16, and it is this brilliantly structured account to which I adhere.

214. On the tangled history of the debate over whether the Jews had the competence to pronounce a death sentence, see Winter, *On the Trial of Jesus*, 66–90; and Brown, *The Gospel According to John, XIII–XXI*, 848–50. There is "impressive cogency" (Brown's words) to support Winter's refutation of Jeremias et al., and to maintain that John is quite correct. The Romans jealously guarded the privilege of pronouncing a death sentence, for otherwise it would have been possible for local authorities to execute pro-Roman parties.

215. The issue of the historicity of Barabbas (which is not a name but simply a designation—"a son of a father") is also hotly contested. Brown, in *The Gospel According to John, XII–XXI*, 871–72, and *The Death of the Messiah*, 811–14, inclines to believe that there was indeed a guerrilla revolutionary named Barabbas, for otherwise it is hard to explain why the story was invented and how it found its way independently into all four Gospel traditions. But it is at least possible that the Barabbas episode (Jn 19,39–40; Mk 15,6–14; Mt 27,15–23; Lk 18,39–40) may have been inserted into the earlier oral, pre-Gospel tradition to heighten Jewish guilt (a motif on which Brown is masterfully perceptive): they prefer a certified crook to Jesus.

215. Similarly, I omit the incident of Pilate sending Jesus over to Herod, which is found only in Lk 23,6–16, and which is very likely more theological than literally historical. See Brown, *The Death of the Messiah*, 760–86.

217. By the time the Gospels were heard by Gentiles—Romans especially—they

could be secure in the knowledge that Jesus was not an anti-Roman criminal, and in fact had been almost defended by a Roman governor!

218. *Look ... I am bringing*　　The passion narrative continues in Jn 19.

218. The complete verse of Jn 19,7—"The Jews answered him, 'We have a law, and according to that law he ought to die because he has claimed to be the Son of God' "—are ironic words put on the lips of the crowd by the evangelist. It is axiomatic that Jesus did not indeed claim to be God's Son in a divine sense during his lifetime—although on several occasions he seems to have expressed a definitely unique meaning for the title "God's son." But neither his language nor his theology had the ability to express a sense of divinity that differentiated him from the Fatherhood of God. In this regard, the Gospel of John, more than any other, represents the settled, late-first-century faith of Christians in Jesus. On this, see, e.g., Brown, *An Introduction to New Testament Christology,* 80–89.

219. Some Johannine texts referring bitterly to "the Jews" in the matter of Jesus' death: 8,31–59; 11,45–57; 19,7, 12, 31, 38.

219. I have already made important references to Josephus in chapters 1, 2 and 4.

220. The Babylonian Talmud, which was begun in the third century A.D. but did not reach its final form until over four hundred years later, speaks of a man named Yeshu (Jesus) who was hanged on the eve of Passover, but there are confusing references to a month-long trial. Yeshu, says this document, was a magician or sorcerer who deceived the people of Israel. As Meier persuasively reasons (*A Marginal Jew,* vol. 1, 96), "the talmudic text is simply reacting to the gospel tradition."

220. *on indictment*　　*Antiquities of the Jews,* 18.3.3, §63–64.

220. *hanging Jesus*　　Babylonian Talmud, *Sanhedrin* 43a.

221. As usual, no scholar is clearer for the general reader on the matter of the Jewish-Christian rift than Brown, in several of his books: see, e.g., *Reading the Gospels with the Church from Christmas Through Easter,* 39–40, 47, 55–64; *Reponses to 101 Questions on the Bible,* 114–16; *A Crucified Christ in Holy Week,* 13–16, 41–42.

222. The proclamation of faith "My Lord and my God" is put on the lips of the famously doubting Thomas: Jn 20,28. And on the lips of Jesus are put several late-first-century affirmations of his divinity—e.g., 5,18; 10,33; and 18,6. When Jesus says, "I am he," the Greek *'egō èimi*=I am [the pronoun "he" is understood]) translates the Hebrew divine name (Yahweh=I am).

222. On the insertion into the Benedictions of the curse against those who believe in Jesus, see Davies, *The Setting of the Sermon on the Mount,* 275 ff., and Martyn, *History and Theology in the Fourth Gospel,* 31 ff.

223. The prayer of Pope John XXIII is reprinted in Appleton, *The Oxford Book of Prayer,* 112.

224. *Slaves, obey* Eph 6,5.

224. *The books of Scripture* *Dei Verbum* (The Dogmatic Constitution on the Divine Revelation), §11.

226. *Jesus of Nazareth, King of the Jews* Jn 19,19–21.

227. More detail on the likelihood of April 7, 30, as the date of Jesus' death may be found in the array of scholars discussed by Meier, *A Marginal Jew*, vol. 1, 431.

228. According to Matthew and Mark, Jesus says only, "Eli, Eli . . ." Luke adds two statements borrowed from his other work (Acts of the Apostles): these are the last words of the first Christian martyr, the deacon Stephen, as he is stoned to death: "Receive my spirit" and "Do not hold this sin against them" (Acts 7,59–60). He also adds Jesus' words to the repentant criminal ("Today you will be with me in Paradise"), consistent with the ministry of the gracious Jesus in Luke. The words spoken by Jesus in John are richly theological but of doubtful historicity. The giving of the mother and disciple into each other's care is an ecclesiastical symbol: Mary and John the apostle are not even named as the mother and disciple—rather they are emblems of the newborn Church and its prototype. The phrase "I thirst" is just as complex, and may recall Ps 22 ("my tongue cleaves to my jaws . . ."). His statement is followed in Jn 19 by the description of the sponge soaked in sour wine, offered on hyssop to Jesus and held to his mouth. In Egypt, the hyssop was used to smear the Israelite doorposts with the blood of the Passover lamb. In addition, John reports that none of Jesus' bones were broken after his death, just as was prescribed for the preparation of the lamb. On all this, see Brown, *Death of the Messiah*, 1008–13 and 1072–73; and his *The Churches the Apostles Left Behind*, 113.

228. Regarding Jesus' cry of Psalm 22 and the bystanders' reaction, see Mk 15,34–36 and Mt 27,46–49. Those who minimize the humanity of Jesus try (rather lamely) to explain this psalm verse by interpreting it as a Messianic claim: the first verse implies the entire psalm, with the speaker finally vindicated. Most serious exegetes rightly dismiss this reading on literary and theological grounds.

228. Regarding the abandonment of Jesus by his family and friends: All four Gospels mention the presence of women at the death of Jesus, but the accounts are impossible to reconcile. Mk 15,40 and Mt 27,55 mention—after recounting the death of Jesus—the nearby presence of women "looking on from a distance," who had served Jesus during his ministry. But they mention only Mary Magdalene, Mary the mother of James and Joseph (Mk: Joses), and (Mt) the mother of the sons of Zebedee (possibly the same as Mk: Salome, who is not called the mother of the sons of Zebedee). Lk 23,49 mentions only the presence "at a distance" of "acquaintances and women who had followed him." There is, then, no mention of Jesus' mother, or of any particular disciple, in the synoptics. The only name that Matthew, Mark and Luke share in common with Jn 19,25–27 is Mary Magdalene. But for his own purposes, John goes further: "Standing near the cross of Jesus were his mother, and his mother's sister, Mary, the wife of Clopas, and Mary

Magdalene." The syntax of this verse in the Greek is ambiguous, as I have tried to represent it also in the translation: are there four women or three? A named pair (Mary the wife of Clopas and Mary Magdalene) and an unnamed pair (Jesus' mother and his mother's sister)? Or three women named Mary (with "his mother's sister" in apposition to "Mary, the wife of Clopas)? "Identifications are easy to conjure but impossible to ascertain," as C. K. Barrett has tersely indicated (*The Gospel According to St. John*, 551). Against the idea of three is the notion that Mary the wife of Clopas would not be "his mother's sister" because two sisters would not have the same name (Mary)—but of course John does not mention the name of Jesus' mother anywhere in his Gospel. Her only other appearance is at Jn 2,1–12 (the wedding at Cana), but there, as in Jn 19, she is unnamed and addressed as "Woman." Serious Johannine scholarship rightly sees that the mother of Jesus is a symbolic figure: if John had wished her two appearances in the narrative to refer to specific historic moments, why not mention her name, which everyone knew? As "Woman," clearly she has a theological significance. John McKenzie is probably quite right in this regard: "The evangelists say clearly that all the disciples had fled and were absent from the death of Jesus; it is not strange that the sources of the gospels were ambiguous on who was actually present, but the synoptics are not ambiguous on the absence of Mary. *We must accept the words of Jesus to Mary and the beloved disciple as a theological construction of John*" (italics his: "The Mother of Jesus in the New Testament," *Concilium* 168 [1983] 8).

CHAPTER 14

232 ff. On the different worlds or spheres of being, there is a vast theological and metaphysical literature; relative to the Resurrection, see, e.g., Macquarrie, *Jesus Christ in Modern Thought*, 406–7.

233. *He is alive now* 2 Cor 13,4. On the Greek preposition *'ek* meaning "with" in the sense of "by means of," see Balz and Schneider, *Exegetical Dictionary*, 403.

233. Of the occurrences of the word "alive" in the New Testament, these are of singular importance: in discussing the past patriarchs of Israel, Jesus says, "He is God not of the dead but of the living, for *to Him all of them are alive*." The Greek is *pantes gar 'autō zōsin*: "all live to [or with reference to] Him," that is, in the realm of God, or with respect to God (a referential dative), all of them are alive. Consider, too, Acts 1,3: of Jesus, it is said "He presented himself alive—*parestēsen 'eauton zōnta*," literally, "he presented himself, living" (*zōnta* is the present participle modifying *'eauton*). Romans 6,11 discusses Christians "dead to sin but alive to God"—*nekrous men tē 'amartia, zōntas de tō theō*," that is, "dead with respect to sin, which means alive with respect to God." Perhaps one of the most exquisite phrases occurs at the end of the New Testament (Rev 1,17–18): "I am the first and the last," says the Risen Jesus, "and the living one. I was dead, and—see!—I am alive forever and ever"—*'egō 'eimi 'o prōtos kai 'o 'eschatos, kai 'o zōn, kai 'egenomēn nekros kai 'idou zōn 'eimi 'eis tous 'aiōnas tōn 'aiōnōn*.

236 ff. An important lecture on the Resurrection was presented at several universities in 1963 by the great German Lutheran theologian Wolfhart Pannenberg: "Did Jesus Really Rise From the Dead?" It is reprinted in *Dialog* 4 (1965) 128–35. As for the spirituality of Resurrection theology, I doubt anyone is more full of faith and feeling (not to say intellectual rigor) than Guardini, *The Lord*, 405–15.

236. Regarding the variations in the Gospel accounts of the arrival of the women at the tomb and of the post-Resurrection appearances of Jesus, see, e.g., Brown, *The Gospel According to John XIII–XXI*, 965–1061, and any of the standard commentaries listed in the Bibliography.

237. *the limitless internal depth*   Schilling, *The New Consciousness*, 118. For the reference to Schilling, and for much of this discussion of the other form of existence, I am indebted to the suggestions of John Macquarrie, *Christian Hope*, 106–29.

237. On the interplay of elementary particles and the "composition" of life, see Rahner, *Foundations of Christian Faith*, 271.

237. *He whom God raised up*   Acts 13,37.

239. *Do not be afraid*   Mt 28,10.

239. The Magdalene story in John is both fascinating and problematic, and it has caused several ingenious and tortured exegeses. As usual, Brown (*Gospel XIII–XXI*, 1011–1015) deals with them all quite firmly. "In telling her not to hold on to him, Jesus indicates that his permanent presence is not by way of appearance, but by way of the gift of the Spirit" (1012). As for the impression the Gospel of John gives, that there is a time frame involved, it is important to see how the writer constructs a narrative. John conceives the Glorification of Jesus as a passage from the Last Supper to Easter Night. The meaning of the injunction not to cling to him, then, is also that this obsession with his *visible presence* impedes the effects of his Glorification on humanity.

240. *You must say*   Mt 28,13–14.

242. The extended Pauline treatment of the risen Jesus and of the risen body is found in 1 Cor 15.

242. On the antiquity and significance of the early Christian memory of the empty tomb, see Campenhausen, *Tradition and Life in the Church*, 42–89, and W. L. Craig in *New Testament Studies* 31 (1985) 39–67.

242. *Nobody believed in Socrates*   Justin Martyr, *Apology* 10, quoted in Deiss, 20.

242. A superb and up-to-date bibligraphy (to 1997) on 1 Corinthians can be found in Brown, *An Introduction to the New Testament*, 538–40.

243. *life-giving spirit*   Jesus has become *pneuma zōopoioun*. See Jn 6,63: correcting those who cannot understand that Jesus can give his flesh and blood in the Eucharist (that is, those who take it for a kind of literal, crass cannibalism), the evangelist remarks that "the spirit gives life, the flesh counts for nothing," and the Greek is remarkably similiar to 1 Cor 15,45: *to pneuma 'estin to zōopoioun*. The phrase *pneuma zōopoioun* is found only here, although there is a parallel in 1 Peter 3,18: Jesus is "put to death so far as the flesh is concerned, but raised to life in the spirit"—*thanatōtheis men sarki, zōopoiētheis de pneumati*. (On 1 Peter 3,18–4,6, see Spoto, *Christ's Preaching to the Dead*.) Paul's reference to the Risen Jesus as a life-giving spirit in verse 45 is linked to the continuation of the Adam/Christ contrast in verse 47: "The first man is of earth, the second of heaven."

243. *spiritual body:*   *Sōma pneumatikon*.

243. Regarding the raising "on the third day in accordance with the Scriptures": See Hos 6,2: "On the third day He will raise us up and we will live in His presence." Gen 22,3: "On the third day, Abraham looked up and saw the place in the distance." Gen 42,18: "On the third day, Joseph said to them, 'Do this and you will live.' " Ex 19,11: "The day after tomorrow, Yahweh will descend on Mount Sinai." 2 Samuel 1,2: "On the third day, a man arrived from Saul's camp." 1 Kings 12,12: "On the third day, Jeroboam and all the people came to Rehoboam in obedience." The third day refers not to a passage of seventy-two hours but to a *turning point* that separates the old from the new. Jn 2,1: "On the third day, there was a wedding at Cana." The third day after *what?* We're not told: this is a literary device, referring to a moment when something crucial occurs. Also, the primitive Church knew of course that the first announcement of Jesus' Resurrection was on a Sunday. So the oral tradition at once picked up the Old Testament phrase "on the third day," finding it literally fulfilled in the redemptive event.

244. The Resurrection is held in far less exalted understanding by the framers of the "Jesus Seminar" (John Dominic Crossan, Burton Mack, Marcus Borg, Robert Funk and even the Episcopalian bishop John Shelby Spong) than it was decades ago by Rudolf Bultmann. For them, Easter faith is variously expressed as a nice idea about Jesus rising up in the hearts of his followers before and then most effectively after his death. For Spong as for the German scholar Willi Marxsen, on the other hand, the Resurrection expresses merely Peter's sudden intuition about Jesus' grandeur, communicated to others. On this, see Johnson, *The Real Jesus*, 137–40, who uses the analogy of the great reduction in the population of European Jewry in 1945 compared with that population in 1932. Something has to account for that, although the Holocaust would not necessarily be the automatic conclusion. Theories of emigration or tourism are not persuasive, and some external force sufficiently great to account for that effect would have to be found. A study of history, then, reveals the tragic cause.

245. *epistemological imperialism*   Johnson, 140.

245. *does not come before*   Quoted in Kenneth L. Woodward, "Rethinking the Resurrection," *Newsweek*, 8 April 1996.

246. *If we have placed our hope*   1 Cor 15,19; translated by the author. The literal rendering: "If we are those having hoped in Christ only in this life, we are more pitiful than all men."

247. *as they were watching*   Acts 1,9.

CHAPTER 15

251. *I was dead*   Rev 1,18

255. *for a thousand years*   Ps 90,4

257. *Truly, You are a hidden God*   Is 45,15.

SELECTIVE BIBLIOGRAPHY

Achtemeier, Paul J., ed., *Harper's Bible Dictionary*. San Francisco: HarperSan-Francisco, 1985.

Alexander, David, and Pat Alexander. *Eerdmans Handbook to the Bible*. Oxford, England: Lion Publishing, 1973.

Alsop, John R., ed. *An Index to the Revised Bauer-Arndt-Gingrich Greek Lexicon* 2nd edition. Grand Rapids, Mich.: Zondervan, 1981.

Appleton, George, ed., *The Oxford Book of Prayer*. Oxford, England: Oxford University Press, 1985.

Balz, Horst, and Gerhard Schneider, eds., *Exegetical Dictionary of the New Testament*. 3 vols. Grand Rapids, Mich.: William B. Eerdmans, 1991–94.

Barrett, C. K. *A Critical and Exegetical Commentary on the Acts of the Apostles*. 2 vols. Edinburgh: T. & T. Clark, 1994.

———. *The Gospel According to St. John*. Philadelphia: Westminster, 1978.

Beare, Francis Wright. *The Gospel According to Matthew: A Commentary*. Oxford, England: Basil Blackwell, 1981.

Blair, Edward P. *The Illustrated Bible Handbook*. Nashville, Tenn.: Abingdon Press, 1987.

Blass, F., and A. Debrunner, *A Greek Grammar of the New Testament and Other Early Christian Literature*. Translated and revised by Robert W. Funk. Chicago: University of Chicago Press, 1961.

Blinzler, Josef. *The Trial of Jesus*. Translated by Isabel and Florence McHugh. Westminster, Md.: The Newman Press, 1959.

Boulding, Maria. *The Coming of God*. London: SPCK, 1982.

———. *Gateway to Hope: An Exploration of Failure*. Petersham, Mass.: St. Bede's Publications, 1985.

Bourke, Myles M. *Passion, Death and Resurrection of Christ*. New York: Paulist Press, 1963.

Bowker, J. *Jesus and the Pharisees*. Cambridge, England: Cambridge University Press, 1973.

Brooks, James A., and Carlton L. Winbery. *Syntax of New Testament Greek*. Lanham, Md.: University Press of America, 1979.

Brown, Raymond E. *An Adult Christ at Christmas*. Collegeville, Minn.: Liturgical Press, 1978.

———. *The Birth of the Messiah*. New York: Doubleday/Anchor Bible Reference Library, 1993 (updated edition of the 1977 original).

———. *The Churches the Apostles Left Behind*. New York: Paulist Press, 1984.

———. *A Coming Christ in Advent*. Collegeville, Minn.: Liturgical Press, 1988.

———. *The Critical Meaning of the Bible*. New York: Paulist Press, 1981.

———. *A Crucified Christ in Holy Week*. Collegeville, Minn: Liturgical Press, 1986.

———. *The Death of the Messiah*. 2 vols. New York: Doubleday/Anchor Bible Reference Library, 1994.

———. *The Gospel According to John I–XII*. Garden City, N.Y.: Doubleday/The Anchor Bible, 1966.

———. *The Gospel According to John XIII–XXI*. New York: Doubleday/The Anchor Bible, 1970.

———. *The Gospel and Epistles of John*. Collegeville, Minn.: Liturgical Press, 1988.

———. *An Introduction to the New Testament*. New York: Doubleday/Anchor Bible Reference Library, 1997.

———. *An Introduction to New Testament Christology*. New York: Paulist Press, 1994.

———. *New Testament Essays*. Milwaukee: Bruce, 1965.

———. *A Once and Coming Spirit at Pentecost*. Collegeville, Minn.: Liturgical Press, 1994.

———. *Reading the Gospel with the Church from Christmas Through Easter*. Cincinnati: St. Anthony Messener Press, 1996.

———. *Responses to 101 Questions on the Bible*. New York: Paulist Press, 1990.

———. *A Risen Christ in Eastertime*. Collegeville, Minn.: Liturgical Press, 1991.

———. *The Virginal Conception and Bodily Resurrection of Jesus*. New York: Paulist Press, 1973.

Brown, Raymond E., Joseph A. Fitzmyer, S. J., and Roland E. Murphy, O.Carm., eds. *The New Jerome Biblical Commentary*. Englewood Cliffs, N. J.: Prentice Hall, 1990.

Campenhausen, H. F. von. *Tradition and Life in the Church*. Philadelphia: Fortress, 1968.

Capon, Robert Farrar. *The Parables of Judgment*. Grand Rapids, Mich.: Eerdmans, 1989.

Collins, John J. *The Scepter and the Star*. New York: Doubleday/Anchor Bible Reference Library, 1995.

Cook, Michael L. *Responses to 101 Questions About Jesus*. New York: Paulist Press, 1993.

Cullmann, Oscar. *Prayer in the New Testament*. Translated by John Bowden. Minneapolis: Fortress Press, 1995.

Daniel-Rops, Henri. *Daily Life in Palestine at the Time of Christ*. London: Weidenfeld and Nicholson, 1962.

Davies, W. D. *A Critical and Exegetical Commentary on the Gospel According to Saint Matthew*. Edinburgh: T. & T. Clark, 1988.

———. *The Setting of the Sermon on the Mount*. Cambridge, England: Cambridge University Press, 1964.

de Caussade, Jean-Pierre *Abandonment to Divine Providence*. Translated by John Beevers. New York: Doubleday Image, 1975.

Deiss, Lucien *Early Sources of the Liturgy*. Translated by Benet Weatherhead. Collegeville, Minn.: Liturgical Press, 1967.

Donahue, John R. *The Gospel in Parable*. Minneapolis: Fortress, 1988.

Ehrman, Bart D., and Michael W. Holmes, eds. *The Text of the New Testament in Contemporary Research*. Grand Rapids, Mich.: Eerdmans, 1995.

Eliot, T. S. *The Complete Poems and Plays, 1909–1950*. New York: Harcourt, Brace & World, 1952.

Fiensy, David A. *The Social History of Palestine in the Herodian Period*. Lewiston, N.Y.: Edwin Mellon Press, 1991.

Fitzmyer, Joseph A., S. J. *A Christological Catechism*. New York: Paulist Press, 1991.

———. *The Gospel According to Luke, I–IX and X–XXIV*. Vols. 28 and 28A of *The Anchor Bible*. Garden City, N.Y.: Doubleday, 1981.

———. *Responses to 101 Questions on the Dead Sea Scrolls*. New York: Paulist Press, 1993.

———. *Scripture and Christology*. London: Geoffrey Chapman, 1986.

———. *To Advance the Gospel: New Testament Studies*. New York: Crossroad, 1981.

Freedman, David Noel, editor-in-chief. *The Anchor Bible Dictionary.* 6 vols. New York: Doubleday, 1992.

Freyne, S. *Galilee from Alexander the Great to Hardian: A Study of Second Temple Judaism.* Wilmington, Del.: Michael Glazier and Notre Dame: Notre Dame Press, 1980.

Fuller, Reginald H. *The Formation of the Resurrection Narratives.* New York: Macmillan, 1971.

————. *Interpreting the Miracles.* London, England, and Naperville, Ill.: SCM Book Club, 1963.

Goold, G. P., ed. *Tacitus: The Annals.* 5 vols. Cambridge, Mass.: Harvard University Press/London: William Heinemann, 1981.

Guardini, Romano. *The Lord.* Chicago: Henry Regnery, 1954.

Guelich, Robert A. *The Sermon on the Mount: A Foundation for Understanding.* Waco, Tex.: Word Books, 1982.

Hamel, Patrick J. *Handbook of Patrology.* Staten Island, N.Y.: Alba House, 1968.

Hamm, Dennis. *The Beatitudes in Context.* Wilmington, Del.: Michael Glazer/Zacchaeus Studies: New Testament, 1990.

Harrington, Daniel. *How to Read the Gospels.* Hyde Park, N.Y.: New City Press, 1996.

Jeremias, Joachim. Cave. *Jerusalem in the Time of Jesus.* Translated by F. H. and C. H. Cave. London: SCM Press, 1969.

————. *New Testament Theology: The Proclamation of Jesus.* New York: Scribner's, 1971.

————. *The Parables of Jesus.* 3rd edition, revised. London: Xpress Reprints/SCM Press, 1995.

————. *Rediscovering the Parables.* London: SCM Press, 1966.

Johnson, Luke Timothy. *The Acts of the Apostles.* Collegeville, Minn.: Michael Glazier/Liturgical Press, 1992.

————. *The Real Jesus: The Misguided Quest for the Historical Jesus and the Truth of the Traditional Gospels.* San Francisco: HarperSanFrancisco, 1996.

Jones, Clifford M. *New Testament Illustrations.* Cambridge, England: Cambridge University Press, 1956.

Julian of Norwich. *Revelations of Divine Love.* Translated by Clifton Wolters. Baltimore: Penguin, 1966.

Karris, Robert J., ed. *The Collegeville Bible Commentary: New Testament.* Collegeville, Minn.: Liturgical Press, 1992.

Kee, Howard Clark. *Understanding the New Testament.* 5th edition. Englewood Cliffs, N.J.: Prentice Hall, 1993.

Kelly, J. N. D. *Early Christian Doctrines.* Revised edition. San Francisco: HarperSanFrancisco, 1976.

Kingsbury, Jack Dean. *Proclamation Commentaries: Jesus Christ in Matthew, Mark and Luke.* Philadelphia: Fortress Press, 1981.

Kloppenborg, John S. *Q Parallels.* Sonoma, Calif.: Polebridge Press, 1988.

Komonchak, Joseph A., Mary Collins and Dermot A. Lane, eds. *The New Dictionary of Theology.* Wilmington, Del.: Michael Glazier, 1987.

Kümmel, Werner Georg. *Introduction to the New Testament.* Translated by Howard Clark Kee. Revised and updated edition. Nashville, Tenn.: Abingdon, 1975.

Küng, Hans. *On Being a Christian.* Translated by Edward Quinn. Garden City, N.Y.: Doubleday, 1976.

Latourelle, René, and Rino Fisichella, eds. *Dictionary of Fundamental Theology.* New York: Crossroad, 1994.

Leclerc, Eloi. *Francis of Assisi: Return to the Gospel.* Translated by Richard Arnandez. Chicago: Franciscan Herald Press, 1981.

Léon-Dufour, Xavier. *Dictionary of Biblical Theology.* Translated by P. Joseph Cahill. New York: Desclee, 1967.

Lienhard, Joseph T. *The Bible, the Church, and Authority.* Collegeville, Minn.: Liturgical Press/Michael Glazier, 1995.

Livingstone, E. A., ed. *The Concise Oxford Dictionary of the Christian Church.* New York: Oxford University Press, 1977.

Macquarrie, John. *Christian Hope.* New York: Seabury Press, 1978.

————. *Jesus Christ in Modern Thought.* London: SCM, 1990.

Malina, Bruce J. *The New Testament World: Insights from Cultural Anthropology.* Atlanta: John Knox, 1981.

Marchione, Margherita. *Yours Is a Precious Witness: Memoirs of Jews and Catholics in Wartime Italy.* New York: Paulist Press, 1997.

Martyn, J. L. *History and Theology in the Fourth Gospel.* New York: Harper & Row, 1968.

Matthews, Victor H. *Manners and Customs in the Bible.* Peabody, Miss.: Hendrickson, 1988.

Mays, James L., ed. *Harper's Bible Commentary.* San Francisco: HarperSanFrancisco, 1988.

McBrien, Richard P. *Catholicism.* San Francisco: HarperSanFrancisco, 1994.

————. *Responses to 101 Questions on the Church.* New York: Paulist Press, 1996.

McBrien, Richard P., ed. *The HarperCollins Encyclopedia of Catholicism.* San Francisco: HarperSanFrancisco, 1995.

McKenzie, John L. *Dictionary of the Bible.* Milwaukee: Bruce, 1965.

McManners, John, ed. *The Oxford Illustrated History of Christianity.* New York: Oxford University Press, 1990.

Meier, John P. *A Marginal Jew,* 2 vols. New York: Doubleday/Anchor Bible Reference Library, 1991 and 1994.

————. *Matthew.* Collegeville, Minn.: Michael Glazier/Liturgical Press, 1980.

Metz, Johannes B. *Poverty of Spirit.* Translated by John Drury. New York: Paulist Press, 1968.

Metzger, Bruce M., and Michael D. Coogan, eds. *The Oxford Companion to the Bible.* New York and Oxford, England: Oxford University Press, 1993.

Meyers, Eric M., and James F. Strange. *Archaeology, the Rabbis, and Early Christianity.* Nashville, Tenn.: Abingdon, 1981.

Murphy, Roland E. *Responses to 101 Questions on the Psalms and Other Writings.* New York: Paulist Press, 1994.

Murphy-O'Connor, Jerome. *Paul—A Critical Life.* Oxford, England: Clarendon, 1996.

Neufeld, Vernon H. *The Earliest Christian Confessions.* Grand Rapids, Mich.: Eerdmans, 1963.

Neusner, Jacob. *From Politics to Piety.* Englewood Cliffs, N.J.: Prentice Hall, 1973.

New Interpreter's Bible, The. 12 vols. Nashville, Tenn.: Abingdon Press, 1995.

Newman, Barclay M., Jr. *A Concise Greek-English Dictionary of the New Testament.* London: United Bible Societies, n.d.

Osborne, Kenan B. *The Resurrection of Jesus.* New York: Paulist Press, 1997.

Pannenberg, Wolfhart. *Jesus—God and Man.* Philadelphia: Westminster Press, 1968.

Perkins, Pheme. *Resurrection.* Garden City, N.Y.: Doubleday, 1984.

Perowne, Stewart. *The Later Herods: The Political Background of the New Testament.* London: Hodder and Stoughton, 1958.

————. *The Life and Times of Herod the Great.* Nashville, Tenn.: Abingdon, 1956.

Pesch, Rudolf. *Das Markusevangelium.* Freiburg/Basel/Vienna: Herder, 1977.

Prejean, Helen, C. S. J., *Dead Man Walking*. New York: Random House, 1993.

Pritchard, James B. *The Harper Concise Atlas of the Bible*. New York: HarperCollins/Times, 1991.

Rahner, Karl, ed. *Encyclopedia of Theology: The Concise Sacramentum Mundi*. New York: Crossroad, 1986.

Rahner, Karl. *Foundations of Christian Faith*. Translated by William V. Dych. New York: Crossroad, 1996.

Rahner, Karl. *The Resurrection of the Body*. Derby, N.Y.: St. Paul Publications, 1967.

Ratzinger, Josef. *Introduction to Christianity*. New York: Herder and Herder, 1969.

Rivkin, E. *A Hidden Revolution: The Pharisees' Search for the Kingdom Within*. Nashville, Tenn.: Abingdon, 1978.

Rousseau, John J., and Rami Arav, *Jesus and His World: An Archaeological and Cultural Dictionary*. Minneapolis: Fortress Press, 1995.

Sandmel, Samuel. *Herod: Profile of a Tyrant*. Philadelphia: Lippincott, 1967.

Schillebeeckx, Edward. *The Language of Faith: Essays on Jesus, Theology, and the Church*. Maryknoll, N.Y.: Orbis, 1995.

Schilling, Harold K. *The New Consciousness in Science and Religion*. Philadelphia: United Church Press, 1973.

Schnackenburg, Rudolf. *All Things Are Possible to Believers: Reflections on the Lord's Prayer and the Sermon on the Mount*. Translated by James S. Currie. Louisville: Westminster John Knox, 1995.

———. *Jesus in the Gospels: A Biblical Christology*. Translated by O. C. Dean, Jr. Louisville: Westminster John Knox Press, 1995.

Schweizer, Eduard *The Good News According to Matthew*. Translated by David E. Green. Atlanta: John Knox, 1975.

Scott, Bernard Brandon. *Hear Then the Parable: A Commentary on the Parables of Jesus*. Minneapolis: Fortress Press, 1989.

Senior, Donald. *The Gospel of Matthew*. Nashville, Tenn.: Abingdon Press, 1997.

———. *Jesus: A Gospel Portrait*. New York: Paulist Press, 1992.

Shuler, Philip L. *A Genre for the Gospels: The Biographical Character of Matthew*. Philadelphia: Fortress Press, 1982.

Spoto, Donald. *Christ's Preaching to the Dead: An Exegesis of I Peter 3,18–4,6*. Dissertation for the Ph.D. degree in the Department of Theology, Fordham University, New York: 1970. Available on University Microfilms, Ann Arbor, Michigan; also in Dissertation Abstracts.

Staniforth, Maxwell, trans. *Early Christian Writings.* London: Penguin, 1968.

Stanton, Graham. *Gospel Truth? New Light on Jesus and the Gospels.* Valley Forge, Pa.: Trinity Press, 1995.

Stone, Michael E. *The Testament of Levi.* Jerusalem: St. James Press, 1969.

Stuhlmueller, Carroll, ed. *The Collegeville Pastoral Dictionary of Biblical Theology.* Collegeville, Minn.: Liturgical Press, 1996.

Theissen, G. *The Miracle Stories of the Early Christian Tradition.* Philadelphia: Fortress, 1983.

Throckmorton, Burton H., Jr. *GospelParallels: A Synopsis of the First Three Gospels.* 3rd edition, revised. Toronto: Thomas Nelson, 1967.

Tillich, Paul. *The Shaking of the Foundations.* New York: Scribner's, 1948.

Ulanov, Ann and Barry. *Primary Speech: A Psychology of Prayer.* Atlanta: John Knox Press, 1982.

Wakefield, Gordon S., ed. *A Dictionary of Christian Spirituality.* London: SCM, 1983.

Ward, Benedicta, trans. *The Prayers and Meditations of St. Anselm.* London: Penguin, 1973.

Wenham, J. W. *The Elements of New Testament Greek.* Cambridge, England: Cambridge University Press, 1965.

Wilson, Ian. *Jesus: The Evidence.* San Francisco: HarperSanFrancisco, 1996.

Winter, Paul. *On the Trial of Jesus.* Berlin and New York: de Gruyter, 1961; and 2nd edition (1974), revised by T. A. Burkill and G. Vermes

Witherington, Ben, III. *The Jesus Quest: The Third Search for the Jew of Nazareth.* Downer's Grove, Ill.: InterVarsity Press, 1995.

Wright, N. T. *What Saint Paul Really Said.* Grand Rapids, Mich.: Eerdmans, 1997.

———. *Who Was Jesus?* Grand Rapids, Mich.: Eerdmans, 1992.

Zerwick, Maximilian. *Biblical Greek.* 4th edition. Translated by Joseph Smith. Rome: Pontifical Biblical Institute, 1963.

INDEX

birth (of Jesus) (*continued*)
John the Baptist and, 8
Joseph, 10–11
as a metaphor, 5–6, 7, 11
Moses, comparison with, 5–6, 7, 11,
21, 190
Saint Francis of Assisi and, 1, 8
the shepherds, 8–9
silence of God, 14–17, 217, 256–57
the star, 4–5
the three wise men, 4
Blondel, Maurice, 127
books
written about Jesus, 161–62, 162
Brown, Raymond E., 71, 204
Brutus, 207
Buddha, 59
burial (of Jesus), 229–30, 230
the empty tomb, 237–38
the empty tomb, angelic proclamation
at, 239–40
the empty tomb, as a fraud, 240–41,
241–42
the empty tomb, gospel accounts, 238–
39
the empty tomb, women at, 238–39,
241–42
final days, mythicizing, 207–9
four Gospels on, 184–85
grave of Joseph of Arimathea, 230, 238
Messianic secret and, 182–83, 183–84

Capernaum, 77
See also Galilee
capital punishment
executioners, anonymity of, 150
Jesus and, 148–49
Catholic Church. *See* Roman Catholic
Church
Cato, 207
census of Augustus, 3–4
Chalk Garden, The (Bagnold), 167
chance, 108
chaos, 108
"Christ"
Messianic secret and, 182–83, 183–84,
214–15, 215–16
as a name, 10
Christianity
and anti-Semitism, 219–21, 221–25

break with Judaism, 208–9, 221–25
and the burning of Rome, 208–9
Constantine and, 223
the empty tomb as a fraud, 240–41
the hidden Jesus, 251–52, 256–57
Jesus as alive and present, 233–35
See also Roman Catholic Church
Christmas, 12–14
Colossians, Letter to the (St. Paul), 14,
142
"compassion"
ethic of love, 147–49
Jesus and, 164
loving your enemy, 143–44, 146, 155
See also forgiveness of sin
conception (of Jesus), 18–36
the ancestry of, 20–21
annunciation, 22, 23–24
Gospel of John on, 30
Gospel of Luke on, 20–21, 23, 26, 27,
33–34, 35
Gospel of Matthew on, 20–21, 26, 27,
30–31, 33–34, 35
Mary and Joseph, 19–20
and the prophesies of Isaiah, 30–31
sexual relations after betrothal, 20
virginal conception, 24–25, 25–27, 27–
29, 29–30, 30–31, 31–33, 34–35
Confucius, 59
Constantine
and Christianity, 223
Corinthians (Paul's letter to), 178
on the last supper, 192
and the Resurrection, 242–43
crucifixion, 226–30, 230
artistic representations of, 208
final days, mythicizing, 207–9
four Gospels on, 184–85, 207, 208
"King of the Jews," 226–27
Messianic secret and, 182–83, 183–84
as a metaphor for the Passover, 227–28
over-familiarity of, 225–26
Simon of Cyrene, 227
the way to the cross, 227
Cyril of Alexandra, Saint, 154

Dante, 9
David, King, 3, 21
birth of, 5
Deuteronomy, 128, 142

ABOUT THE AUTHOR

Donald Spoto earned his B.A. degree *summa cum laude* in Greek and Latin from Iona College. He then received M.A. and Ph.D. degrees in theology from Fordham University, where he concentrated in New Testament Studies under the mentorship of Myles M. Bourke. His dissertation for the doctorate, *Christ's Preaching to the Dead: An Exegesis of I Peter 3,18–4,6*, examined Bible verses that suggest an early Christian belief in the possibility of conversion after death.

Dr. Spoto taught theology, Christian mysticism and biblical literature on the university level for twenty years before turning to full-time writing. Since 1976, his sixteen books have included internationally best-selling biographies of Alfred Hitchcock, Tennessee Williams, Laurence Olivier and Ingrid Bergman, as well as a dynastic history of the Royal Family of England. He lives in Los Angeles.